LEVITICUS, NUMBERS, DEUTERONOMY

BERIT OLAM
Studies in Hebrew Narrative & Poetry

Leviticus, Numbers, Deuteronomy

Stephen K. Sherwood, C.M.F.

David W. Cotter, O.S.B.
Editor

Chris Franke
Jerome T. Walsh
Associate Editors

M G

A Michael Glazier Book

THE LITURGICAL PRESS
Collegeville, Minnesota

www.litpress.org

A Michael Glazier Book published by The Liturgical Press.

Cover design by Ann Blattner.

1 2 3 4 5 6 7 8 9

Library of Congress Cataloging-in-Publication Data

Sherwood, Stephen K., 1943–
Leviticus, Numbers, Deuteronomy / Stephen K. Sherwood.
p. cm. — (Berit olam)
"A Michael Glazier book."
Includes bibliographical references and index.
ISBN 0-8146-5046-5 (alk. paper)
1. Bible. O.T. Leviticus—Language, style. 2. Bible. O.T. Numbers—Language, style. 3. Bible. O.T. Deuteronomy—Language, style. 4. Narration in the Bible. I. Title. II. Series.

BS1255.5 .S54 2001
222'.1066—dc21 2001033747

CONTENTS

ACKNOWLEDGMENTS

I would like to express my sincere thanks to Fr. Bill Morell, O.M.I., President, Sister Marcella Hoesl, M.M., Dean, and my colleagues on the faculty of Oblate School of Theology for allowing me a two-semester sabbatical in which to complete this work.

ABBREVIATIONS

ABD	*Anchor Bible Dictionary*
ASV	American Standard Version
BDB	Brown, Driver, Briggs *Hebrew and English Lexicon of the Old Testament*
BLA	Biblia Latino-americana
BHS	*Biblia Hebraica Stuttgartensia*
CCB	Christian Community Bible
DHHoy	Dios Habla Hoy
HALOT	*Hebrew/Aramaic Lexicon of the Old Testament*
Hamp	*Die Heilige Schrift* 1964
Holladay	*A Concise Hebrew and Aramaic Lexicon of the Old Testament*
IDB	*Interpreter's Dictionary of the Bible*
LXX	The Septuagint (The Greek version of the Old Testament)
Magaña Mendez	*Sagrada Biblia* 1980
MT	Masoretic Text (The traditional Hebrew text)
NAB	New American Bible
NASB	New American Standard Bible
NJB	New Jerusalem Bible
NJPS	New Jewish Publication Society version (TANAKH)

NRSV	New Revised Standard Version
PL	Patrologia Latina (Migne)
SB	The Schocken Bible (Everett Fox)
TLOT	*Theological Lexicon of the Old Testament*
TOB	Traduction Oecuménique de la Bible
Vg	The Latin Bible

GENERAL INTRODUCTION

The Method

This work represents an attempt to apply the techniques of narrative criticism to the biblical books of Leviticus, Numbers, and Deuteronomy. In doing so, I have taken as my guide the introduction by Jean-Louis Ska, S.J. *"Our Fathers Have Told Us": Introduction to the Analysis of Hebrew Narratives.*[1]

Simply put, this book is a discussion of the narrative art of these three books of the Bible, an investigation of their literary properties, a search for devices such as *inclusio* (the repetition of a word, idea, or form at the beginning and end of a unit) and chiastic (X-shaped) or concentric (onion-like) structures, elevated language, irony, and allusion; in short, all the devices that ancient literary works employ, searching for any artful artifice that would betoken careful crafting and purposeful arrangement.

But are these works narrative? Definitely yes. These three books are works of narrative art not only because they contain such colorful stories as the deaths of Nadab and Abihu, the Sabbath breaker, the threat from Sihon and Og, the story of Balaam, the bronze serpent, Aaron's rod, Miriam's leprosy, water from the rock, and others, but also because they (especially Leviticus and Deuteronomy) contain extended discourses made by characters in the story. These discourses are part of a story and contribute to the characterization of their speakers. As several authors have shown, it is somewhat misleading to think of these books primarily as collections of laws. For one thing, one would expect a law code to be unified and complete. But that is not the case with these books. The sections of instruction in our three books sometimes overlap

[1] Jean-Louis Ska, S.J., *"Our Fathers Have Told Us": Introduction to the Analysis of Hebrew Narratives* (Rome: Editrice Pontificio Instituto Biblico, 1990).

and at other times complement one another, but, as Mary Douglas has pointed out, even when taken together the laws of Exodus, Leviticus, Numbers, and Deuteronomy in no way represent a complete, unified code of law. What Douglas says of the book of Numbers applies as well to Leviticus and Deuteronomy:

> Even if Numbers is taken as sharing the account of law with Exodus and Leviticus, in so far as they are to be seen as parts of a single law book, the combined laws give a very incomplete coverage. . . . We cannot explain the curious selection and incompleteness of the laws in each book as due to the rest of the topic having been covered in one of the others (1993a, 144–45).

The fact that so much that one would expect to find in a law code is not found in these books is an indication that they were not intended to be a handbook for a court official (Grabbe 1993, 25). Nor do they contain all that a priest would need to know in order to carry out his functions. For example, there is no treatment of drink offerings (Grabbe 1993, 38). The incompleteness of the laws points to a purpose other than complete codification.

Another reason for not considering these books as law codes is precisely their narrative character. It has long been recognized that the *halakah* (instruction on worship and morality) has been set within a matrix of *haggadah* (story-telling). So, do we have in these books a separable combination of law code and story? Not necessarily. Why not regard the *halakah* as part of the *haggadah*? The instruction put on the lips of a character in a narrative contributes to the way the reader construes that character. The extended speeches of the character YHWH in Leviticus contribute greatly to the reader's perception of who YHWH is, what YHWH does, and what YHWH wants or does not want. Moses' particular way of retelling the events that the reader has witnessed in the previous books of the Pentateuch affects the characterization of Moses.

Finally, our three books are unlike Ancient Near Eastern collections of law in their use of language that is more characteristic of literature than of law.

> [They] exhibit numerous non-legal literary features: varied formulations, peculiar contexts, extraordinary word choice and terminology with semantic power far exceeding the strict demand of legal precision, explanatory and motivational clauses of all types, repetitions and legally illogical omissions, exhortations and admonitions woven in the very fiber of the legal statement (Schwartz 1991, 34–35).

Whereas ancient Near Eastern law codes contain little in the way of motive clauses, the instructions of Leviticus, Numbers, and Deuteronomy feature a large number of motive clauses (Gemser 1953, 62). This high proportion of motive clauses points to the performative aspect of these texts. They are designed to be read publicly and listened to by people. They are designed to move these listeners to act in accord with the instructions contained in these books.

The Structure of This Book

After this general introduction there is an introduction to each book, followed in turn by notes. The introductions address overall literary considerations, while the notes make observations on the literary quality of smaller units of the book.

The Introductions

In each introduction I will discuss the name of the book and the interest that it may have for readers. For Christian readers I will make some remarks on its importance as background for the New Testament. This is reflected in the amount of the text that is allotted for reading in worship in the Christian liturgies. A discussion of why the book begins and ends where it does will be next. This is followed by some observations on the language of the book. There follow remarks on time (pace and order), plot (especially tension and its resolution), structure, characterization, voices, symbolism and imagery, reading positions (the manipulation of knowledge by the narrator), and point of view. Not all of these items are treated for every book, but only those that prove fruitful in discovering the literary quality of a particular book.

In treating characterization I have tried to give a synthetic presentation of the major characters in each book by gathering together statements that the persons make about themselves (if any) and what is said about them by others (whether by the narrator or other characters in the story). While gathering this material together, I have tried to avoid steering it in any particular direction (i.e., by expressing any summary or conclusion about a particular character).

Similarly, I have gathered together the various images found in the book (imagery being broadly understood as anything that might evoke an image in the mind of the reader). Such a collection may prove particularly useful in overcoming the perception that these books are dry, since it shows that there is a surprising amount of imagery of various kinds in each book.

In discussing plot I have focused on the formal structure and narrative tension in each of the three books. Granted that Freitag's Pyramid (a model of narrative tension) does not rise to great heights in these books, they are certainly not without any narrative tension. In treating Leviticus and Deuteronomy I have experimented with bringing out the implied narrative tension contained in some case law.

Regarding structure, I have looked at various proposed structures both for the books as a whole and for parts of the books, but have not found any of the proposals for entire books convincing. Those for parts of books that I have found persuasive have been included.

The Notes

The notes take the form of an outline of the book (in bold type) filled in with observations, either my own or those gathered from the literature on these books that contribute to an understanding of them as works of narrative art.

Intended Audience

I have tried to write a commentary that any interested reader could use as a companion to the text. Many issues of interpretation—many important questions that will no doubt arise in the mind of the reader—have not been addressed. This is because the aim of this work is to focus only on the literary aspects of the text.

A Word about the Main Character in the Three Books

By far the major character in the three books is YHWH/Elohim, as can be seen by plotting the number of occurrences of the name compared to those of other characters:

Hits per 100 words

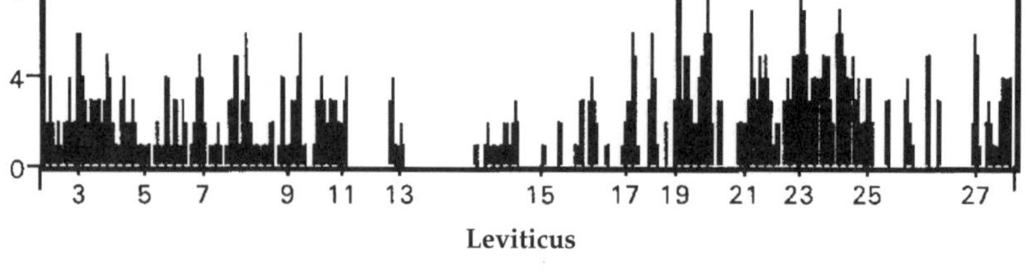

Distribution of "YHWH" or "Elohim" in Leviticus (MT)

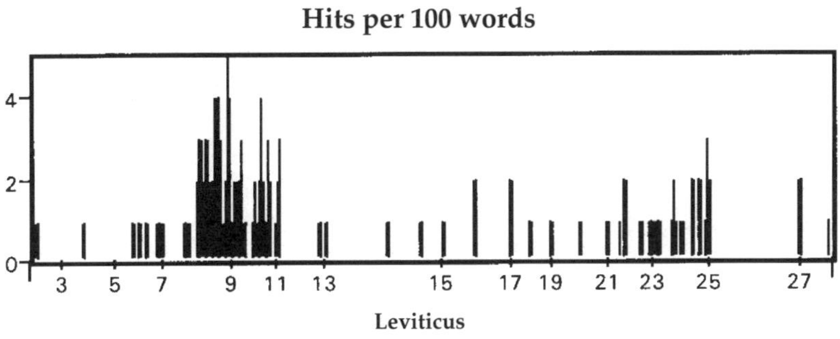

Hits per 100 words

Leviticus

Distribution of "Moses" in Leviticus (MT)

Hits per 100 words

Numbers

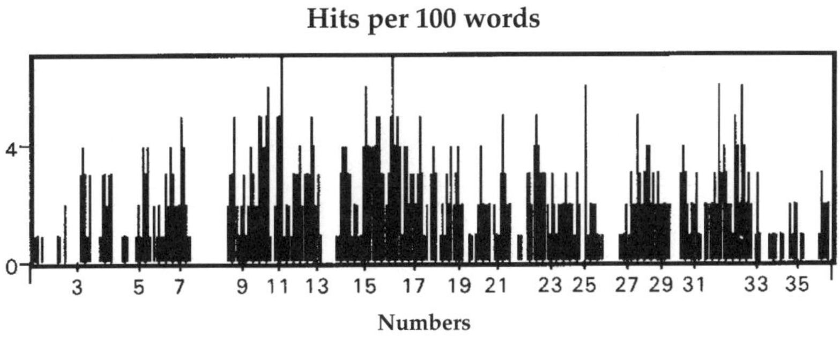

Distribution of "YHWH" or "Elohim" in Numbers (MT)

Hits per 100 words

Numbers

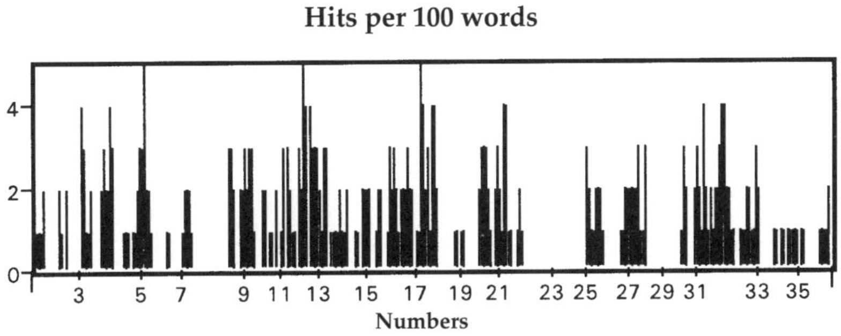

Distribution of "Moses" in Numbers (MT)

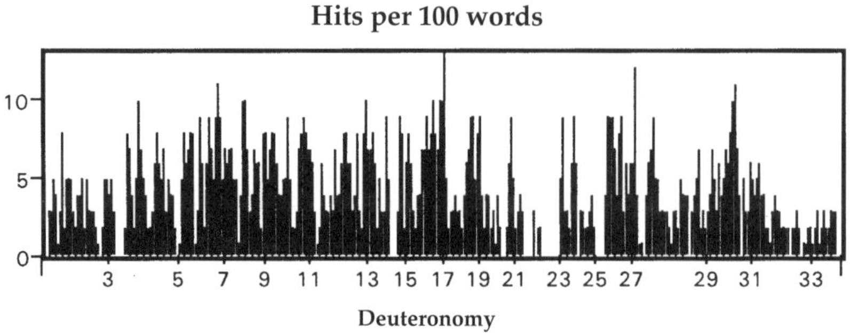

Distribution of "YHWH" or "Elohim" in Deuteronomy (MT)

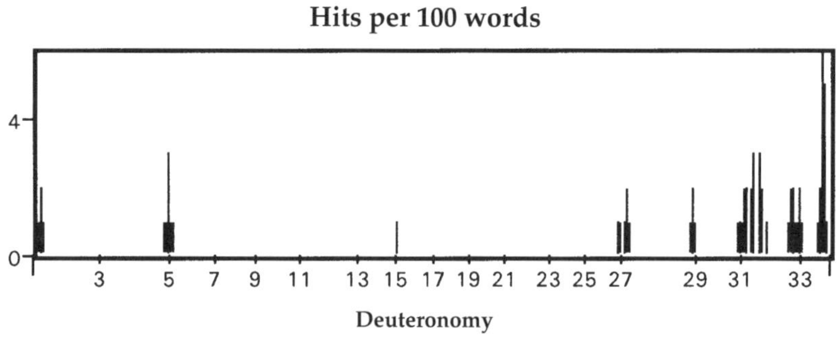

Distribution of "Moses" in Deuteronomy (MT)

These three books are in every sense books of theology—works of narrative art in which the main character is YHWH/God.

A Word about the Translation

Although the commentaries in the Berit Olam series often refer to the NRSV, it must be borne in mind that the series is actually a commentary on the Hebrew text. I sometimes point out instances where the NRSV rendering is at some remove from the Hebrew or give a more literal translation in order to bring out the flavor of the Hebrew.

FOR FURTHER READING

Alter, Robert, and Frank Kermode, eds. *The Literary Guide to the Bible.* Cambridge, Mass.: Belknap Press, 1987.

Arden, Eugene. "How Moses Failed God." *JBL* 76 (1957) 50–52.

Bal, Mieke. *Narratology. Introduction to the Theory of Narrative.* 2nd ed. Toronto: University of Toronto, 1997.

Baumgarten, Albert I. "The Paradox of the Red Heifer." *VT* 43 (1993) 442–51.

Bloom, Harold. "'Before Moses Was, I Am': The Original and Belated Testaments." Pages 3–14 in *Notebooks in Cultural Analysis: An Annual Review.* Edited by Norman F. Cantor. Durham, N.C.: Duke University Press, 1984.

Brunner, Hellmut. "Gerechtichkeit als Fundament des Thrones." *VT* 8 (1958) 426–28.

Buth, Randall. "The Hebrew Verb in Current Discussions." *Journal of Translation and Textlinguistics* 5,2 (1992) 91–105.

Butler, Trent C. "An Anti-Moses Tradition." *JSOT* 12 (1979) 9–15.

Fowler, Jeaneane D. *Theophoric Personal Names in Ancient Hebrew: A Comparative Study*. JSOTSup 49. Sheffield: JSOT, 1988.

Gane, Roy. "'Bread of the Presence' and Creator-in-Residence." *VT* 42 (1992) 179–203.

Gemser, B. "The Importance of the Motive Clause in Old Testament Law." Pages 50–66 in *Congress Volume Copenhagen, 1953.* VTSup 1. Leiden: Brill, 1953.

Gottcent, John H. *The Bible as Literature: A Selective Bibliography.* Boston: Hall, 1979.

Graetz, Naomi, "Miriam: Guilty or Not Guilty?" *Judaism* 40 (Spr 1991) 184–92.

Hirsch, Raphael Samuel. *The Pentateuch. Translated and Explained*. London: L. Honig and Sons, 1964.

Laffey, Alice L. *An Introduction to the Old Testament: A Feminist Perspective.* Philadelphia: Fortress, 1988.

_____. *The Pentateuch: A Liberation-Critical Reading.* Minneapolis: Augsburg, 1998.

Mann, Thomas, W. *The Book of the Torah: The Narrative Integrity of the Pentateuch.* Atlanta: John Knox, 1988.

Minor, Mark. *Literary-Critical Approaches to the Bible: An Annotated Bibliography.* West Cornwall, Conn.: Locust Hill Press, 1992.

Morris, Peter M. K., and Edward James. *A Critical Word Book of Leviticus, Numbers, Deuteronomy.* Computer Bible 8. Wooster, Ohio: Scholars Press and Biblical Research Associates, Inc., 1975.

North, Robert. "Yahweh's Asherah." Pages 118–37 in *To Touch the Text: Biblical and Related Studies in Honor of Joseph A. Fitzmyer, S.J.* Edited by M. Horgan and P. Kobelski. New York: Crossroad, 1989.

Noth, Martin. *Die Israelitischen Personennamen im Rahmen der Gemeinsemitischen Namengebung.* BWANT 46. Stuttgart: Kohlhammer, 1928.

Pons, Jacques. "La Référence au séjour en Egypte et à la sortie d'Egypte dans les codes de loi de l'Ancien Testament." *ETR* 63 (1988) 169–82.

Powell, Mark Alan. *The Bible and Modern Literary Criticism: A Critical Assessment and Annotated Bibliography.* New York: Greenwood Press, 1992.

Propp, William H. "The Rod of Aaron and the Sin of Moses." *JBL* 107 (1988) 19–26.

Revell, E. J. "The Repetition of Introductions to Speech as a Feature of Biblical Hebrew." *VT* 47 (1997) 91–110.

Robinson, Bernard P. "The Jealousy of Miriam." *ZAW* 101 (1989) 428–32.

Rosenberg, David, ed. *Congregation: Contemporary Writers Read the Jewish Bible.* San Diego, Calif.: Harcourt Brace Jovanovich, 1987.

Seters, John van. "The Conquest of Sihon's Kingdom: A Literary Examination." *JBL* 91 (1972) 182–97.

Smend, Rudolf. *Yahweh War and Tribal Confederation: Reflections upon Israel's Earliest History.* Nashville: Abingdon, 1970.

Wold, Donald. "The Kareth Penalty in P: Rationale and Cases." *SBL Seminar Papers* 1 (1979) 1–45.

Wold, Donald John. *The Meaning of the Biblical Penalty Kareth.* Ph.D. diss., UC Berkeley, 1986.

Wright, David P., David Noel Freedman, and Avi Hurvitz, *Pomegranates and Golden Bells: Studies in Biblical, Jewish, and Near Eastern Ritual, Law, and Literature in Honor of Jacob Milgrom.* Winona Lake, Ind.: Eisenbrauns, 1995.

LEVITICUS

INTRODUCTION

Name

The name that is given to this book in English, Leviticus, comes to us from Greek via Latin. It means "the levitical [book]," that is, the book that deals with what the Levites do. Such a title is apparently based on an assessment of the contents of the book—that it constitutes a manual for priests—a collection of laws pertaining to priests.

While it is true that the Hebrew word *kōhēn,* priest, is one of the most common in the book, the word "levite" itself only occurs four times in Leviticus (in two verses). So the name "Leviticus" may be somewhat misleading. In the first place, it is not only about priests. One can see this, for example, in the first seven chapters, which detail the various types of sacrifices and the manner in which they are to be offered. Much of the activity (except in the case of bird sacrifices) is performed by the person offering the sacrifice. Many of the laws in Leviticus are given in the third person and begin with words such as "a person" (*ʾādām, nepeš*), "anyone" (*ʾîš ʾîš*), "a woman" (*ʾiššâ*).

Second, it would be a mistake to see Leviticus as an attempt to codify all law regarding the cult. We can see that this is not the case because other laws governing worship are found elsewhere in the Pentateuch, i.e., outside Leviticus, and there are important aspects of the cult (e.g., tithes) that are scarcely treated in Leviticus.

In Hebrew this book is known by its first word, *wayyiqrāʾ,* "he called." Since this form of the verb indicates that it is part of a larger narrative context this name, more than the name "Leviticus," highlights the narrative character of the book as well as its continuity with what has come before.

Another reason why this book should be seen as a literary work more than as a law code is its language—the use of such literary devices as *chiasmus*, *inclusio*, and repetition give the text a more poetic and rhetorical character. It is not simply the dry list of commands and prohibitions that it may seem to be on the surface.

Part of the problem in understanding the nature of the book comes from the translation of "Torah" as "law" rather than as "instruction."

Not a "Page Turner"

For Christians, many a good intention to read the whole Bible from cover to cover has foundered on Leviticus. One author describes it as "gristle." It seems so dry, so technical, so unnourishing, and so utterly unrelated to our lives. Unless we belong to a group that wants to rebuild the Temple and reinstitute the sacrificial cult, it is exceedingly difficult to work up much enthusiasm for this text.

Consider the amount of space given to Leviticus in the Lectionary of the Roman Catholic Church. Of the 156 Sundays of the three-year cycle, pericopes from Leviticus are read on one Sunday of Year A, one of Year B and none of Year C. Texts from Leviticus make up only 1.3% of the Sunday readings. The total number of verses from Leviticus that is read on these two Sundays is a mere nine, or 1.05% of Leviticus' 859 verses. Leviticus fares no better in the weekday cycle. Of the 624 available slots, Leviticus fills four (0.64%). These four readings cover only twenty-five verses (2.9%) of Leviticus.

Yet this text has been of great importance to the Jewish people for more than two thousand years even though for much of that time there has been no possibility of offering animal sacrifices in Jerusalem. In Jewish tradition one begins the study of Torah with the chapters on sacrifice in the book of Leviticus (Munk 4, citing *Wayyiqra Rabba*).

Structurally, Leviticus is at the heart of the Pentateuch. Not only is it the middle book of the Pentateuch but, as we are told in the marginal notes in the Hebrew Bible, it contains the middle verse (8:8), the middle word ("sin" in 10:16), and the middle letter (the *waw* in *gāḥôn*, "belly," in 11:42) in the Pentateuch.

Leviticus is also the midpoint in the larger narrative that extends out on either side of it—the so-called "Sinai pericope" (Smith 1996, 18), i.e., the events that took place between the arrival at Mount Sinai (Exod 19:2) and the departure from there (Num 10:11).

Furthermore, Leviticus provides very important background for the New Testament. The Letter to the Hebrews would be incomprehensible without Leviticus. Some allusions to Leviticus in the New Testament:

Lev 1:2 This verse contains the first of eighty-nine instances of the use of *hiqrîb*, "bring near," in Leviticus. This symbolism of "bringing near" is alluded to in Eph 2:13, "But now in Christ Jesus you who once were far off have been brought near by the blood of Christ." The same is true in Heb 7:19, "(for the law made nothing perfect); there is, on the other hand, the introduction of a better hope, through which we approach God," and Jas 4:8, "Draw near to God, and he will draw near to you . . ."

Lev 1:4 The use of *rṣh* Niphal ("be acceptable") is alluded to both in Rom 15:16, where Paul refers to the grace given him by God "to be a minister of Christ Jesus to the Gentiles in the priestly service of the gospel of God, so that the offering of the Gentiles may be acceptable, sanctified by the Holy Spirit," and in 1 Pet 2:5, ". . . like living stones, let yourselves be built into a spiritual house, to be a holy priesthood, to offer spiritual sacrifices acceptable to God through Jesus Christ."

Lev 1:9 This is the first of seventeen occurrences of the expression "a pleasing odor" in reference to sacrifice. This expression is picked up by Paul in Phil 4:18, ". . . I am fully satisfied, now that I have received from Epaphroditus the gifts you sent, a fragrant offering, a sacrifice acceptable and pleasing to God." [But *rêᵃḥ nîḥôᵃḥ* and *rṣh* or *rāṣôn* do not appear together in Leviticus.] See also Eph 5:2, ". . . live in love, as Christ loved us and gave himself up for us, a fragrant offering and sacrifice to God," and Rom 12:1, "I appeal to you therefore, brothers and sisters, by the mercies of God, to present your bodies as a living sacrifice, holy and acceptable to God, which is your spiritual worship."

Lev 4:12, 21; 8:17; 9:11 "For the bodies of those animals whose blood is brought into the sanctuary by the high priest as a sacrifice for sin are burned outside the camp." See Heb 13:11.

Lev 4:25, 34; 5:9; 6:30; 16:15, 27 The use of blood in rituals that remove the guilt of sin is referred to in 1 John 1:7, "but if we walk in the light as he himself is in the light, we have fellowship with one another, and the blood of Jesus his Son cleanses us from all sin," Eph 1:7, "In him we have redemption through his blood, the forgiveness of our trespasses . . .," and Rom 3:25, "whom God put forward as a sacrifice of atonement by his blood . . ."

Lev 5:11 A pair of turtledoves or two pigeons is the sacrifice prescribed for the poor (cf. Luke 2:24).

Lev 6:16, 18, 26; 7:61 "Do you not know that those who are employed in the temple service get their food from the temple, and those who serve at the altar share in what is sacrificed on the altar?" (1 Cor 9:13).

Lev 6:22 ". . . The priest, anointed from among Aaron's descendants as a successor . . ." and Heb 7:23, ". . . the former priests were many in number, because they were prevented by death from continuing in office . . ." should be read in light of the text from Leviticus.

Lev 7:20 This is the first of thirteen instances of the so-called *kareth* penalty (see the note on this verse for an explanation of the penalty). Paul alludes to it in Rom 11:22, "Note then the kindness and the severity of God: severity toward those who have fallen, but God's kindness toward you, provided you continue in his kindness; otherwise you also *will be cut off*."

Lev 10:10; 11:47; 20:24-26 The question of separation from the Gentiles comes up in Gal 2:12, "for until certain people came from James, he used to eat with the Gentiles. But after they came, he drew back and kept himself separate for fear of the circumcision faction . . ." Paul himself uses this image in reference to separation from pagans in 2 Cor 6:17, "Therefore come out from them, and be separate from them, says the Lord, and touch nothing unclean; then I will welcome you . . ."

Leviticus 11 The dietary laws and the theme of separation are the background for Peter's dream in Acts 10:15, "The voice said to him again, a second time, 'What God has made clean, you must not call profane.'"

Lev 11:4 Matthew 23:24 says that the ". . . blind guides strain out the gnat but swallow a camel." While the gnat is indeed unclean, the camel is equally so according to Leviticus.

Lev 14:1-32 This text describes a ritual for restoration to the community of a person who has been healed of "leprosy." Compare this to Matt 8:4, "Go, show yourself to the priest, and offer the gift that Moses commanded, as a testimony to them." See also Luke 17:14.

Lev 15:25 Matthew's readers would understand that the hemorrhaging woman of Matt 9:20 was ritually unclean.

Lev 16:1-15 The Narrator first recalls the death of Aaron's two sons. Then YHWH tells Moses to tell Aaron that if he enters the sanctuary when he is not supposed to he will die. He is to come with the blood of the sacrificial goat. Compare this with Heb 10:19, "Therefore, my friends, since we have confidence to enter the sanctuary by the blood of Jesus . . ." See also Heb 9:12, "he entered once for all into the Holy Place, not with the blood of goats and calves, but with his own blood, thus obtaining eternal redemption."

Lev 16:29 The fast referred to in Acts 27:9 is that prescribed in Leviticus.

Lev 17:10-14 Gentile Christians should refrain from eating blood, Acts 15:20.

Lev 18:16; 20:21 In Matt 14:4 John the Baptist told Herod that it was not lawful to marry his brother's wife.

Lev 18:22; 20:13 A prohibition of homosexual relations appears also in Rom 1:27.

Lev 19:23-25 The owner should not expect fruit from trees in the first three years; cf. Luke 13:7.

Lev 19:33-34 The question "who is my neighbor?" (Luke 10:29) ignores the command to love the alien as oneself.

Lev 20:10 John's readers would recognize that the statement of those who brought the adulteress to Jesus, "Moses commanded us to stone such women" (John 8:5), was only halftrue. Leviticus requires the stoning of both the adulterer and the adulteress.

Lev 21:1 "Moses is to tell the priests, 'No one shall defile himself for a dead person among his relatives.'" Compare the command with Luke 10:31, "Now by chance a priest was going down that road; and when he saw him, he passed by on the other side."

Lev 21:10 In tearing his robes, the high priest in Matt 26:65 violates the law.

Lev 21:18 Compare Matt 11:5 where the blind receive their sight and the lame walk. "Blemishes" that excluded from priestly service are removed.

Lev 24:5-9 Matthew 12:4 describes the moment when David ". . . entered the house of God and ate the bread of the Presence, which it was not lawful for him or his companions to eat, but only for the priests."

Lev 25:10 Jesus proclaims the Jubilee in Luke 4:19.

Leviticus as Narrative?

When I tell colleagues and confreres that I am writing a commentary on Leviticus as narrative, they usually do a double take. "Leviticus as *narrative*?!" But, actually, I think that a good case can be made for Leviticus as narrative. After all, what else is it? It is part of a larger story. It is also the heart of that story. Leviticus creates a story world in which the priesthood and the sacrificial cult are instituted and in which the character "YHWH," in a series of speeches, lays out the conditions (both ritual and ethical) under which he, the Holy One, will dwell in the midst of the people.

Delimitation of Text— Where Does It Begin and End and Why?

We take as a given the present canonical shape of the book. It begins with the Lord calling Moses from the tent and ends with the narrator's conclusion: "These are the commandments that the LORD gave to Moses for the people of Israel on Mount Sinai" (Lev 27:34). But, apart from that, can Leviticus be treated as a literary unity? After all, Leviticus is not much separated from its surroundings. It even begins with a form of the verb *(wayyiqtol)* that assumes continuity with some previous narrative.

What happens before Leviticus begins? The book of Exodus ends with a narration of how Moses assembled all the materials for the cult including the tent. Once the tent is in place we are ready for the next step, which is the establishment of the priesthood and the ritual—and this is what we find in Leviticus.

What happens after Leviticus ends? Once the cult has been established, the people are ready to leave Mount Sinai—and this is what happens in the Book of Numbers, which begins with a census in preparation for establishing the order of march.

The Language of Leviticus

One reason for *not* treating Leviticus as a narrative could be the relative absence of a form of the Hebrew verb that is usually associated with narrative. This Hebrew verb form, called *wayyiqtol,* or "*waw* consecutive," is characteristic of narrative. The number of *wayyiqtol* forms in Leviticus is 188 (in 108 verses).

When the number of *wayyiqtol* verbs in Leviticus is compared with the number of the same form in Genesis (2113), Numbers (755), and Deuteronomy (252), we see that the narrative verb form is relatively scarce in Leviticus.

Many of the *wayyiqtol* verbs in Leviticus simply introduce speech. That is, many instances are simply the verb "he said" and not an action performed by a character in the story. If we eliminate these occurrences from our count of the typical narrative verb form, we end up with an even smaller number of *wayyiqtol* verb forms.

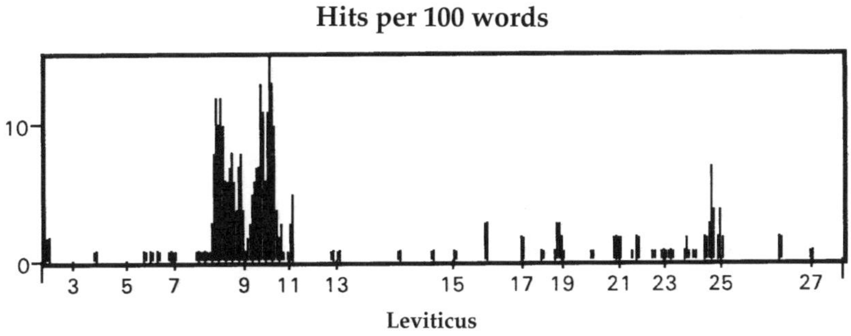

Total *Wayyiqtol* Verbs in Leviticus

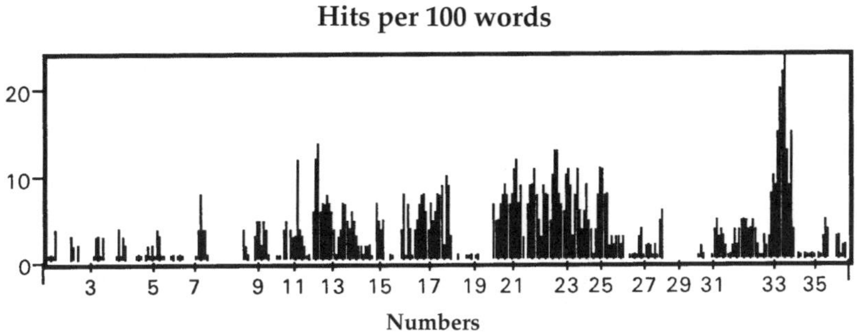

Wayyiqtol Verbs in Numbers

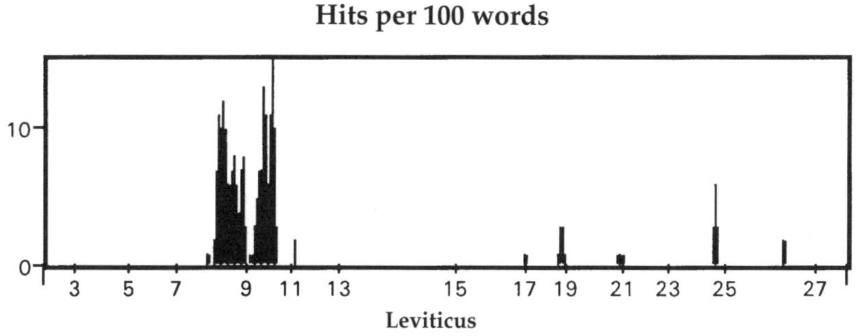

Wayyiqtol Verbs in Leviticus Minus *dbr* and *ʾmr*

As the graphics illustrate, most of these narrative forms occur in chapters 8-10, which narrate the ordination of the priests and the institution of the sacrificial cult. If, then, Leviticus can be treated as a narrative at all, it is one that has little action aside from the extended speeches made by one of the characters (YHWH). So the main focus of a narratological investigation must be on what these speeches contribute to the characterization of YHWH (Mann 1988, 116).

The Dearth of Descriptive Adjectives

Eighty-five adjectives occur a total of six hundred times in Leviticus, but most of these are numbers and demonstratives ("this," "that," "these"). Descriptive adjectives are relatively scarce in Leviticus (about forty-five vocables), but this is typical of biblical narrative in general. The more frequently occurring adjectives will help illustrate the interests of Leviticus:

tāmîm	whole	23x	sacrificial animals
ṭāhôr	clean	21x	
qdwš	holy	20x	
ṭmʾ	unclean	46x	
ymny	right	20x	
ḥy	living	23x	
lbn	white	20x	all in chapter 13 (scale disease)

Verbs

In Leviticus 272 different verbs are used 2,515 times. Apart from the most common words (be, make, give, come, say, speak, take), one may note a significantly high number of occurrences of words such as "approach/bring near" (*qrb* 102x), "to be unclean" (*ṭmʾ* 85x), "make atonement" (*kpr* 49x), "to purify" (*ṭhr* 43x), "to slaughter" (*šḥṭ* 36x), "to command" (*ṣwh* 35x), "to turn into smoke" (*qṭr* 33x).

About sixty vocables (twenty-seven of which only occur once) are used in participial form in Leviticus. The most common is *zwb* (flowing, 14x).

According to Sawyer (1996, 16) there is a remarkable dearth of the imperatives one might expect in a book of law; only forty-one, in fact. However, some of those are followed by perfect-tense verbs that continue the imperative meaning and there are 129 instances of *lôʾ* followed by a second-person imperfect (prohibition). Even at that, Sawyer is right. The number is low.

Nouns

There are relatively few personal names in Leviticus—about 19 out of a total of 25 proper nouns as opposed to 459 proper nouns in Genesis, 410 in Numbers, and 156 in Deuteronomy.

The most commonly occurring nouns are "priest" (194x), "son" (160x), "day" (113x), "blood" (88x), "altar" (87x), "land" (82x), "sin" (82x), "holocaust" (62x), "year" (59x), "house" (53x), "skin" (53x), "fat" (48x), "tent" (44x), "water" (43x), "people" (43x), "offering by fire" (42x), "offering" (*qorbān* 40x), "gift" (*minḥâ* 36x), "wife" (35x), "sacrifice" (35x), "fire" (32x), "nakedness" (32x).

Rhetorical Questions

There are only three questions in Leviticus, and two of these are clearly not rhetorical (10:17; 25:20). Possibly, but not necessarily, 10:19, "If I had eaten the sin offering today, would it have been agreeable to the LORD?" is a rhetorical question.

Time

Pace

When a writer tells the story of an event, there is a ratio between the actual time length of the event itself (the time it took to happen, called narrative time) and the time it takes to tell it (called narration time). This ratio can vary depending on the effect the writer wants to create.

In the case of Leviticus, since most of the book consists of speech, the ratio of narration time to narrated time is about even. In other words, the time it would take to happen and the time it takes to tell it are about the same (setting aside individual differences in the rate of speaking or reading).

The effect that this creates is that the reader seems to witness the event as it happens, as if in real time. Specifically, the reader is listening in as the Lord tells Moses (or Aaron) what to say to the people and the priests.

The narrative time = narration time ratio holds for most of the book, but there are some exceptions: for example, the summary statements that someone did as Moses or the Lord had commanded (8:4, 36), or that the people stoned the blasphemer (24:23). These take less time to tell than to do (narrative time is greater than narration time). The same is true of Moses' actions during the ordination ceremony in Leviticus 8–10.

Order

Jewish tradition sees at least the ordination ceremony of Leviticus 8–10 as a flashback *(analepsis)* that chronologically would come before Exodus 40 (Rosenbaum and Silverman 1946, 30). See also the commentary on 16:3-4.

Past, Present, Future

The divine speech narrated in Leviticus has already taken place in the past. This is indicated by the *waydabbēr* "[the Lord] spoke" with which each speech begins. We are being told what the Lord said to Moses. But what the Lord said was for Moses to speak to someone else. We are told in 21:24 that Moses did this. Likewise, in 23:44 Moses declared the appointed festivals to the people and in 24:23 Moses relayed the Lord's decision concerning the blasphemer to the people. Can we assume on the basis of 21:24 that Moses has passed on all the instructions that we have heard the Lord give to Moses? In reference to pace, these summary statements obviously take less narration time than would a narration that repeats every detail of the instruction (as one sometimes finds in the Septuagint).

Within the divine speech there are a few references to events prior to the divine speech. Among these there is one reference to the period of Egyptian servitude ("you were aliens in the land of Egypt," 19:34) and several references to the deliverance from Egypt (11:45; 19:36; 22:33, 43; 25:38, 42, 55; 26:13, 45). There are references to the abhorrent practices for which the Canaanites are being vomited out by the land (20:22-23). There is a reference to past worship of satyrs by the Israelites (17:7). And in 26:42 the patriarchs Abraham, Isaac, and Jacob are named (in reverse chronological order).

In a sense the whole narrative looks to the future inasmuch as it is setting up rituals that will continue to be carried out in the future. Some other indications of future orientation are the mention of houses (14:34; 25:29-33; 27:14-15), the name Canaan (14:34; 25:38), the expression *ḥoq/ḥuqqat ʿôlām* (perpetual statute, 17x), the use of *taḥtāyw* (in his place) in 6:15 (NRSV 6:22), which implies anointed priests who succeed Aaron (likewise 16:32), the words "When you come to the land and plant trees . . ." (19:23), and the reference to future exile ("I will scatter you among the nations . . ." (26:33; see also 38, 39, 41, 44,).

The story world portrays the character "the LORD" as one who foresees future conditions and makes provision for them.

Plot

If one understands plot in terms of the creation and resolution of tension, there is not much plot in Leviticus—but there is some:

Tension:

–the death of Nadab and Abihu (10:2) naturally creates tension

–the confrontation between Moses and Aaron over eating the sin-offering (at the end of Leviticus 10)

–the fate of the blasphemer must await Moses' consultation with the Lord (24:12)

–the pattern of command-fulfillment creates tension—will the pattern continue or will it be broken? (8:4, 36; 16:34; 24:23)

–will people be killed for failing to separate the holy from the profane?

–will the people be able to learn what is holy and what is profane so as to be able to keep them separate?

–will the people be able to avoid provoking YHWH to anger *(qṣp)*?

Another way of looking at plot is to ask the question: "What has changed between the beginning of the story and its end?" In Leviticus there are changes in character and changes in knowledge. Aaron and his sons are ordained and consecrated as priests and initiated into the cult. They and the people are instructed in matters of sacrifice, ritual purity, sanctification of time, and morality.

The death of Nadab and Abihu gives an object lesson in the vital necessity of properly separating the sacred from the profane in that it provokes YHWH's anger, which, in turn, leads to punishment.

Perhaps the fundamental tension in Leviticus revolves around the question: "How can the all-holy Lord, who cannot tolerate the unholy, dwell in the midst of a people who are, by the very nature of things, subject to contamination by the profane" (see 16:16)? The answer is a system of purification and atonement that will prevent the kind of explosive reaction that killed two of Aaron's sons (Mann 1988, 114–15).

This is only a partial resolution of tension—the people now know what to do, but will they do it? This second tension is reinforced by the command-fulfillment pattern in the narration but is itself left unresolved, thus providing a rhetorical challenge to the reader to complete the pattern by fulfilling the prescriptions of the law.

Moments

It does not appear that we can analyze the book of Leviticus according to the classic "moments" of the plot. However, it is worth noting that Mary Douglas (1995, 248) uses the term "exposition" in reference to chapters 1–7. According to Douglas these chapters enunciate the major themes that will be treated in the rest of the book.

Implied Narrative Structure of Laws

Even the individual laws have within them an implied narrative structure and are probably best described as problem-solution. That is, although they prescind from concrete instances, the laws can easily be imagined as involving a drama in which a problem arises for which the law is the solution. The problem creates tension and the solution resolves that tension:

1–3 A person wants to offer *(hiqrîb)* an offering *(qorbān)*. How is this to be done in a way that is acceptable to YHWH *(lirṣōnô lipnê yhwh* 3; *wᵊnirṣâ lô* 4*)* so that it will be an appeasing odor *(rêaḥ nîḥôaḥ)* to YHWH? The solution to this problem comes from the prescriptions for sacrifice.

4 Problem: A person or group of persons commits an inadvertent sin *(ḥṭʾ bišgāgâ)*. Solution: A means of atonement. This principle is first stated generally, and then specific cases are taken up: the high priest (3), the whole congregation (13), the ruler (*nāśîʾ* 22), a lay person (27).

Some sacrifices respond to the need to atone for sin and have an implied problem-solution narrative structure.

5:11-13 Problem: A person wants to atone for his/her sin, but cannot afford the cost of the prescribed sacrifice. Solution: A bird offering.

5:20-26 Problem: A person has sinned against a neighbor. Solution: Restitution and sacrifice (25-26).

6 Perhaps we could see the laws of Leviticus 6 in terms of a plot of knowledge. The tension is created by the implied need to know how to perform the various kinds of sacrifices in accordance with the will and holiness of the deity (so as to avoid the potentially lethal divine displeasure).

While some laws presume the good will of the subject, others are in the form of sanctions, such as the following:

7:20-21 Problem: A person in a state of ritual defilement eats some meat from a well-being sacrifice. Solution: Application of the *kārēth* penalty. (This term is explained in the note on this verse.)

7:25 Problem: A person eats fat. Solution: *kārēth.*

7:27 Problem: A person eats blood. Solution: *kārēth* (also 17:10-12).

11 Problem: Which animals can be eaten for food? Solution: Criteria for discerning cleanness or uncleanness.

12 Problem: How is a woman to be restored to ritual purity after childbirth? Solution: A ritual of restoration.

13 Problem: How is "leprosy" to be recognized? Solution: Criteria for diagnosis.

14 Problem: How is a cured "leper" to be restored to the worshiping community? Solution: A ritual of restoration.

14:21 Problem: The former "leper" is ready to be restored to the community but cannot afford the prescribed sacrifice for restoration. Solution: A less expensive (bird) offering.

14:33 Problem: How is "leprosy" in houses to be recognized and treated? Solution: Criteria for diagnosis and ritual prescriptions.

15 Problem: A person has a discharge and wishes to be restored to a state of ritual purity. Solution: A ritual of restoration.

16 Problem: The community needs to rid itself of the guilt of sin. Solution: The scapegoat.

17:1-9 Problem: How can the people be prevented from sacrificing to satyrs? Solution: Slaughtered domestic animals must be brought to the door of the tent of meeting. Further problem: Someone does not do this. Solution: *kārēth.*

17:13 Problem: What to do with the blood of an animal killed in a hunt. Solution: Pour the blood on the ground.

17:14b Problem: Someone eats the blood of an animal killed in a hunt. Solution: *kārēth.*

17:15 Problem: How to regain ritual purity after eating carrion. Solution: Bathe and wait until evening.

17:16 Problem: A person made ritually unclean by eating carrion does not bathe. Solution: He will bear his guilt.

18 Problem: What is YHWH's will regarding sexual morality (and child sacrifice to Molech, 18:21)? Solution: Instruction.

18:29 Problem: Someone commits abomination in the area of sexual morality. Solution: *kārēth.*

19:8 Problem: Someone eats sacrificial meat on the third day after the sacrifice. Solution: *kārēth.*

19:9-10 (also 23:22) Problem: How are the poor to be fed? Solution: Leave gleanings.

19:16b Problem: A person sees a neighbor in peril (whatever "standing by the blood" means) and must decide whether to help him or not. Solution: Do not stand by.

19:20-22 Problem: A man has sexual relations with a female slave who has been designated for another man. Solution: No indemnity; ritual atonement.

19:23-25 Problem: When can the fruit of a newly planted tree be eaten? Solution: In the fifth year.

20:2-5 Problem: Someone gives a child to Molech. Solution: Execution by stoning and *kārēth*. Further complication: People do not enforce the penalty. Solution: YHWH will enforce *kārēth* in any case.

20:6 Problem: Someone consults ghosts and spirits. Solution: *kārēth.*

20:9 Problem: Someone curses father or mother. Solution: Execution.

20:10 Problem: People commit adultery. Solution: Execution of both.

20:11 Problem: Someone commits incest with his father's wife. Solution: Execution of both.

20:12 Problem: Someone commits incest with his daughter-in-law. Solution: Execution.

20:13 Problem: Someone has sex with a person of the same gender. Solution: Execution.

20:14 Problem: A man takes a wife and her mother. Solution: Death by burning.

20:15-16 Problem: A man or a woman has sex with an animal. Solution: Execution.

20:17 Problem: A man commits incest with his sister. Solution: *kārēth* and *nśʾ ʿwn* (bearing guilt).

20:18 Problem: A man has sexual relations with a woman during her monthly period. Solution: *kārēth.*

20:19 Problem: A man has sexual relations with the sister of his father or mother. Solution: *nśʾ ʿwn* (bearing guilt).

20:20 Problem: A man has sexual relations with his uncle's wife. Solution: *nś' ḥṭ't* (bearing sin).

20:21 Problem: A man has sexual relations with his brother's wife. Solution: Childlessness.

20:27 Problem: A man or woman consults a necromancer. Solution: Execution by stoning.

21:1-6, 10-12 Problem: How shall the priests maintain ritual purity, especially when they mourn their dead? Solution: Avoid contact with the dead except in the case of one's nearest kin.

21:7-8, 13-15 Problem: What shall the priest look for in a wife? Solution: Negative and positive criteria.

21:9 Problem: A priest's daughter "plays the harlot." Solution: Death by burning.

21:16-23 Problem: A man of priestly lineage has a physical defect. Solution: He may not serve.

21:18-20 Problem: What physical defects exclude a man of priestly lineage from serving? Solution: A list of criteria.

22:3 Problem: A priest comes near holy things in a state of uncleanness. Solution: *kārēth.*

22:4-9 Problem: What uncleanness disqualifies a priest from serving and how is such a priest to be restored to a state of ritual cleanness? Solution: List of criteria and ritual of restoration.

22:10-16 Problem: Who in the priest's household may eat the holy things? Solution: A list of criteria.

22:17-25 Problem: What defects make animals unacceptable for sacrifice? Solution: A list of criteria.

23 Problem: How is time to be sanctified? Solution: The ritual calendar.

25 Problem: How can it be assured that equality is not undermined by differences in ability or good fortune? Solution: Forgiveness of debts and manumission of slaves every seven years with return of family property every fifty years.

25:20-21 Problem: If people let the land lie fallow in the seventh year, what will they eat? Solution: YHWH will provide an increase in food the year before the sabbatical year.

25:25-28 Problem: A brother becomes poor and has to sell property to pay his debts, resulting in an alienation of tribal land holdings. Solution: His redeemer *(gōʾēl)* will redeem the property. Further complication: He has no *gōʾēl,* but earns enough to buy his property back. Solution: He compensates for the number of harvests remaining till the Jubilee Year. Another scenario: Problem: He cannot afford to buy back the property. Solution: His property reverts to him in the Jubilee Year.

25:35-38 Problem: A "brother" becomes dependent on another. Solution: Let him live as a resident alien. Do not charge him interest on a loan.

25:39-43 Problem: A "brother" sells himself to a fellow Israelite. Solution: He is to be treated as a hired laborer and not as a slave. He is to be released in the Jubilee Year.

25:47-55 Problem: A "brother" sells himself to a non-Israelite. Solution: Redemption by kin or by self. If not, release will follow in the Jubilee Year.

27 Problem: A person wants to redeem someone or something vowed. Solution: He replaces the monetary value.

As tedious as it is, there is an implied narrative in each condition.

Structure

Christopher Smith (1996) proposes a seven-member structure of alternating laws and narrative:

Chapter	Genre	Topic
1–7	laws	ritual offerings
8–10	narrative	need to distinguish holy/profane
11–15	laws	reparable uncleanness
16	narrative	Day of Atonement
17:1–24:9	laws	holiness
24:10-23	narrative	the blasphemer
25–27	law	redemption

There is much to like in Smith's proposal and much useful insight to be found in his article. However, while Smith rightly points out that the root *gʾl* occurs seventeen times in chapter 25 and twelve times in chapter 27 but nowhere else in the rest of Leviticus, he has some difficulty in explaining chapter 26. Also, the attempt to read chapter 16 as narrative is not very convincing.

Structuring Elements of Leviticus

One clear structuring element is the formula "The Lord spoke to Moses" *(wayydabbēr yhwh ʾel-mōšeh),* which occurs thirty-five times in Leviticus.

Verse	Verse before	Preceding Conclusion	Beginning	Audience
1:1	none		*dabbēr*	children of Israel
4:1	3:17	yes: *ḥuqqat ʿôlām*	*dabbēr*	children of Israel
5:14	5:13	yes: *wᵊkipper hakkōhēn*	*nepeš kî*	
5:20	5:19	yes: *ʾāšām hûʾ*	*nepeš kî*	
6:1	5:26	yes: *wᵊkipper hakkōhēn*	*ṣaw*	Aaron and sons
6:12	6:11		*zeh qorban*	
6:17	6:16		*dabbēr*	Aaron and sons
7:22	7:21		*dabbēr*	children of Israel
7:28	7:27	yes: *kārēth* formula	*dabbēr*	children of Israel
8:1	7:35-38	yes: summary	*qaḥ*	Aaron and sons
11:1	10:20	yes: conclusion	*dabbᵊrû*	children of Israel
12:1	11:46-47	yes: summary	*dabbēr*	children of Israel
13:1	12:8	yes: *wᵊkipper hakkōhēn*	*ʾādām kî*	
14:1	13:59	yes: summary	*zōʾt tihyeh*	
14:33	14:32	yes: summary	*kî tābōʾû*	
15:1	14:54-57	yes: summary	*dabbᵊrû*	children of Israel
16:1	15:32-33	yes: summary	*dabbēr*	Aaron your brother
17:1	16:34b	yes: fulfillment	*dabbēr*	Aaron, sons, and Israel
18:1	17:16	yes: *wᵊnāśāʾ ʿăwōnô*	*dabbēr*	children of Israel
19:1	18:30	yes: *ʾănî yhwh*	*dabbēr*	children of Israel
20:1	19:37	yes: *ʾănî yhwh*	*wᵊʾel bᵊnê*	
21:16	21:15	yes: *ʾănî yhwh*	*dabbēr*	Aaron
22:1	21:23	yes: *ʾănî yhwh*	*dabbēr*	Aaron and sons
22:17	22:16	yes: *ʾănî yhwh*	*dabbēr*	Aaron and sons
22:26	22:25		*šôrʾ ô keśeb*	
23:1	22:32b-33	yes: *ʾănî yhwh*	*dabbēr*	children of Israel
23:9	23:8		*dabbēr*	children of Israel

23:23	23:22	yes: *ʾănî yhwh*	*dabbēr*	children of Israel
23:26	23:25		*ʾak beʿāśôr*	
23:33	23:32		*dabbēr*	children of Israel
24:1	23:44	yes: fulfillment	*ṣaw*	children of Israel
24:13	24:12		*hôṣē*	
25:1	24:23	yes: execution	*dabbēr*	children of Israel
27:1	26:46	yes: summary	*dabbēr*	children of Israel

Subsections are sometimes marked by *wᵊʾim.* The phrase *ḥuqqat* (or *ḥoq*) *ʿôlām* occurs seventeen times in Leviticus (at the end of the verse in 7:36; 10:9; 16:31; and 24:9); *wᵊkipper* occurs twenty-seven times, frequently with words such as *ʿālāyw hakkōhēn wᵊnislaḥ lô* (eleven times at the end of a verse); *wᵊnikrᵊtâ hannepeš* occurs nine times (seven at the end of a verse); *nśʾ ʿwn* about seven times; *ʾănî yhwh* fifty-two times (often at the end of a verse); *môt yûmāt* twelve times (twice at the end of a verse); *lōʾ yērāṣeh* four times. Other concluding formulae are "It is an x" (Hebrew: x *hûʾ/hîʾ*), "this is the instruction on x" *(zōʾt tôrat* x*),* "it will be forgiven" *(nislaḥ),* "he will atone" *(wᵊkippēr),* "it is acceptable" *(yērāṣeh),* and "a pleasing odor to YHWH" *(rēᵃḥ nîḥôᵃḥ lyhwh).*

Another structuring element in Leviticus is the use of various introductory formulae: *ʾādām kî* 1:2; 13:2; *nepeš kî* 2:1; 4:2; 5:1; 5:4, 15, 17, 21; 7:21; *ʾiššâ kî* 12:2; 13:29, 38; 15:19, 25; 20:27; *ʾîš kî* 13:40; 15:2, 16; 19:20; 22:14, 21; 24:15, 17, 19; 25:26, 29; 27:2, 14; *bat kōhēn kî* 22:12, 13; *kōhēn kî* 22:11; *ʾîš ʾîš* 15:2; 17:3, 8, 10, 13; 18:6; 20:2, 9; 22:4, 18; 24:15.

Smith (1996, 18) points out that Leviticus is framed by an *inclusio* that consists of the designation of the tent of meeting as the place from which God spoke (a designation only found in Lev 1:1 and Num 1:1).

Characterization

In General

Only twenty characters are named in Leviticus (including YHWH, the Levites, the Israelites, Azazel, and Molech). Of these twenty names, eleven occur only once.[1] Of the rest, Eleazar, Ithamar, and Azazel occur three times each, Molech four times, and the Levites are mentioned four times (in two verses). The people/assembly and the priests also function corporately as characters in the story.

[1] Nadab, Abihu, Mishael, Elzaphan, Uzziel, Shlomith, Dibri, Dan, Jacob, Isaac, Abraham. Nadab and Abihu are referred to as "the sons of Aaron" in 16:1.

The main characters in Leviticus are YHWH, Moses, and Aaron. Of these, it is significant that YHWH's name occurs 311 times compared with Moses (86x) and Aaron (80x). After them come the Israelites (65x).

YHWH

As Mann (1996, 116) points out, Leviticus is of supreme importance in the characterization of YHWH.

Words and Deeds

Self-Characterization

Certainly, the most authoritative characterizations of YHWH are those he makes of himself. YHWH characterizes himself as "holy" *(qādôš)* (11:45; 19:2; 20:26; 21:8). He shows himself holy in those who are near him (10:3). YHWH wants the people to be holy as he is holy (19:2). To this end he separates them from other peoples (20:24, 26) and sanctifies them (20:8; 21:8, 15, 23; 22:9, 16, 32). They, in turn, are to learn to separate the clean from the unclean (20:25).

Speaking to the people, he calls himself "your (singular or plural) God" (2:13; 18:2, 4, 21, 30; 19:2, 3, 4, 10, 12, 14, 25, 31, 32, 34, 36; 20:7, 24; 21:8; 22:25; 23:14, 22, 28, 40, 43; 24:22; 25:17, 36, 38, 43, 55; 26:1, 13). He is the One who brought the people out of Egypt (*yṣʾ* Hiphil 19:36; 22:33, 43; 25:38, 42, 55; 26:13, 45; *ʿlh* Hiphil 11:45). In doing so, he broke the bars of their yoke, thus enabling them to stand upright (26:13). He is bringing the people to Canaan (18:3) from which he is expelling the previous inhabitants whom he abhors on account of their immoral practices (18:24; 20:23). He is giving Canaan to the children of Israel (20:24; 23:10; 25:2, 38). But the land remains his (25:23). The people are his servants (25:42, 55).

YHWH's Commands

YHWH wants the people to fear him who is their God (25:17). YHWH is one who gives commands (*ṣwh* 33x; *miṣwâ* 10x). YHWH commands what he regards as acceptable (*ḥšb* Niphal 7:18; 17:4) and pleasing (*rṣh* Niphal, *rāṣôn* 1:3, 4; 7:18; 19:5, 7; 22:19, 20, 21, 23, 25, 27, 29; 23:11). Specified sacrificial animals without physical defects (*tāmîm* 23x; without *mûm* 3x) are to be slaughtered before him (1:5, 11; 3:8, 13; 4:4, 15, 24; 6:18). The burnt portion of the sacrifice is food offered to YHWH (3:11) and the fat (suet: *peder* 3x; *ḥēleb* 49x) is his (3:16), as is the tithe (27:30). The sacrifices are to be turned into smoke (*hiqtîr* 32x), which makes an appeasing odor to YHWH (*rêaḥ nîḥôaḥ* 16x).

In several instances YHWH makes particular provision for the poor either by mitigating the requirements for sacrifice (5:7, 11; 12:8; 14:21) or by instructing that harvesters leave grain and grapes for the poor to glean (19:9-10; 23:22).

YHWH also gives portions of what the people offer him to the priests, who have no land from which to earn income. YHWH gives a portion *[ḥēleq]* of the offerings he receives to the priests (6:17; 7:33; 8:29 *[mānâ]*; 7:35 *[mišḥâ]*; 7:34). YHWH gives the breast of the *tᵊnûpâ* (Milgrom 1991a, 461-73, "elevation offering") and the thigh of the *tᵊrûmâ* (Milgrom 1991a, 415-6, "contribution") to Aaron and his children (cf. 10:14-15).

In Leviticus 11 YHWH instructs the people as to which animals are clean and can legitimately be eaten. He provides them with the means by which anyone who has been defiled can return to a state of cleanness (11:26ff). He provides for the purification of a woman after childbirth (Leviticus 12) and orders the circumcision of the male children (12:3). He also instructs the people on "leprosy" (Milgrom 1991a, 774-6, "scale disease") in persons and in things (Leviticus 13–14).

YHWH provides for the sanctification of time by organizing the calendar and designating days of feast (Leviticus 23), fast (16:29, 31; 23:27, 29, 32), abstention from work (16:29; 23:7, 8, 21, 25, 35, 36), and rejoicing (23:40). He provides for a sabbatical year (24:4) every seven years and a Jubilee Year every forty-nine years (25:8-16), at which time liberty is to be proclaimed (25:10) and land that has been alienated is to be redeemed (25:24).

He commands the people to cleanse themselves from their sins (16:30) and prescribes the use of blood as an agent for atonement (17:11).

In everyday human affairs YHWH requires that reverence for YHWH *(yrʾ)* manifest itself in reverence for one's father and mother (19:3), not shaming the deaf or the blind (19:14), respect for the aged (19:32), not cheating (25:17), not taking interest (*nešek, tarbît, marbît* 25:36), and not treating indentured servants harshly (25:43).

YHWH also prescribes the use of just weights and measures (19:36) as well as the application of the law of the talion (24:19-20). YHWH requires that the laws apply equally to native and foreigner (19:34; 24:22), but allows the purchase of foreigners as slaves (25:44) while requiring the redemption of Hebrew slaves (25:47-55). YHWH specifies the monetary value of persons who are sold (Leviticus 27).

YHWH details the penalties for failure to comply with his laws (20:9ff), and imposes penalties for breaches of the law, including the death penalty. In imposing the death penalty YHWH sometimes specifies the method of execution (stoning: 20:2, 27; 24:14, 16, 23; burning: 20:14; 21:9).

YHWH's Prohibitions

YHWH's name must not be profaned (22:32). Such profanation occurs when people offer their children to Molech through fire (18:21) or when they swear falsely in YHWH's name (19:12) or when the priests do not properly administer sacred donations (22:2).

YHWH forbids dishonesty in human affairs, which he regards as a breach of faith with himself (6:1-5; 25:17). He prohibits eating sacrificial meat on the third day (7:18), eating unclean animals (11), sacrificing to satyrs in the fields (17:5, 7), doing as the Egyptians and Canaanites (18:3), illicit sexual unions (18:6ff), swearing falsely (19:12), illicit mixtures of species, seed and cloth (19:19 also 18:23 and 20:12 *tebel*), augury and witchcraft (19:26), self-laceration and tattoos (19:28; 21:5 gashes), priests with bodily defects approaching the altar (21:17, 18, 21, 23), interest on loans (25:36-37), idols (26:1, also 19:4), and redemption of a doomed person (*ḥērem* 27:29).

There are things that are offensive (*piggûl* 7:18; 19:7) or an abomination to YHWH (*tôʿēbâ* 18:22, 26, 27, 29, 30; 20:13). He has, in fact, abhorred (*qûṣ*) the nations that he cast out of Canaan on account of their deeds (20:23).

YHWH's Punishments

YHWH will exact *kārēth* (17x, beginning in 7:20; of those, 13 Niphal, 4 Hiphil). Defilement of YHWH's house brings death (15:31). YHWH will set his face against the guilty person (*ntn pānîm* 17:10; 20:3, 6, 34; 26:17). YHWH will cause to perish (*ʾbd* Hiphil) the person who works on the Day of Atonement (23:30). YHWH will set his face against and cut off the person who offers his children to Molech or anyone who does not take actions against such a person (20:3-4) or who whores after mediums (20:6).

YHWH's Promises

YHWH promises to provide extra food for the fallow Sabbath year (25:21). Leviticus 26:3-13 lists a series of blessings which YHWH promises if the people are faithful in observing YHWH's statutes, in fulfillment of the covenant: rain, produce, fruit, over-abundance of food, peace, freedom from dangerous animals, freedom from the sword, victory over enemies, numerous progeny. All of these culminate in YHWH's presence in the midst of his people.

YHWH's Threats

But if the people are not faithful, 26:14-36 details a series of punishments (said four times to be multiplied sevenfold) that will take the blessings listed above and reverse them: terror, consumption, fever, pining, food stolen by enemies, defeat in battle, being ruled over by enemies, lack of rain, lack of food, destruction of livestock and children by wild animals, the sword, pestilence, starvation and cannibalism in time of siege, destruction, refusal by YHWH to accept sacrifices, exile, faintness, and skittishness.

But these threats are not the end of the story, for, if the people repent, YHWH will remember his covenant with Jacob, Isaac, and Abraham (26:40-45).

Other Traits

YHWH's Speech

YHWH is someone who calls (1:1) and speaks (*waydabbēr yhwh* 35x) with Moses and Aaron. He gives commands (*ṣwh* or *miṣwâ* 45x), regulations (*mišpāt* 14x), and statutes (*ḥoq* 11x; *ḥuqqâ* 26x). His statutes are eternal (3:17; 7:36; 10:9; 16:29, 31, 34; 17:7; 23:14, 21, 31, 41; 24:3) and they bring life (18:5).

Since most of Leviticus is YHWH's speech, one can get an idea of what the character's interests are by studying the most frequently occurring words. Among these would be: priest (196x), bring near (170x), holy (152x), unclean (150x), sacrifice (130x), sin (116x), to face (112x), to eat (106x), blood (88x), clean (74x), flesh (61x), year (59x), atone (*kpr* 49x), fat (49x), guilt (38x), smoke (38x), slaughter (36x), offering (*minḥâ* 36x).

YHWH's personal investment in his discourse is indicated by his speaking in the first person. This is especially true of the concluding exhortation in chapter 26. (See the list of first-person YHWH speeches in the section on voices.)

YHWH's Actions

YHWH's glory appears to the people in 9:23 and YHWH appears in a cloud over the *kapporet* (16:2). This appearance is potentially lethal.

Fire comes out from YHWH's presence *(millipnê yhwh)* and consumes the first sacrifice (9:24) but also, at another time, the fire consumes Nadab and Abihu, two of Aaron's sons (10:2, 6).

YHWH Uses the Theological Passive

Niphal

rṣh "it will be treated (by YHWH) as acceptable" 1:4; 7:18; 19:7; 22:25, 27.

slḥ "it will be forgiven (by YHWH)" 4:20, 26, 31, 35; 5:10, 13, 16, 18, 26; 19:22.

ḥšb "it is reckoned (by YHWH) as . . ." 7:18; 17:4.

krt "to be cut off (by YHWH) from one's kin" 7:20, 21, 25, 27; 17:4, 9, 14; 18:29; 19:8; 20:17, 18; 22:3, 29.

ntn "given (by YHWH)" 10:14; 26:25.

Pual

mᵊṣōrâ one struck (by YHWH?) with scale disease.

Hophal

hôdaᶜ when the sin is made known (by YHWH?) 4:23, 28.

Moses

Action

Perhaps the most salient characteristic of Moses in Leviticus is that he does as YHWH has commanded (8:4; 16:34; 23:44; 24:33). Moses is a person to whom YHWH calls and with whom he speaks (1:1). He is able to pass on YHWH's commands to Aaron and his sons (6:9; 9:7). Moses suddenly bursts into a flurry of activity in 8:6-30 (the ordination ceremony), where he is the subject of fifty-one *wayyiqtol* verbs. He and Aaron enter the tent, then come out and bless the people (9:23). Moses makes careful inquiry *(dārōš dāraš)* about the goat for the sin offering and is angry *(wayyiqṣōp)* when he discovers that it has not been consumed, but accepts Aaron's explanation (10:20).

Speech

All the speeches of Moses in Leviticus take place in chapters 8–10 and consist of giving instruction to the priests on ritual matters to be observed. Moses speaks for the first time in 8:5, immediately before the intense activity of 8:6-30. In 8:31-35 he gives directions to the priests during their ordination. A peculiarity of this section that touches on the characterization of Moses is the verb *ṣiwwêtî* "I commanded" in verse 31 (see the note on this verse). Even though it is clear that the commands Moses conveys are ultimately YHWH's, if one takes the Hebrew text at face value it seems that YHWH speaks through Moses to such an extent that Moses can speak of commands that he gives. See also the discussion on the melding of voices in Leviticus.

The voice of Moses is also heard in 9:2-4, 6-7, again giving directions to Aaron about matters of ritual.

Moses speaks next in 10:3 where he quotes (a hitherto unknown) saying of YHWH to explain the death of Aaron's sons. In 10:4 he orders the removal of the bodies of Nadab and Abihu and in 10:6-7 he orders the priests neither to perform the customary mourning nor to depart from the tent. In 10:12-15 he gives further rubrical instructions and in verses 17-18 asks why the sin offering has not been consumed. These are the last words of Moses in Leviticus.

Aaron

Aaron becomes a man of action in 9:8-22, where he is the subject of twenty-two *wayyiqtol* verbs and his sons are the subject of an additional four verbs, all having to do with the initiation of the sacrificial cult.

Aaron is specifically said to have carried out the Lord's commandments (8:36; 9:8, 12; 10:7, the last being the command not to mourn the death of his sons Nadab and Abihu).

On one occasion YHWH, who usually relays commands through Moses, does so through Aaron (10:8). In 13:1 Aaron joins Moses to receive instruction from YHWH on "leprosy."

Aaron lifts his hands toward the people and blesses them (9:22). He then enters the tent with Moses, leaves it, and the two of them bless the people.

When Moses angrily questions Aaron's sons Ithamar and Eleazar about why they have not consumed the goat offered as a sin offering, Aaron responds to the question (10:19).

One puzzling aspect of the characterization of Aaron comes in 10:3 due to the occurrence of a homophone. After two of Aaron's sons, Nadab and Abihu, have been consumed by fire, Moses gives Aaron a word from YHWH that interprets the event. The word that then describes Aaron's reaction can be read in two ways. It can either mean "he kept still" or "he wailed." There are advocates for both interpretations. If the former is adopted, then Aaron might be characterized as stoic, accepting YHWH's will, etc. If the latter is chosen, then Moses' command not to mourn (10:6) receives its motivation.

Nadab and Abihu

Nadab and Abihu are sons of Aaron who offered illicit fire (*ʾēš zārâ*), which the Lord had not commanded (10:1). As a result they were consumed by fire that came out from the presence of YHWH. Their bodies were carried outside the camp. The phrase "which the Lord did not command" may suggest idol worship (Deut 17:3; Jer 7:31; 19:5; 32:35; cf. Milgrom 1991a, 628–33).

The People/Congregation

YHWH characterizes the people as sojourners *(gērîm)* and foreigners *(tôšābîm)* in his land (25:23), as his servants (25:55), but also as "uncircumcised of ear" (26:41), who once sacrificed to satyrs in open fields (17:5, 7). In 9:5 the congregation draws near and stands before YHWH. When they see YHWH's glory, they shout (*rnn*—probably a joyful sound) and fall on their faces (9:24). They carry out YHWH's order to stone the blasphemer (24:23).

Azazel

Azazel is apparently thought of as a being (although some commentators doubt this) that inhabits the wilderness (16:10) and to whom the goat bearing the people's guilt is sent (Milgrom 1991a, 1020–21).

Molech

Molech is conceived of as a being to whom people give *(ntn)* their children. In one verse (18:21) this giving is also characterized by the verb *ʿbr* Hiphil, "to cause to cross." Elsewhere in the Bible this passing is said to be through fire (2 Kgs 23:10). Some interpret this as simply passing the child through fire, but most understand it as referring to child sacrifice.

The Blasphemer

The blasphemer is the son of an Israelite woman and an Egyptian father (an example of the kind of illicit mixing that Leviticus wants to avoid). He goes out among the people and quarrels with a man of Israel in the camp (24:10). He blasphemes the name and curses (24:11). At this point the narrator informs us that the blasphemer's mother's name was Shelomith, daughter of Dibri of the tribe of Dan. Since the man's name is not given, we may wonder if the mother's name is meant to have some symbolic meaning. Does the name Shelomith suggest devotion to the Canaanite god Shalem, thereby portraying the family as less than loyal Yahwists? Or is the name related to the story, and so intended to be read as meaning something like: PAY-BACK, daughter of MY WORD, son of [THE DEITY] HAS JUDGED?

Egypt/Canaan/The Men of the Land

The Egyptians and Canaanites are characterized by the immoral practices listed in 18:6-23. Since this characterization comes from YHWH, it is supremely authoritative. The men of the land (i.e., the previous inhabitants of Canaan who, elsewhere, are said to have been vomited out by the land) are characterized as committing abominations (18:27).

The Land

The land vomits out its inhabitants (18:25, 28 [2x]; 20:22). It also flows with milk and honey (20:24).

Voices

The story is highly mediated. That is, we hear the narrator telling what the Lord told Moses to tell the people (or Aaron and his sons). These levels of mediation imitate (in reverse direction) the mediation found in the cult—i.e., people bring their sacrifices to the priest who places them on the altar to turn them into smoke (which ascends to God).

Of the 859 verses in Leviticus, about 21 (2%) are spoken by Moses; in 110 (13%) we hear the voice of the narrator; 727 (85%) are spoken by the Lord. In addition, Aaron speaks in 10:19.

The Narrator

The whole book of Leviticus is a third-person narrative in which the narrator tells us what the Lord or Moses or Aaron or the people said or did. The first and last voice we hear in Leviticus is that of the narrator. Most of the time the narrator simply tells us who is speaking.

Of the 859 verses in Leviticus, a maximum of 115, or roughly 13%, can be assigned to the narrator directly; in these verses the narrator speaks with his own voice rather than reporting the speech of a character in the narrative.

The interventions of the narrator can be classified as follows:

1) indication of speaker (48 verses);

2) report of fulfillment of command (6 verses);

3) summary conclusion (6 verses);

4) narrative (two narratives totaling about 53 verses).

There is some ambiguity as to the identity of the speaker in the summary statements at 7:35-38; 11:46-47; 13:59; 14:32, 54-57; 15:32-33; 26:46; 27:34. In several of these it is not clear whether they represent the end of the Lord's speech or the narrator's conclusion. In fact they have been treated differently by various translations. In the following, "yes" means that the verse(s) is/are included within quotation marks as part of the divine speech; "no" means that they are not included and, therefore, presumably are attributed to the narrator. In one case (15:32-33 in NJB) the verses are treated as a quotation within a quotation.

Verse	NAB	NJB	CCB	TOB	BLA	Magaña	DHHoy	Hamp	NASB
7:35-38	no	no	no	part	yes	no	no	no	part
11:46-47	yes	no	yes	no	?	yes	no	yes	no
13:49	yes	yes	yes	no	yes	yes	no	yes	no
14:32	yes	yes	yes	no	yes	yes	no	yes	yes
15:32-33	yes	“ ‘ ’ ”	yes	no	yes	yes	no	yes	no
26:46	no	no	no	no	no	no	no	no	no
27:34	no	no	no	no	no	no	no	no	no

If one studies the use of *zōʾt* or *zōʾt tôrat* in Leviticus, the formula can credibly be attributed to the divine voice in all verses except 27:34, where it can scarcely be attributed to the Lord. Since 27:34 is clearly not part of the divine speech, but must be attributed to the narrator, the same can plausibly be said of the other concluding formulas. However, there is also the distinct possibility that the ambiguity in identifying the voice of these passages reflects a deliberate strategy to meld the voices of the divine speaker and the narrator. This would, at one and the same time, both bolster the authority of the text and signify its inadequacy as but a mediated reflection of the divine will. In revelation, the divine is simultaneously hidden and revealed.

So, it is important to remember that throughout the book we are listening on the top level to the voice of the narrator. The fact that some editions use quotation-within-quotation marks for the words that YHWH tells Moses to speak indicates the layering of voices. The melding of voices can be seen in YHWH's frequent references to himself in the third person.

The Divine Speeches

YHWH's speech is a mixture of third-person case-type regulations (if someone wants to x, let them y, z) mixed with direct second-person (singular and plural) address. Often the Lord's speech takes on a more personal aspect with the use of first-person references. In the following list the chapter number comes first, followed by the number of instances of first-person speech by YHWH in that chapter, and then the chapter and verse citations.

First-Person Speech by YHWH in Leviticus

01-0
02-0
03-0
04-0
05-0
06-1: 6:10 I have given . . . from my offerings
07-1: 7:34 I have taken . . . and I have given
08-0
09-0
10-0 [YHWH quoted by Moses]
11-2: 11:44 For I am YHWH your God . . . for holy am I
11:45 For I am YHWH who brought you up from the land of Egypt to be your God . . . for holy am I
12-0
13-0
14-1: 14:34 The land of Canaan which I have given to you . . . I will set the plague of leprosy on a house of your possession
15-1: 15:31 my dwelling
16-1: 16:2 In the cloud I will appear over the cover
17-4: 17:10 I will set my face against the soul that eats blood and I will cut it off from the midst of its people
17:11 I have set it for you on the altar
17:12 I said
17:14 I said
18-10: 18:2 I am YHWH your God
18:3 I brought you from there
18:4 my decisions . . . my statutes . . . I am YHWH your God
18:5 my statutes . . . my decisions . . . I am YHWH
18:6 I am YHWH
18:21 I am YHWH
18:24 I am casting out before you
18:25 I visited its guilt upon it
18:26 my statutes . . . my decisions
18:30 my charge . . . I am YHWH your God
19-17: 19:2 for holy am I YHWH your God
19:3 I am YHWH your God

19:4 I am YHWH your God
19:10 I am YHWH your God
19:12 In my name . . . I am YHWH
19:14 I am YHWH
19:16 I am YHWH
19:18 I am YHWH
19:19 my statutes
19:25 I am YHWH your God
19:28 I am YHWH
19:30 my sanctuary . . . I am YHWH
19:31 I am YHWH your God
19:32 I am YHWH
19:34 I am YHWH your God
19:36 I am YHWH your God who brought you out from the land of Egypt
19:37 my statutes . . . my decisions . . . I am YHWH

20-9: 20:3 I will set my face against that man and I will cut him off from the midst of his people . . . my sanctuary . . . my holy name
20:5 I will set my face against that man and his clan and I will cut him off, and all who whore after him by whoring after Molech from the midst of their people
20:6 I will set my face against that soul and I will cut him off from the midst of his people
20:8 my statutes . . . I am YHWH who sanctify you
20:22 my statutes . . . my decisions . . . I brought you there
20:23 I am casting out before you . . . I abhorred them
20:24 I said to you . . . I will give it . . .
I am YHWH your God who have separated you from the peoples
20:25 I separated
20:26 You will be to me holy for holy am I YHWH
I separated you from the peoples to belong to me

21-4: 21:8 for holy am I YHWH who sanctify you
21:12 I am YHWH
21:15 for I YHWH sanctify him
21:23 . . . my sanctuary for I YHWH sanctify them

22-9: 22:2 my holy name . . . [they dedicate] to me; I am YHWH
22:3 from before me I am YHWH
22:8 I am YHWH
22:9 my charge . . . I YHWH sanctify them
22:16 for I YHWH sanctify them

22:30 I am YHWH
22:31 my commandments . . . I am YHWH
22:32 my holy name that I may be sanctified . . . I am YHWH who sanctify you
22:33 who brought you out from the land of Egypt to be your God I YHWH

23-5: 23:2 my festivals
23:10 which I gave to you
23:22 I am YHWH your God
23:30 I will destroy that soul from the midst of her people
23:43 I made them dwell . . . when I brought them out from the land of Egypt I YHWH your God

24-1: 24:22 for I am YHWH your God

25-8: 25:2 the land that I am giving to you
25:17 for I am YHWH your God
25:18 my statutes . . . my decisions
25:21 I will command my blessing
25:23 for mine is the land since you are sojourners and aliens with me
25:38 I am YHWH your God
who brought you out from the land of Egypt
to give you the land of Canaan to be your God
25:42 for they are my slaves whom I brought out from the land of Egypt
25:55 for to me the children of Israel are slaves; my slaves are they whom I brought out from the land of Egypt; I YHWH

26-34: 26:1 for I am YHWH your God
26:2 my Sabbaths shall you observe and my sanctuary shall you reverence I YHWH
26:3 my statutes . . . my commandments
26:4 I will give your rains in their time
26:6 I will set peace in the land . . . I will remove evil animals from the land
26:9 I will turn to you and make you fruitful and numerous I will fulfill my covenant with you
26:11 I will put my dwelling in your midst and my soul will not abhor you
26:12 I will be walking in your midst and I will be to you God and you will be to me a people
26:13 I am YHWH your God who brought you out from the land of Egypt from being their slaves and I broke the bars of your yoke and caused you to walk upright

26:14 *lî* to me
26:15 my statutes . . . my decisions . . . my commandments . . . my covenant
26:16 I for my part will do this to you: I will bring terror on you
26:17 I will set my face against you
26:18 If you will not listen to me I will continue . . .
26:19 I will break your proud strength and I will make your skies like iron and your land like copper
26:21 If you oppose me and are not willing to heed me I will continue to plague you . . .
26:22 I will send against you the animals of the field
26:23 If you do not turn back to me . . . but oppose me
26:24 I for my part will oppose you and I myself will strike you
26:25 I will bring a sword against you . . . I will send pestilence into you
26:26 When I break your staff of bread
26:27 If you will not heed me . . . and oppose me . . .
26:28 I will oppose you furiously and I will punish you myself, I will
26:30 I will destroy your high-places and I will cut down your incense altars; I will put your corpses on the corpses of your idols and my soul will abhor you
26:31 I will make your cities rubble and desolate your sanctuaries and I will not inhale your soothing aromas
26:32 I will desolate the land
26:33 and as for you I will scatter you among the nations and I will unsheathe behind you a sword
26:36 I will send despondency into their hearts
26:40 their treachery against me and opposition to me
26:41 I for my part opposed them and I brought them into the land of their enemies
26:42 I will remember my covenant with Jacob and my covenant with Abraham I will remember and the land I will remember
26:43 my decisions . . . my statutes
26:44 I will not spurn them and I will not abhor them so as to destroy them utterly and break my covenant with them for I am YHWH their God
26:45 I will remember for them the covenant of the first ones whom I brought from the land of Egypt before the eyes of the peoples to be their God I YHWH

27-0

Such personal investment in the speech is particularly evident in chapter 26, which functions as a kind of peroration to the book.

The speeches sometimes begin with a second-person plural form and then proceed to third-person case-type style. At other times they begin by stating a general principle in second-plural address and then move to second-singular specifications.

Numeruswechsel

Commentators have sought some rationale for the switching between singular and plural in the second-person addresses (sometimes referred to by the German term *Numeruswechsel*). In some cases it seems that a speech begins with an address to the whole people (plural) in an introductory general statement and then moves to address the people as individuals for rhetorical effect. Sometimes the second-person introduction is followed by third-person case law. This phenomenon can be illustrated from the KJV since it preserves the distinction between singular and plural second-person forms in English.

The following list is based on a computer check of the KJV but has been checked against the Hebrew. The only example missing from KJV is Lev 25:46 (see below).

Lev 10:9 Do not drink wine nor strong drink, *thou*, nor *thy* sons with *thee*, when *ye* go into the tabernacle of the congregation, lest *ye* die: it shall be a statute for ever throughout *your* generations.

Lev 10:14 And the wave breast and heave shoulder shall *ye* eat in a clean place; *thou*, and *thy* sons, and *thy* daughters with *thee:* for they be *thy* due, and *thy* sons' due, which are given out of the sacrifices of peace offerings of the children of Israel.

Lev 19:9 And when *ye* reap the harvest of *your* land, *thou* shalt not wholly reap the corners of *thy* field, neither shalt *thou* gather the gleanings of *thy* harvest.

Lev 19:10 And *thou* shalt not glean *thy* vineyard, neither shalt *thou* gather every grape of *thy* vineyard; *thou* shalt leave them for the poor and stranger: I am the LORD *your* God.

Lev 19:12 And *ye* shall not swear by my name falsely, neither shalt *thou* profane the name of *thy* God: I am the LORD.

Lev 19:15 *Ye* shall do no unrighteousness in judgment: *thou* shalt not respect the person of the poor, nor honour the person of the mighty: but in righteousness shalt *thou* judge *thy* neighbour.

Lev 19:19 *Ye* shall keep my statutes. *Thou* shalt not let *thy* cattle gender with a diverse kind: *thou* shalt not sow *thy* field with mingled seed: neither shall a garment mingled of linen and woollen come upon *thee.*

Lev 19:27 *Ye* shall not round the corners of *your* heads, neither shalt *thou* mar the corners of *thy* beard.

Lev 19:33 And if a stranger sojourn with *thee* in *your* land, *ye* shall not vex him.

Lev 19:34 But the stranger that dwelleth with *you* shall be unto *you* as one born among *you*, and *thou* shalt love him as *thyself;* for *ye* were strangers in the land of Egypt: I am the LORD *your* God.

Lev 21:8 *Thou* shalt sanctify him therefore; for he offereth the bread of *thy* God: he shall be holy unto *thee:* for I the LORD, which sanctify *you*, am holy.

Lev 23:22 And when *ye* reap the harvest of *your* land, *thou* shalt not make clean riddance of the corners of *thy* field when *thou* reapest, neither shalt *thou* gather any gleaning of *thy* harvest: *thou* shalt leave them unto the poor, and to the stranger: I am the LORD *your* God.

Lev 25:6 And the sabbath of the land shall be meat for *you;* for *thee*, and for *thy* servant, and for *thy* maid, and for *thy* hired servant, and for *thy* stranger that sojourneth with *thee.*

Lev 25:9 Then shalt *thou* cause the trumpet of the jubilee to sound on the tenth day of the seventh month, in the day of atonement shall *ye* make the trumpet sound throughout all *your* land.

Lev 25:14 And if *thou* sell ought unto *thy* neighbour, or buyest ought of *thy* neighbour's hand, *ye* shall not oppress one another.

Lev 25:17 *Ye* shall not therefore oppress one another; but *thou* shalt fear *thy* God: for I am the LORD *your* God.

Lev 25:44 Both *thy* bondmen, and *thy* bondmaids, which *thou* shalt have, shall be of the heathen that are round about *you;* of them shall *ye* buy bondmen and bondmaids.

To this list should be added 25:46 where KJV unaccountably renders *lōʾ tirdeh* as "ye shall not rule . . ."

Joosten (1997, 4–5) has suggested that in chapters 17–26 the plural forms are used for matters that affect the community as a whole while the singular is used for matters of private morality. He points out that terms such as *môšābôt* (dwellings), *dôrôt* (generations), and *ʿārîm* (cities) appear in you-plural contexts while terms such as *kerem* (vineyard) *bəhēmâ* (animal), *ʿebed* (slave), *rēaʿ* and *ʿāmît* (two words for "neighbor") are found in you-singular contexts. However, as Joosten himself admits in his footnote 14, this usage is not consistent; e.g., Lev 25:6-9 uses the singular in a passage that is obviously addressed to the group. So far it seems that no consistent rationale has been discerned for the *Numeruswechsel* in Leviticus.

Symbolism and Imagery

Spatial symbolism plays an important role in Leviticus. The text creates a world in which physical proximity to the divine presence in the tent is correlated with ritual purity and holiness. A key concept here is separation (*bdl* Hiphil 10:10; 11:47; 20:24-26). Use of the word *hibdîl* (to separate) may be meant to echo the story of Creation in which God separates light from darkness (Gen 1:4, 18), day and night (1:14), and the waters above and below the earth (1:6-7). Thus the separation of Israel from the nations and the separation of the holy/clean from the profane/unclean would be seen as part of the created world order.

Israel is to separate itself from the other nations so as not to become polluted by the practices that have caused the land to vomit out its inhabitants.

The spatial symbolism of separation is horizontal. Other horizontal symbolism has to do with the set inside/outside. The text creates a set of concentric circles that move from pollution to increasing holiness: the nations, the wilderness, outside the camp, the altar, the door of the tent, the inside of the tent, inside the veil.

Sacrifice involves a combination of horizontal and vertical symbolism. The action of the layperson offering the sacrifice as well as that of the priest is expressed by the word *qrb* Hiphil which means "to bring near," and the offering itself is referred to as *qorbān* (from the same root). The layperson brings the sacrificial animal or cereal offering to the priest who, in turn, brings it to the altar. There the priest "turns it into smoke" *(hiqṭîr)*—a vertical image.

If the sacrifice is a whole burnt offering, it is called an *ʿôlă* (from the root *ʿlh* meaning "to go up")—another vertical symbol. The verbal form of *ʿlh* is used in 14:20 and 17:8 in reference to sacrifice. Of course "up" is where the Lord is (though his presence is also in the tent, before which the sacrifices are offered).

The altar is within the sacred space that the layperson may not enter. The priests are set apart to function within the sacred space so that it cannot be contaminated—i.e., as long as the priests observe the rules of ritual purity that pertain to them.

What has been said about symbolism can also apply to imagery. Various actions associated with sacrifice easily conjure up images in the mind: pinching off the head of a bird and removing its crop (*mlq* 1:15-16; 5:8), slaughtering an animal in front of the tent (3:2, 8, 13) before the Lord (1:5, 11; 4:4, 15, 24; 6:25), collecting and manipulating its blood (see above), flaying (*pšṭ* 1:6), removing suet/fat (*peder* 1:8, 12; 8:20; *ḥēleb* 49x),[2] cutting into pieces (*ntḥ* 1:6, 8, 12; 8:20; 9:13), arranging (*ʿrk* 1:8, 12; 6:5), washing (*rḥṣ* 1:9, 13; 8:21; 9:14), bringing near (*qrb* Hiphil 89x), turning into smoke (*qṭr* Hiphil 32x), boiling (*bšl* 6:21; 8:31), disposing of skin and entrails (4:11; 8:17; 9:11; 16:27), a pleasing aroma to the Lord (17x).

Some other actions that evoke images would be:

YHWH calling or speaking to Moses and/or Aaron.

A person bringing an offering to the door of the tent (1:3; 4:4; 14:23; 15:14, 29; 17:4-5, 9; 19:21).

Laying hands (leaning) on a sacrificial victim (also 3:2, 8, 13; 4:4, 15, 24, 29, 33; 8:14, 18, 22) or on a person condemned to death (24:14).

Manipulation of blood: sprinkling (*nzh* 15x), dashing against the altar (*zrq* 12x), draining (*mṣh* 1:15; 5:9), pouring out (*špk* 4:7, 18, 25, 30, 34), bringing near (*qrb* Hiphil 7:33; 9:9), dipping into (*ṭbl* 14:6). Blood is sometimes put on the right earlobe, thumb and big toe of persons (8:23; 14:14, 25). At other times, the blood is put on the horns of the altar (4:7, 18, 25, 34; 8:15; 9:9; 16:18).

Grain offerings cooked in oven, griddle, or pan (2:4-5, 7; 6:21; 7:9; 11:35; 26:26).

Manipulation of oil: mixing (*bll* 8x), sprinkling (14:16, 27), anointing (*mšḥ* 2:4; 7:12; 8:10, 12), pouring (*yṣq* 2:1, 6; 8:12; 14:15, 26; 21:10).

The use of *gzl* (to tear off or away) in the sense of "to rob" (5:21, 23; 19:13).

The idiomatic use of the expression "The hand not being able to reach something" in the sense of "not being able to afford it" (5:7, 11; 12:8; 14:21, 22, 30, 32; 27:8).

Other images that appear in Leviticus are:

A fire kept always burning (6:9).

[2] There is some dispute as to whether *peder* refers only to suet while *ḥēleb* covers other fat. Such precision is not likely according to Milgrom (1991a, 159).

YHWH giving a portion (*ḥēleq*–only here) of the sacrifice to the priests (6:17).

Boiling meat in an earthen vessel (6:28).

Breaking an earthen vessel (6:28).

The whole congregation assembled at the door of the tent of meeting (8:3; 9:5).

Moses washing the priests (8:6).

Investiture (8:7, 13) *(lbš; ḥgr)*.

Aaron lifting his hands and blessing the people (9:22).

Fire coming out from the Lord and consuming the burnt offering (9:24).

Fire coming out from the Lord and devouring Nadab and Abihu (10:2).

Carrying the dead sons of Aaron out of the camp in their cloaks (10:5).

Circumcision (12:3).

A swelling eruption or a spot on the skin (13:2).

Hair turned white (13:3).

Raw flesh (13:10).

A reddish-white spot (13:19).

A burn on the skin (13:24).

The hair of the beard turns yellow and thin (13:30).

The leper wearing torn clothes, letting his hair hang loose, covering his upper lip and crying "unclean, unclean" (13:45-46).

A leprous disease in a garment (13:47).

The sacrifice offered after being cured of leprosy: two birds, cedar wood, and scarlet thread. One bird killed over running water. Dipping the living bird, the cedar wood . . . (14:1-7).

A cured leper shaving head, beard, and eyebrows (14:9).

A man coming to report a possible outbreak of leprosy in his house (14:35).

The priest ordering the house emptied (14:36).

Removing leprous stones from a house (14:40).

Scraping the plaster off the inside of a house and then replastering (14:41-42).

Breaking down a house and removing it to an unclean place (14:45).

Bodily discharges (15).

YHWH appearing in a cloud on the *kapporet* (the cover of the ark, 16:2).

Casting lots over two goats (16:8).

Sending a goat to the wilderness to Azazel (16:10).

A cloud of incense covering the *kapporet* (16:13).

Playing the harlot (17:7).

Eating blood (17:10).

Pouring out the blood of an animal and covering it with dust (17:13).

Uncovering nakedness (18).

Devoting children to Molech by fire (18:21).

Homosexual sex (18:22).

Lying with an animal (18:23).

YHWH throwing the former inhabitants out of Canaan (18:24).

The land vomiting out its inhabitants (18:25, 28; 20:22).

Making molten gods (19:4).

Turning to idols (19:4).

Gleaning (19:9).

Reaping a field to its border (19:9; 23:22).

Gathering fallen grapes (19:10).

Stripping a vineyard bare (19:10).

Putting a stumbling block in front of a blind person (19:14).

A garment made of two types of cloth (19:19).

Letting cattle of different kinds interbreed (19:19).

Sowing a field with two kinds of seed (19:19).

Planting trees (19:23).

Rounding off the hair of one's temples (19:27).

Self-laceration (19:28).

Tattoo (19:28).

Honoring the face of an old man (19:32).

Rising up before the hoary head (19:32).

Execution by stoning (20:2, 27; 24:16, 23).

YHWH turning his face against a person (20:3).

People hiding their eyes (from evil) (20:4).

"Their blood is upon them" (20:9, 11, 12, 13, 16, 26) always in reference to capital punishment.

Execution by burning (20:14; 21:9).

Making naked a fountain; uncovering a fountain of blood (20:18).

Dying childless (20:20).

A land flowing with milk and honey (20:24).

Separating from other peoples (20:24).

Shaving off the edges of beards (21:5).

Tonsure (21:5).

Physical defects in priests: blind, lame, mutilated face, limb too long, injured foot or hand, hunchback, dwarf, defective in sight, itching disease, scabs, crushed testicles (21:20).

Physical defects in animals (22:22-24).

Eating unleavened bread for seven days (23:6).

Bringing the sheaf of the first fruits (23:10).

Trumpet blast (23:24; 25:9).

Carrying fruit and branches of trees (23:40).

Dwelling in booths (23:42).

A lamplight kept burning continually (24:2).

A walled city (25:29).

Unwalled villages (25:31).

Taking interest (bite) (25:36).

The sword (26:6).

Five people chasing a hundred; a hundred chasing ten thousand (26:8).

Breaking the bars of a yoke so that one can walk upright (26:13).

One's crops being eaten by one's enemies (26:16).

Heavens like iron; earth like brass (26:19).

Abandoned roads (26:22).

Wild beasts rob people of their children and destroy cattle (26:22).

Breaking the staff of bread (26:26).

Eating the flesh of sons and daughters (26:29).

Heaping up corpses on idols (26:30).

Deserted sanctuaries (26:31).

The Lord refusing to smell the aroma of sacrifices (26:31).

People scattered (26:33).

YHWH unsheathing a sword against the people (26:33).

People so skittish that they are panicked at the sound of a wind-blown leaf (26:36).

Not having the strength to withstand one's enemies (26:37).

People stumbling over one another in panic (26:37).

Being eaten up by the land of one's enemies (26:38).

Uncircumcised heart (26:41).

Herd animals passing under the herdsman's staff (27:32).

Manipulation of Knowledge/Reading Positions

In general, all the speeches are a communication of knowledge from the Lord to the people: Knowledge of what is pleasing and acceptable *(rṣh, rāṣôn),* of how to avoid the Lord's anger, of how not to encroach, of how to have things brought near to the Lord, of how to atone for sins, of how to maintain ritual purity and how to restore it when it is lost. Knowledge of what is clean and unclean, of what brings guilt and how this burden of guilt is to be removed, and calculation of sacred time is communicated as well.

In a way one can say that the plot of Leviticus is a plot of knowledge. The tension then is over whether God will let the people know how to avoid God's anger by keeping separate the holy and the profane, the ritually pure and impure.

Some Texts in Which Manipulation of Knowledge Plays a Role

The treatment of sins committed unintentionally *(bišgāgâ)* in chapters 4 and 5 implies a situation in which one character (the sinner) does not know that he/she has sinned (it has escaped notice [*ʿlm* Niphal]), whereas another character (YHWH) does know. This in itself creates a certain amount of dramatic tension since it implies a possible danger to the community should the offence provoke a flare-up of divine wrath. The Holy One cannot tolerate what is ritually unclean even when this contact is unintentional. Here the contrast in knowledge is between YHWH and the people. The individual or the assembly is not aware of the potential danger but the Lord knows.

But then somehow the sinner becomes aware of the sin (4:13-14) and of the need to make amends. In this, the reading position is character elevating since the reader is not told how it is that the sinner comes to know that an unintentional offence has been committed.

The implied reader would be more preoccupied by this *šᵊgāgâ* (inadvertence) than us moderns, who would tend to think that God judges people by their intentions (in biblical imagery, their heart).

5:1 In this instance the law deals with the case of a potential witness in a lawsuit who has knowledge relevant to the case but does not come forward. The character who has knowledge relevant to the case is elevated over other characters. The reader is elevated to a lesser extent since she knows that someone possesses important information but does not know what that information is. However, this is simply due to the fact that the law is not about a particular case but generalizes about any case.

10:1 There is a certain character elevation here since the reader sees Nadab and Abihu offer alien fire but does not know why they do so.

10:11 Aaron and his sons are to teach *(yrh)* the Israelites. They have knowledge which other characters do not have but which the priests are to communicate.

10:16 By using the reinforcing infinitive absolute the narrator communicates that there is a certain intensity to Moses' inquiry as reflected in the translations by words like "searching inquiry" (REB) or "inquired carefully" (NJB). This seems to be a case of character elevation since the cause of his anxiety, and subsequent anger, is not known to the reader. In verse 16 the narrator leads the reader to expect that the problem is that the goat has been burned rather than eaten. But in verse 17 we hear Moses protesting about their not eating it in the sanctuary. If the complaint was made to Eleazar and Ithamar, why was the response given by Aaron? And what is the logic of Aaron's argument? Whatever it was, it was sufficient to persuade Moses.

14:34 Character elevation: The character "YHWH" says that he might put "leprosy" in a house. The reader does not know why the character "YHWH" would choose to take this action.

14:35 "There seems to me to be some sort of disease in my house." The man who suspects that there is "leprosy" in his house speaks circumspectly since that judgment belongs to the priest. The homeowner does not know for certain whether his house is infected until he hears definitively from the priest.

21:18-20 The term "blemish" is specified with respect to the priests; i.e., the term has been used before in the narrative without any specification as to its meaning. Now the character "YHWH" passes on to the characters in the narrative (and to the reader) the knowledge of what constitutes a "blemish." The same applies to 22:18-25 where the meaning of "blemish" as it applies to animals is specified.

24:11 Character elevation: the reader does not know why or how the character blasphemed the name.

24:11 Knowledge that has been withheld from the reader is now conveyed: the woman's name was Shelomith, daughter of Dibri of the tribe of Dan. This delayed exposition may aim at further discrediting the blasphemer by associating him with a tribe that had a reputation for idolatry.

24:12 The people do not know what to do with the blasphemer. They must seek a word from the Lord.

25:20 The character "YHWH" anticipates a question that the people would raise concerning what they are to eat during the seventh (fallow) year. YHWH informs them that he will increase the produce threefold in the sixth year.

Point of View

In general, nothing much need be said about point of view in Leviticus. Most of the text consists in the narrator's report of what YHWH or other characters in the story said or did. However, there are in Leviticus twenty-five examples of the combination of *rʾh,* "to see," and *hinnēh,* "behold." In Hebrew narrative this combination is often used to signal a shift in point of view, especially a shift from the viewpoint of the narrator to that of a character in the narration. This is the case of the examples in Leviticus, all of which occur in the two chapters that deal with "leprosy" (Leviticus 13–14). All of the examples indicate a shift to the perspective of the priest as he inspects surfaces (including people's skin) to determine whether they are "leprous" or not.

A Note on Verse Numbering

There is a difference in the numbering of verses between the MT and the NRSV in chapters 5 and 6.

MT	NRSV
5:20	6:1
5:26	6:7
6:1	6:8
6:23	6:30
7:1	7:1

NOTES

Leviticus 1

1:1–3:17 Speak to the Children of Israel

ʾādām kî yaqrîb When one would offer . . .

Sacrifices

Whole Burnt Offering

Introduction 1:1-2

1:1 "The Lord summoned Moses and spoke to him . . ." More literally, "He called and spoke, the Lord did." The identification of the subject of the verb "called" and "spoke" is delayed until after the second verb, contrary to the usual pattern (Auld 1996, 42). The place from which the Lord speaks is no longer the summit of Mount Sinai as it has been until now, but the so-called "tent of meeting." The change of place is an indication that a new scene begins here.

1:2 YHWH commands Moses to speak to the Israelites. The message that Moses is to deliver begins and ends with the root *qrb*, "bring near," forming an *inclusio* using a word that is key in Leviticus. It starts in the third person (whoever would bring . . .) but then switches to the second person plural (you may bring). The offerer is referred to as *ʾādām,* a human person, as opposed to the other designations used in Leviticus *(ʾîš, nepeš).* The double use of a cognate accusative (*hiqrîb qorbān* first in the third person singular and then in the second person plural) lends a poetic quality to the verse. In the root *qrb* there is an implied spatial imagery of bringing something near to the deity. This is reinforced in the next verse by defining the space in which the sacrifice takes place as "before the face of YHWH"—an expression that occurs some seventy times in Leviticus.

ʾim Whole Burnt Offering from Large Cattle 1:3-9

1:3 "If the offering *(qorbān)* is a burnt offering *(ʿōlā)* from the herd . . ." Bovines and sheep may be offered. The various types of sacrifices are now detailed, beginning with the whole burnt offering.

1:3 "You shall bring it . . ." Hebrew: "[The offerer] shall bring it . . ." The grammatical person reverts to third singular (not reflected in NRSV translation).

1:3 "The entrance of the tent . . ." This expression is found twenty-three times in Leviticus. This is the boundary between the space occupied by humans and the dwelling place of the deity, and is where much of the liturgical action in Leviticus takes place: "The place where the sacred intersects the life of the people in ritual" (Gorman 1993, 61).

1:3 "For acceptance of your [Hebrew: his] behalf." The word *lirṣōnô* ("for his pleasure") implies that the Lord will find the devotee's offering acceptable. The noun *raṣōn* appears exactly seven times in Leviticus (which may be by design since the question of how to please YHWH is a key concern) and the verb formed with the same root *(rṣh)* is used six times in a theologically passive sense (Niphal), the first of which is in the next verse.

1:4 "It shall be acceptable." The root *rṣh* (pleasure) is repeated from the previous verse, this time as a verb and again in a roundabout way (an impersonal Niphal in a theological sense, as indicated above) referring to the divine pleasure.

1:4 "As atonement for you [Hebrew: third person]." Just what imagery lies behind the use of the word *kpr* is a topic of some debate.[1] It comes down to a choice between "cover" and "uproot." Douglas (1993, 118) suggests a nuance of repairing a cover.

1:5 "The bull shall be slaughtered . . ." Hebrew: "[The offerer] will slaughter it . . ." The NRSV's passive hides the fact that it is the offerer who slaughters the animal (not the priest). The lay person has an important role (full, active participation) to play in the sacrifice. The animal to be slaughtered is referred to as "son of the herd," an expression

[1] See F. Maass s.v. *kpr* in *TLOT*, Grabbe (1993, 40–41).

that occurs six times in Leviticus. The slaughtering is conceived of as taking place spatially "in YHWH's presence." There is a certain emphasis put on the blood by repeating the word, "Aaron's sons bring the blood near and dash the blood . . ." The reference to YHWH in the third person may indicate that we are now hearing the voice of Moses or it may simply be that YHWH refers to himself in the third person (as happens elsewhere in the Pentateuch).

1:7-8 Aaron's sons arrange the wood and pieces of the victim on the altar. A certain emphasis is put on the act of arranging the wood and the pieces by the repetition of *ʾrk*. In the description of the arrangement there is a movement from top to bottom, which would also be temporally from last to first. This downward description counterpoints the upward movement of the same elements once they are turned into smoke (next verse).

1:9 The priest turns the offering into smoke. We meet here the first instance of *hiqṭîr* which the NRSV rightly renders "turn into smoke." It seems that this word also contains implied spatial imagery; the smoke rises to where YHWH is so that YHWH can smell it and be soothed. So the spatial symbolism of the sacrifice has both a horizontal (bringing the offering to the altar) as well as a vertical (turning it into smoke) dimension. This section (1:3-9) on large-cattle holocausts ends with what will become a refrain in the section of Leviticus dealing with sacrifices, "an offering of pleasing odor to the Lord." Holladay (1971) would render *nîḥōaḥ* as "soothing," and others suggest "appeasing," both of which cause one to wonder why YHWH would need soothing. There may be an echo here of Gen 8:21 where God smells the pleasing odor (*rēaḥ hannîḥôaḥ*, the same expression used here) of Noah's sacrifice and resolves never again to curse the ground or to destroy all living creatures.[2]

It is the Lord himself—the most reliable authority possible—who instructs Moses to tell the people what they need to do to please him

[2] The NRSV renders *ʾiššeh* as "an offering by fire" as if the word were related to *ʾēš*, fire. This has been the traditional interpretation. However, several authors have questioned the connection between the two words. They point to texts where, they say, the *ʾiššeh* is not burned (Deut 18:1; Josh 13:14; 1 Sam 2:28, and Num 15:10, where the *ʾiššeh* is wine) and to a Ugaritic cognate *ʾiṯt* meaning "generous gift." I note that the NRSV is not consistent in its usage, rendering "offerings by fire" in 1 Sam 2:28 and Josh 13:14 but simply "sacrifices" in Deut 18:1. See J. Hoftijzer, "Das sogennante Feueropfer," SVT 16 (1967) 114–34; G. R. Driver, "Ugaritic and Hebrew Words," *Ugaritica* 6 (1969) 181–84; Grabbe (1993, 30). Both KB[3] and the *Dictionary of Classical Hebrew* retain "offering by fire" or the like.

and offer a soothing fragrance. In other words, YHWH recognizes his "need" to be soothed as well as humanity's need or desire to soothe the deity. The phrase presupposes a situation in which humans will need or want to soothe God (note also the presence of the root *kpr* in v. 4 and *rṣh* Niphal in vv. 3 and 4). The presence of the All Holy One in the midst of uncleanness is potentially dangerous since such uncleanness necessarily provokes the wrath of the All Holy. Therefore this wrath must be soothed.

wᵊʾim Whole Burnt Offering from Small Cattle 1:10-13

The procedure in this instance is, with the exception of some small differences, similar to that for large cattle. The repetition of many phrases from 1:3-9 creates a somewhat poetic effect, ending with the refrain, "an offering of pleasing odor to the Lord."

1:13 "It is a burnt offering . . ." Here we have the first appearance of a device frequently used in Leviticus, especially as a concluding formula or as part of a concluding formula. This is the use of a noun clause with pronominal predicate, "It is an x . . ." In this case the phrase is *ʿōlă hûʾ*, "It is a whole burnt offering." This is followed by the "soothing fragrance" formula that we saw in verse 9.

wᵊʾim Whole Burnt Offering of Birds 1:14-17

This section ends with the concluding formula, "it is a whole burnt offering" *(ʿōlă hûʾ)*, as in verse 13.

Leviticus 2

Cereal Offerings 2:1-16

Introduction 2:1-3

2:1 "When anyone presents . . ." The offerer in this instance is referred to as a *nepeš*. This word means, among other things, "throat," as well as the sound of air in the throat. Traditionally, it has been rendered "soul." However, one should understand that *nepeš* does not have the same connotations as the English word "soul." This can be seen from the fact that it sometimes refers to a corpse (19:28; 21:1, 11; 22:4). It has a nuance of appetite and desire—a nuance that may induce some narrative tension as to whether the desire (in this case, to offer an acceptable sacrifice) will be fulfilled. The instructions are given in the third person, as is reflected in the NRSV.

2:2 The refrain "an offering of pleasing odor to the Lord" is repeated here even though we are not yet at the conclusion of the section (see next verse).

2:3 What remains of the grain offering is given to Aaron and his sons. It is most holy. Before this section ends we encounter a new refrain that will be taken up a total of twelve times in the course of the book. The portion of the cereal offering that is given to the priests is called "a most holy part of the offerings to YHWH" *(qōdeš qŏdāšîm mēʾiššēh yhwh).*

Cereal Offering Baked in an Oven 2:4

2:4 "When you present . . ." There is a change of address to the second person singular, which continues in the following verses.

wəʾim Cereal Offering Cooked on a Griddle 2:5-6

2:6 "It is a grain offering" *(minḥâ hîʾ):* an "it is x" concluding formula.

wəʾim Cereal Offering Cooked in a Pan 2:7

2:7 The instruction continues addressing the offerer directly.

Cereal Offering—General Norms 2:8-16

2:8 "You shall bring . . . the priest . . . shall take it to . . ." Here the choice of words changes. Instead of *qrb* Hiphil (bring near), the word *bwʾ* Hiphil is used of the offerer ("you will bring") and *ngš* Hiphil (another word that means "cause to approach") of the priest.

2:9 As with the animal sacrifices detailed above, the priest takes the cereal offering and "turns it into smoke." The familiar refrain "an offering of pleasing odor to the Lord" is repeated. This repetition takes on the character of a refrain, as does the repetition of 2:3 in the following verse (2:10).

2:11 "No grain offering that you bring." Here there is a switch of grammatical person to second plural "you."

2:13 Here the speaker jumps back from "you" to "thou." This verse has the quality of a solemn proclamation divisible into three parts, the first positive, the second negative, and the third positive again (not reflected in the NRSV):

> "Every cereal offering of thine,
> with salt shalt thou salt it
>
> and thou shalt not omit
> the salt of the covenant of thy God
> from thy cereal offering
>
> with all of thine offerings
> thou shalt offer salt."

wᵊʾim First Fruits 2:14-16

2:14 "If you bring a grain offering of first fruits . . ." The implied reader will know that the bringing of first fruits honors the Lord as "landlord"—the true owner of the land to whom rent must be paid (Joosten 1997, 6).

2:15 This and the previous verse continue the address to the individual offerer, ending with an "it is x" formula, *minḥâ hîʾ*, "It is a cereal offering."

Leviticus 3

The Well-Being Sacrifice 3:1-17

wᵊʾim From the Herd 3:1-5

3:1 "If the offering is a sacrifice of well-being . . ." *wᵊʾim* "and if" is often used in Leviticus as a structuring element. The sacrifice is here called *zebaḥ,* which is one eaten by the offerer (Grabbe 1993, 33). The speech reverts to the third person (not reflected in the NRSV).

3:3 "The fat that covers the entrails . . ." In offering the fat, Israel is offering the best of what it has. *ḥēleb,* "fat," connotes that which is the best. In Num 18:12 the expression *ḥēleb yiṣhār*, "the fat of the oil," means "the best oil." In Ps 81:17;[3] 147:14, "the fat of the wheat" means "the best wheat." Sirach 47:2 compares David to the fat of sacrifice.

3:5 "An offering by fire of pleasing odor to the Lord." This verse combines two formulae (by now familiar to the reader) first seen in 1:8, 9.

The sacrifice is put "on the burnt offering, which is on the wood, which is on the fire"—a description moving from top to bottom which counterpoints the upward movement of the smoke of the sacrifice (see 1:8).

wᵊʾim A Well-Being Sacrifice from the Flock 3:6-17

A Sheep 3:7-11

3:9 This verse is framed by an *inclusio: hiqrîb . . . qereb.*

3:11 This is a variation of the familiar formula. Instead of "an offering by fire to the Lord *(ʾiššeh lᵊyhwh),*" the word *leḥem* (food) is added, "a food offering to the Lord *(leḥem ʾiššeh lᵊyhwh)*"—an expression that is repeated in 3:16. Is the sacrifice conceived of as food for YHWH? Other passages in the Bible would deny this (e.g., Ps 50:13 "Do I eat the flesh of bulls, or drink the blood of goats?"). Is this a remnant of a "more primitive" view? If so, why was it left in the text (surely not due to carelessness)?

3:14 This verse is framed by the *inclusio hiqrîb . . . qereb.*

A Goat 3:12-16

3:16-17 Verse 16 concludes with yet another variation on the familiar formula, namely, "a food offering for a pleasing odor" followed by a statement that all fat is the Lord's. This last statement is expanded in the next verse, which is a solemn statement that concludes this part of the instruction on sacrifices. This statement is made in the second person plural, "your generations," "your dwellings," "you shall not eat." The pairing of "generations" and "dwellings" extends the instruction through time and space.

[3] Rendered literally in the Vulgate: Ps 80:17 *et cibavit eos de adipe frumenti . . .*

Leviticus 4

4:1–5:13 Speak to the Children of Israel

nepeš kî teḥĕṭāʾ bišgāgă A person who sins inadvertently . . .

Atonement for Inadvertent Sin

4:2 "When anyone sins unintentionally . . ." This section begins in the third person with the formula *nepeš kî,* "when a person . . ." The identity of this person will be specified in the following verses.

4:2 There is a certain element of suspense in the fact that the offence is known to the character who is offended (YHWH) but not to the offender. This is a potentially lethal situation of which the person would be totally unaware. Ancient readers (if not modern ones) may have felt a sense of relief at being provided with a means to expiate inadvertent offenses.

For the Anointed Priest 4:3-12

4:3 "If it is the anointed priest who sins . . ." The first *nepeš* to be considered is the "anointed priest." It is significant that the priest is treated before the prince since the cases are apparently treated in hierarchical order. Since it is YHWH who is speaking, this would mean that such an ordering of society is of divine origin. The implied reader would understand that the anointed priest's sin brings guilt on the people and that this sin must be atoned for.

4:3 "As a sin offering to the Lord." Milgrom (1991a, 253–54; see also Grabbe 1993, 34) would prefer the term "purificatory offering" to "sin offering" (as in the NRSV), pointing out that a *ḥaṭṭāʾt* is sometimes prescribed when no sin is involved (as in Lev 12:6).

wᵊʾim For the Whole Congregation 4:13-21

4:20 "It will be forgiven them" is an example of the use of theological passive as an indirect way of saying that YHWH will forgive. One may wonder why the character YHWH has chosen to put the matter so indirectly rather than say "YHWH will forgive," or even "I will forgive." This paraphrastic use of *slḥ,* "forgive," is found ten times in Leviticus, mostly in chapters 4 and 5.

For the Ruler 4:22-26

4:22 "When a ruler sins . . ." Traditional Jewish exegesis points out that, whereas with the other classes of sinner the expression "if x sins" is used, when it comes to the ruler it is not a question of "if" but of "when." The choice of words seems to presuppose that persons wielding power will sin.

wᵊʾim For Any Person 4:27-35

4:27 The ordinary individual is here called *nepeš ʾaḥat . . . mēʿam hāʾāreṣ* "a single soul from the people of the land."

wᵊʾim If It Is a Sheep 4:32-35

Leviticus 5

Other Specific Offences for Which Atonement Must Be Made

On the difference in numbering of verses between the Hebrew and the NRSV in this chapter see the introduction.

5:1 "When a person sins . . ." This section begins with *wᵊnepeš kî* and then goes on to name three kinds of offence for which atonement must be made. The character YHWH takes care to be very specific about how things are to be done.

wᵊʾim "If he cannot afford . . ." 5:7-10

wᵊʾim "If he cannot afford . . ." 5:11-13

5:14-19

nepeš kî timʿol maʿal A person who commits a trespass.

wᵊʾim Inadvertent Sin 5:17-19

5:19 The section ends with a triple repetition of the root *ʾšm ʾāšām hûʾ ʾāšōm ʾāšam lyhwh.* "It is *asham,* he has committed *asham, asham* I say."

5:20-26 [NRSV 6:1-7]

nepeš kî teḥĕṭāʾ A person who sins

5:23 (NRSV 6:4) This verse uses a series of cognate accusatives for effect *(haggəzēlâ ʾăšer gāzāl . . . hāʿōšeq ʾăšer ʿāšāq . . . happiqqādôn ʾăšer hopqad).* The word for "robbery" *(gəzēlâ)* means literally "to rip off" (as in American slang).

Leviticus 6

6:1-11 [NRSV 6:8-18] Command Aaron and His Sons

zōʾt tôrat hāʿôlâ This is the instruction on the whole burnt offering.

The Whole Burnt Offering: Rules for Priests

6:2 [NRSV 6:9] "This is the ritual of the burnt offering." The formula *zōʾt tôrat* x ("this is the instruction on x") is used here as an introductory formula that also prepares for a return to the subject of the holocaust in verses 2-6 with more specific regulations for the priests. Some emphasis seems to be put on clothing.

6:2 "Burnt offering." The Hebrew word *ʿôlâ,* rendered "burnt offering" in NRSV, was traditionally translated "holocaust" (based on the rendering of *ʿôlâ* in the LXX), which denotes a sacrifice that is completely burned. But the Hebrew word connotes a sacrifice that goes up—an example of spatial symbolism. The verb *ʿlh* is also used in the Hiphil in reference to sacrifices (14:20; 17:8).

6:12-16 [NRSV: 6:19-23]

zeh qorban ʾahărōn This is the offering of Aaron.

Grain Offering 6:14-11 [NRSV 6:14-18]

Anointing Offering 6:12-15 [NRSV 6:19-23]

6:15 [NRSV 6:22] "As a successor." *taḥtāyw,* "in his place," implies the future; the anointed priest(s) who will succeed Aaron.

6:17–7:21 [NRSV 6:24–7:21] To Aaron

zōʾt tôrat haḥaṭṭāʾt This is the instruction on the sin offering.

Sin Offering 6:17-23 [NRSV 6:24-30]

6:19 [NRSV 6:26] "The priest who offers the sin offering shall eat of it." Milgrom (1991a, 638) interprets the symbolism of the priest consuming the sin offering to mean that "holiness has swallowed impurity; life can defeat death." This would be a reversal of the image of Sheol swallowing the dead.

Leviticus 7

Guilt Offering: Rules for Priests 7:1-10

Well-Being Offering 7:11-36

***wᵊʾim* Votive Offering (7:16-17)**

***wᵊʾim* Meat Eaten on the Third Day (7:18)**

7:18 By a somewhat solemn pronouncement, this verse strengthens the prohibition in the previous verse that the flesh of the sacrifice that is left over on the third day after the sacrifice is to be burned.

> If there is eaten, I say eaten
> any of the flesh of one's sacrifice of well-being on the third day
> one will not be looked at favorably, the one bringing it near
> it will not be reckoned to him
> dead meat it is
> and the soul that eats from it will bear her guilt

One must conclude that this is something that the Lord regards very seriously, and/or that it was an abuse practiced among the original target audience of the book.

It seems clear here that it is YHWH who makes the evaluation of the acceptability of the offering. Therefore the use of *rṣh* and *ḥšb* Niphal can be taken as theological passive. This opens up the possibility that other instances of these verbs in the Niphal, as well as the Niphal of *slḥ*, can also be read as theological passives. Such a usage puts a buffer zone between YHWH, on the one hand, and the ritual, on the other, suggesting that the efficacy of the ritual is not automatic. YHWH does not say, "I will take pleasure/consider/forgive" but rather "it will be looked at with pleasure/considered/forgiven."

7:20 "Shall be cut off from their kin" *(wᵊnikrᵊtâ hannepeš hahiwʾ mēʿammehā)*. This verse provides us with the first instance of the *kareth* penalty, which occurs thirteen times in Leviticus. Although the imagery of being cut off is clear enough, there has been much discussion as to whether this penalty is enforced by the community or the deity and what precisely "being cut off from one's kin" consists of. Some see it as denial of descendants, others as denial of the afterlife (Milgrom 1991a, 457–60).

7:22-27 Speak to the Children of Israel

kol-ḥēleb All fat.

This short section begins with a prohibition against eating fat (which repeats the prohibition found in 3:16-17) and ends with a prohibition of eating blood, concluding with the *kareth* formula.

7:28-38 Speak to the Children of Israel

hammaqrîb et zebaḥ šᵊlāmîm The one bringing a well-being sacrifice.

The People's Role 7:28-36

7:35 "This is the portion allotted to Aaron . . ." The perquisites accruing to Aaron as High Priest are referred to as *mišḥat ʾahărôn,* literally "the anointing of Aaron" (NRSV: "portion"). There is word play on the root *qrb* Hiphil, "to bring near." The priests will bring sacrifice near to the Lord; the Lord brings Aaron and his sons near to serve as priests *(lᵊkahēn).* This prepares for the next chapters, which will narrate the ordination ritual.

Conclusion: 7:37-38

7:37-38 "This is the ritual . . ." A concluding Torah colophon (Fishbane 1980, 440) *(zōʾt hattôrâ lāʿōlâ lamminḥâ wᵊlaḥaṭṭāʾt wᵊlāʿāšām wᵊlammillûʾîm ûlᵊzebaḥ haššᵊlāmîm)* sums up the previous material on the various types of sacrifices, adding a new term: *wᵊlammillûʾîm* "ordination sacrifice." The root of this word has to do with being full or filling, perhaps in reference to receiving the sacrificial victims to be placed on the altar (Milgrom 1991a, 538–40).

Leviticus 8

8:1–10:30 Take Aaron and His Sons

qaḥ ʾet-ʾahărōn wᵉʾet bānāyw Take Aaron and his sons . . .

The Ordination of the Priests

8:1-5 Introduction

The fact that the ordination ceremony that takes place now has already been prescribed in Exodus 29 gives our present narrative the quality of a "climactic moment at which the entire liturgical structure and activity of the people is consummated" (Mann 1988, 114).

The narrative of the ordination ceremony is punctuated seven times by the refrain "as YHWH commanded" (vv. 4, 9, 13, 17, 21, 29, 36. Milgrom 1991a, 273; Gorman 1993, 60. See also the proposal of Gerald Klingbeil [1996] concerning chiastic structure in Leviticus 8).

This chapter features a change in pace. Until now everything has been speech (during which narrative time equals real time), but now the description of Moses' actions takes less time than their accomplishment in real time.

8:3 The spatial setting for the ceremony is the door of the tent, "the place where the sacred intersects the life of the people in ritual" (Gorman 1993, 61).

8:4 The formula "as YHWH commanded" occurs fifteen times in Leviticus. Of those fifteen, thirteen occur in chapters 8 to 10. This emphasis on the ritual being carried out exactly as commanded makes a strong contrast with the offense of Nadab and Abihu, who brought strange fire *which the Lord had not commanded* (Lev 10:1).

8:6 Washing Aaron and His Sons

8:6 Since *qrb* Hiphil is so often used in reference to offering sacrifice, its use here with reference to Aaron and his sons may have an overtone of sacrificial offering. This does not seem to be the case a few verses later (v. 24), but at least one can say that there is some word play on *qrb* Hiphil. There is also a parallel in the washing of the priests and the washing of sacrificial victims.

8:7-9 Investiture of Aaron

8:10-12 Anointing of Aaron

8:13 Investiture of Aaron's Sons

8:14-17 The Bull for the Sin Offering

8:15 "Purifying the altar . . . to make atonement for it" *(wayḥaṭṭēʾ ʾet-hammizbēaḥ . . . ləkappēr ʿālāyw)*. Contamination due to sin is removed. The altar is de-sinned and both the sanctuary and the priests are transferred to the realm of the sacred.

8:18-21 The Ram for the Burnt Offering

8:22-29 The Second Ram for Ordination

8:22-24 Blood is put on the earlobe, thumb, and big toe. The anointing of the priests' extremities is similar to what is done for a healed "leper" who is being restored to the community (14:14). Both instances involve a transition from one state to another (Gorman 1993, 63).

8:30 Sprinkling with Oil and Blood

8:31-36 Consumption of Ordination Sacrifice; Quarantine

8:31-33 The translation reads "as I was commanded," whereas the Hebrew says "as I commanded." The identification of the speaker is problematic in these verses. In verse 31 the words "as I commanded" seem to be spoken by Moses, but fit YHWH better, even though Moses does command in 9:5, 21 and 10:18. That this is a problem can be seen from a footnote in the NJPS which suggests reading *ṣuwwêtî* "I was commanded," which is the reading adopted by the NRSV. The difficulty continues in verses 32-33 where the words are again attributed to Moses but fit divine speech better. The NRSV's "it will take seven days to ordain you" masks a difficulty in identifying the subject of *yəmallēʾ ʾet-yedkem*, which literally means "he will fill your hands." Is there a deliberate melding of YHWH's and Moses' speech?

8:35 The phrase "They will not die" introduces the theme of death in anticipation of the death of Nadab and Abihu in chapter 10.

Leviticus 9

Ordination: The Eighth Day

9:2-3 "Take a bull calf . . ." Since this is the only instance where a calf is prescribed as the sacrificial victim, later Jewish exegesis saw this detail of the sacrifice as betokening atonement for the participation of Aaron in the episode of the Golden Calf (Exodus 32, Harrison 1980, 104).

9:5 "The whole congregation drew near and stood before the Lord." Now that the priesthood is functioning, the assembly can safely approach the divine presence and stand before the Lord.

9:24 Fire came from before the Lord (the reader wonders where this fire came from: the tent? heaven?) and consumed the holocaust and the fat on the altar. All the people saw it. They shouted *(rnn)* and fell on their faces. First the narrator tells what happened, in his own voice, and then he records the people's perception of the event and their reaction. This certainly forms a dramatic conclusion to the sacrificial ritual—more than the reader may have been led to expect. What does it mean? Is the reader to take this as a sign of divine acceptance of the sacrifice? Anyone who has read the story of the contest on Mount Carmel would think so, and is probably correct in doing so, but the fire here also prepares for the death of Nadab and Abihu in the next chapter.

Leviticus 10

The Death of Nadab and Abihu 10:1-11

10:1 "Which the Lord had not commanded . . ." The pattern of command-fulfillment that was so carefully established in chapters 8 and 9 is here broken—with tragic consequences—but soon restored in verses 4-7 (Wenham 1979, 154).

10:1 "Aaron's sons, Nadab and Abihu . . ." Aberbach and Smolar claim to identify thirteen points of similarity between the portrayal of Aaron in the Golden Calf incident recounted in Exodus 32 and Jeroboam in 1 Kings 12, in which golden calves are set up at Bethel and Dan after the split between the northern and southern kingdoms (Israel and Judah). I do not find many of these proposed links convincing, but it is intriguing that Jeroboam's sons were named Nadab and Abijah.

Ancient readers may have perceived some irony in the clash between the names "Nadab" and "Abihu" and their actions in this story. The name Nadab may connote generosity and nobility. As an adjective, *nādāb* is used in parallel with *ṣaddîq* (upright) in Prov 17:7, 26 and is contrasted with *nābāl* (foolish) in Isa 32:5, 8. Offering incense to idols would, of course, be the height of unrighteousness and foolishness. The name Abihu means "He is my father." There may be some irony in the name since, as 1 Chr 24:2 points out, neither Nadab nor Abihu had sons. The characters Nadab and Abihu first appear in the Bible in the notice of their birth in Exod 6:23. In Exod 24:10 they are among a group that go up the mountain and see the God of Israel. In some Jewish exegesis their death is seen as a punishment for looking at God—no one can see God and live. In Exod 28:1 the Lord commands Moses to have his brother Aaron and his sons Nadab, Abihu, Eleazar, and Ithamar brought to Moses so that they may act as YHWH's priests.

10:1 "Unholy fire." The sense of *ʾēš zārâ* is specified in what follows: *ʾăšer lōʾ ṣiwwâ ʾōtām* "such as he had not commanded them." The phrase only occurs here in Leviticus, but it is found twice in Deuteronomy and four times in Jeremiah. All but one of these instances concerns the worship of other gods. In other words, the language of this verse implies that Nadab and Abihu were worshiping other gods. This would also explain the severity of the punishment (Aberbach and Smolar 1967, 139). Laughlin (1976, 564) cites a Zoroastrian ritual in which two priests carried holy fire into the sanctuary on censers and enthroned it.

10:2 Is the fiery death of Nadab and Abihu to be construed as punishment? The fact that the fire they use is called *ʾēš zārâ* and the statement that it was not commanded make a strong case for seeing the fire as punishment for idolatrous worship—those who sinned by fire are punished by fire (Wis 11:16; Milgrom 1991a, 599). But the similarity in language and proximity to 9:24, where the similarly worded consumption of the sacrifice by fire from YHWH is seen as a sign of acceptance, might argue for a more favorable interpretation of the death of Nadab and Abihu. As a matter of fact, both readings have a long history.[4] Philo praises Nadab and Abihu and interprets the fire that consumed them as sign of favor. He interprets *zar* to mean that the fire was foreign in the sense of being "alien to creation, but akin to God" (*Somn.* 2.6-7). This positive assessment finds support in a minor tradition in rabbinic literature recorded in *Sipra,* Milluʾim Shemini 22 and 32. This holds that "Nadab and Abihu consecrated the Tabernacle by their deaths and thereby sanctified the divine name. . . . For their zeal in attempting to hasten the theophany by offering incense to God with impure fire, God rewarded them by consuming them with his pure fire" (cited in Milgrom 1991a, 634–35; Ginzburg 6:74–75 notes 382–86). Milgrom sees the story as a kind of *a fortiori* polemic against the idolatrous incense burning in

[4] See Robert Kirchner, "The Rabbinic and Philonic Exegesis of the Nadab and Abihu Incident (Lev. 10:1-6)," *JQR* 73,4 (April 1983) 375–93. This article is a response to Richard D. Hecht, "Patterns of Exegesis in Philo's Interpretation of Leviticus," *Studia Philonica* 6 (1979/80) 77–155.

private homes for which there is ample archaeological evidence. See also 1 Kgs 13:2; Jer 19:4; 32:29; 44:17-19, 25 (in all of which the NRSV translation "making offerings" or the like corresponds to the verb *qṭr*, "smoke"). After all, Nadab and Abihu were not laymen, or Levites, or even ordinary priests, but sons of Aaron. They were authorized to offer incense. And the incense they offered was not illegitimate but perfectly legal. They offered it in the sanctuary and not outside. If, despite all this, they were struck down for using fire from the wrong source, how much more lay people ought to fear to offer incense in their homes! (Milgrom 1991a, 628).

10:3 "This is what the Lord meant when he said . . ." Nowhere in the story world has YHWH said, "Through those who are near me I will show myself holy" *(biqrōbay ʾeqqādēš)*, so the reader must understand this as a flashback; i.e., the reader now learns that YHWH had said this. Segal (1989, 93) wants to read *biqrōbay* in the sense of encroachment, "In those who trespass upon me I will show myself holy"; namely, through the punishment meted out directly and at once upon anyone who encroaches on the sanctuary. Taking a different tack, Levine (1989, 59) cites Esth 1:14 and Ezek 23:12 to the effect that *qᵊrōbîm* here means that the priests are members of YHWH's inner circle analogous to governors and provincial rulers at an imperial court.

10:3 "Aaron was silent." Some authors want to read the less common *dmm* II "to moan, wail, mourn" rather than *dmm* I "to be still, silent" (Levine 1993). Such a reading would have the advantage of motivating Moses' command not to mourn in verse 6.

10:4 "Mishael." The name means "Who is what God is?" but could also be read "Who asked for it?" This would be an ironic reference to the incense YHWH had not commanded.

10:4 "Carry your kinsmen . . . to a place outside the camp." Having the remains of Nadab and Abihu carried outside the camp creates a parallel with the whole burnt offering (6:11, but notice that our present verse does not specify that the place outside the camp be clean). Wenham sees this in a negative light, "They are treated like the useless parts of the sacrificial animals" (1979, 158). But it may also be possible to read this verse in a positive light—Nadab and Abihu are acceptable to YHWH as was the sacrifice.

10:5 They carried them in their tunics. Are we meant to marvel that they were burned, but not their clothing? If so, what is the significance? The tunic is mentioned in 8:13 when the priests are invested. It may be ironic that they are carried out in the tunics with which they were only recently invested, presumably to serve for some time into the future.

10:9 "Drink no wine or strong drink . . ." The reader may wonder if there is any connection between this instruction that priests not serve while intoxicated and the previous episode of the death of Nadab and Abihu. If so, the strategy of the narrator might not be to explain that Nadab and Abihu offered unholy fire because they were drunk, but rather to support the idea that what is involved is idolatry, since drunkenness did feature in some pagan worship, specifically in the worship of the Golden Calf (Exod 32:6. See also Milgrom 1991a, 612; *ANET*[3] 66; *Enuma Elish* 3.134-38).

10:10 "You are to distinguish between the holy and the common . . ." The injunction to separate the holy from the profane looks both forward and backward in time. It echoes God's separation of light from darkness in the Genesis narrative (Gen 1:4), of the waters above and below the dome of heaven (Gen 1:6-7), and of night from day (Gen 1:14), thereby suggesting that the purity laws which follow are part of the structure of creation. Failure to separate will lead to tragedies such as the fiery death of Nadab and Abihu. The priests are not only to observe these vital distinctions themselves but to instruct (*lᵊhôrôt,* same root as Torah) the people in them.

Continuation of the Ordination Ceremony 10:12-15

10:13 "For so I am commanded . . ." (*ṣuwwêtî,* i.e., by YHWH) is an example of the use of the theological passive.

10:14 "They have been assigned . . ." (*nittᵊnû,* i.e., by YHWH—another theological passive).

10:15 "To raise for an elevation offering . . ." This verse uses repetition, cognate accusative, and alliteration *(lᵊhānîp tᵊnûpâ lipnê)* to give a certain solemn form to the conclusion of this section on the priests' portion of the sacrifice.

The Uneaten Sin Offering 10:16-20

This incident consists in a miniature drama. Moses questions what has happened to the goat. When he learns that it had been burned he becomes angry and expresses that anger to Eleazar and Ithamar. This creates tension because the reader wants to know how the two will respond and whether Moses' anger will be assuaged. Moses is answered not by the two sons but by their father. Moses is satisfied with his answer and the crisis ends.

10:19-20 "They offered their sin offering . . . yet such things have befallen me!" The logic of Aaron's response is difficult to follow (see Milgrom 1991a, 635–40). Is the reader meant to infer that Moses accepted a lame excuse and did not press the issue? Would he thereby be compromising on issues that were of vital importance?

Leviticus 11

11:1–11:47 Speak to the Children of Israel

zōʾt haḥayyâ These Are the Animals . . .

Instruction on Diet

11:1 Many attempts, going back to ancient times, have been made to find a rationale for the dietary laws. The *Letter of Aristeas* tried to tie the forbidden animals to moral qualities. For example, birds that dominate by their own strength or steal their food from other birds are forbidden in order to teach people not to act in such a way (*Let. Aris.* 142-51). "Even in antiquity it was argued that the rules were purely arbitrary, designed by God simply to teach discipline to the Jews and to set them apart" (Grabbe 1993, 54).

In narrative terms we might speak of a character-elevating reading position regarding knowledge communicated by the narrator to the reader. The character YHWH presumably knows the rationale for the purity laws but the reader does not.

The fact that in the dietary laws the order in which various animals are discussed is the same order used in the creation story (Douglas 1993, 16), as well as the use of *lᵊmînāh,* "according to its kind" in this verse contribute to the elements tying the purity laws to the order of the cosmos (see comment on 10:10).

This chapter has an unusually high number of second-person plural forms. The laws of purity are addressed to the people as a whole.

11:2-8 Land Animals

11:9-12 Water Creatures

11:9 "These you may eat . . . such you may eat." Note the *inclusio*: *ʾet-zeh tōʾkᵊlû . . . ʾōtām tōʾkēlû,* perhaps even a *chiasm* if one is willing to overlook the additional words:

ʾet-zeh tōʾkᵉlû	*bammayim*	
	bammayim	*ʾōtām tōʾkēlû*

11:11 The NRSV has been able to reproduce the *inclusio šeqeṣ . . . tᵉšaqqēṣû* by placing the word "detestable" at the beginning and end of the verse.

11:13-19 Birds

11:20-23 *šereṣ* Things that Swarm

11:24-28 Carcasses

11:29-30 *šereṣ* Things that Swarm (Again)

11:31-40 Carcasses (Again)

11:41-45 *šereṣ* Things that Swarm—Peroration

11:44 "Be holy, for I am holy." The reader is now told the reason for the foregoing regulations—Israel must be holy because YHWH is holy. God's otherness is mirrored by Israel's separateness from other nations. Israel's separation from the nations is an *imitatio Dei.*

11:45 "For I am the Lord who brought you up from the land of Egypt . . ." Rendsburg (1993) suggests that the exceptional use of the verb *ʿlh* here ("brought you up") as opposed to the usual *hôṣîʾ* ("brought you out") is meant to form an *inclusio* with the use of the same verb in reference to animals that chew the cud (first instance: 11:3), thereby framing all the dietary laws.

The personal nature of YHWH's speech here is highlighted by the *inclusio* formed by placing "I" *(ʾănî)* at the beginning and end of the verse. The personal investment in this particular topic shows the importance that it has for YHWH.

Torah Colophon 11:46-47

11:46-47 "This is the law . . ." The dietary laws end with a solemn Torah colophon.

Leviticus 12

12:1-8 Speak to the Children of Israel

ʾiššâ kî tizrîaʿ A woman who produces seed . . .

Restoration of a Woman to Ritual Purity after Childbirth

The purity laws of chapters 12–15 seem to have as a common denominator the symbolism of life and death. Vaginal blood and semen are elements of the life force and their loss symbolizes death, while skin diseases are symbolic of death. When Miriam is struck with "leprosy" she is compared to a stillborn infant.

12:2 "A woman who produces seed" is an unusual expression and is rendered in a variety of fashions in modern translations. It attracts attention. BDB notes a metaphorical usage in Psa 126:5 which may shed some light. Here the phrase "Those who sow in tears, in joy will reap" is used metaphorically of distress followed by joy, possibly to refer to labor pains.

wᵊʾim "If a female . . ." (12:5)

12:7 "Clean from her flow of blood." The word rendered "flow" *(māqôr)* is literally a spring or well. This is a striking metaphor. (See Sherwood 1990, 56–57 and the literature cited there, also Eslinger 1987.)

wᵊʾim "If she cannot afford . . ." (12:8)

Leviticus 13

13:1-59

ʾādām kî yihyeh One who has on his skin . . .

"Leprosy"—Rules for Detection

13:2 There is a certain artistic arrangement even of the material on "leprosy." Verse 2 speaks of (1) discoloration of skin, (2) pustule, and (3) inflammation. In the following discussion in vv. 3-17 the terms recur in the order 3, 2, 1. In vv. 18-23 the order is 1, 2, 3, and in vv. 24-28 it is 3,

2, 1. (See Fishbane 1980, 442–43; a useful discussion of the history of the term "leprosy" can be found in John G. Anderson, "Leprosy in Translations of the Bible," *BT* 31 [1980] 207–12.)

***wᵊʾim* "If there is a white spot . . ." (13:4)**

***wᵊʾim* "If the scab spreads . . ." (13:7-8)**

***wᵊʾim* "If the disease spreads . . ." (13:12-17)**

13:52 This verse is framed by the word "burn" *(śrp).*

Leviticus 14

zōʾt tihyeh tôrat hamᵊṣōrāʿ This will be the instruction on "leprosy."

"Leprosy"—Rules for Purification 14:1-32

Quite a bit of attention is given to the return of the excluded member to the community (Grabbe 1993, 52). Normally, what is given much space is what is regarded as most important to the narrator.

14:2 hûbāʾ "It/he is caused to come." The NJPS renders "when it is reported" referring to the news of the "leprosy" rather than "when he is brought" referring to the "leper." This makes better sense here in view of the next verse in which the priest goes out of the camp to inspect the leper. The NRSV reads, "He [the leprous person] shall be brought to the priest."

14:11-20 Milgrom (1991, 846–87, based on Lund 53–55) has proposed the following chiastic structure:

11 A *khn, ṭhr*

12-13 B *šmn, lipnê yhwh,* 13 *ḥṭʾt, ʿôlâ, šḥṭ*

14 C *dm ʾšm*

D *ntn khn tᵊnûk ʾôzen miṭṭahēr ymny, bōhen yd, rgl*

15 E *šemen, kap*

16 X *šemen, kap, lipnê yhwh*

17 E' *šemen, kap*

D' *ntn khn t*ᵊ*nk* ᵓ*ōzen miṭṭahēr, ymny bōhen, yd, regel*

C' *dm* ᵓ*šm*

18-19 B' *šemen, lipnê yhwh,* 19 *ḥaṭṭā*ᵓ*t, šḥṭ,* ᶜ*ôlâ*

20 A' *khn, ṭhr*

Such a proposal is intriguing, but can be accepted only if one ignores the occurrences of words or phrases that have not been considered to form part of the structure; *kōhēn* also occurs in 12, 13 (which Milgrom excludes as a gloss), 14 (2x), 15 (2x), 16, 18 (2x), and 19, *lipnê yhwh* in 11, ᶜ*ōlâ* in 20, and *kap* in 18.

wᵊᵓ***im*** **"If he is poor . . ." (14:21-32)**

14:21-32 Milgrom (1991, 859–60, based on Lund 55–56) proposes the following chiastic structure:

21 A ᵓ*ên yaddô maśśeget*

21-23 B *kpr, minḥâ, tōrîm, b*ᵊ*nê yônâ, nśg yd,* 22 *ṭhr,* ᶜ*ôlâ,* 23 *khn, lipnê yhwh*

24 C *khn, šemen, lipnê yhwh*

25 D *dm,* ᵓ*šm*

E ᵓ*ōzen, ymyn, miṭṭahēr, bōhen*

26 F *khn, šemen, kap*

27 X *khn, šemen, kap, lipnê yhwh*

28 F' *khn, šemen, kap*

E' *t*ᵊ*nûk* ᵓ*ōzen, ymyn, bōhen, regel*

D' *dm,* ᵓ*šm*

29 C' *šemen, khn, lipnê yhwh*

30-31 B' *tōrîm, b*ᵊ*nê yônâ, nśg yd, ḥaṭṭā*ᵓ*t,* ᶜ*ōlâ, minḥâ, khn, kpr, lipnê yhwh*

32 A' *nśg yd*

This proposal has only a few words that do not fit within its structure; *kpr* is not counted in 29 nor *khn* in 25.

14:32 "This is the ritual (Hebrew: *tôrâ*) . . ." The unit is punctuated by a Torah colophon.

14:33-57 The Lord spoke to Moses and Aaron

kî tābōʾû ʾel-ʾereṣ kᵊnaʿan When you enter the land of Canaan . . .

"Leprosy"—in a House 14:34-53

14:34 "When you come into the land of Canaan . . ." This instruction looks to the time when the people will no longer be living in tents but in houses. YHWH is portrayed as giving Moses and Aaron (neither of whom will enter the land, much less build houses) instruction for a future time.

wᵊʾim "If the infection spreads again . . ." (14:43-45)

wᵊʾim "If the priest comes . . ." (14:48)

14:48 In narrative, *hinneh* (traditionally rendered "behold" but not represented in modern translations) is often used to indicate a change in point of view from that of the narrator to that of a character. So here: the *hinneh* indicates the shift to the priest's perception.

14:51-52 Milgrom (1991a, 880) proposes the following chiastic structure:

A *ʿēṣ-hāʾerez ʾēzōb šᵊnî hattôlaʿat*
  B *ṣippōr ḥayyâ*
    C *dam ṣippōr . . . mayim ḥayyîm*
      D *wᵊhizzâ ʾel habbayit*
        X *šebaʿ pᵊʿāmîm*
      D' *wᵊḥiṭṭēʾ ʾet-habbayit*
    C' *dam ṣippōr . . . mayim ḥayyîm*
  B' *ṣippōr ḥayyâ*
A' *ʿēṣ hāʾerez ʾēzōb šᵊnî hattôlaʿat*

14:54-57 These verses constitute the Torah colophon (*tôrâ* is rendered "ritual" in the NRSV) to the preceding section. The four verses are framed by the *inclusio*: *zōʾt hattôrâ lᵊkol-negaʿ haṣṣāraʿat*, "this is the instruction concerning any affliction of scale-disease," in verse 54 and *zōʾt tôrat haṣṣāraʿat*, "this is the instruction on scale disease," in verse 57. Are these words spoken by YHWH or by the narrator? The versions treat them variously. The NAB and NJB include these verses in quotation marks as part of the divine speech. The TOB excludes them. The JPS and NJPS do not use quotation marks at all here. It seems to me on the basis of 27:34, where the voice is clearly that of the narrator, that all such endings should be attributed to the narrator. There may be an attempt here to meld the speech of YHWH and of the narrator.

Leviticus 15

15:1-33 Speak to the Children of Israel

ʾîš ʾîš kî yihyeh zāb If anyone has a discharge . . .

Restoration to Ritual Purity after Bodily Discharges

Whitekettle (1991, 35-8), building on the work of Wenham (1979), sees the structure of the chapter delineated according to whether the discharges are long- or short-term and whether male or female, but also by a series of conditional phrases: *ʾîš kî* or *ʾiššâ kî*. But he also wants to read *ʾăšer* in verse 18 as a conditional particle (citing Joüon, 515 [§167j]), which marks it as a distinct unit along with the other conditional clauses in the chapter. According to Whitekettle this would yield the following structure:

	verses	*duration*	*gender*	*physiological integrity*	*systemic function*
A	vv. 2b-15	long term	male	abnormal	abnormal
B	vv. 16-17	transient	male	typical	dysfunctional
C	v. 18	intercourse	male/female	normal	normal
B'	vv. 19-24	transient	female	typical	dysfunctional
A'	vv. 25-30	long term	female	abnormal	abnormal

15:13 Stress is placed on cleansing, by the threefold repetition of the root *ṭhr* and by placement of this root at the beginning and end of the verse.

15:20 "Everything also upon which she sits shall be unclean." The reader might recall both the suspense and the comedy of Gen 31:34-35 where Rachel sits on Laban's teraphim and claims menstruation as her reason for not rising (see Sherwood 323-30).

wᵊʾim "And if she is cleansed . . ." (15:28-30)

15:28 The *inclusio ṭāhŏrâ . . . tiṭhār* frames this verse (see 13).

15:31 "Thus you shall keep the people of Israel separate from their uncleanness, so that they do not die . . ." This verse is important in stating the purpose of the purity laws. The preceding verses have been divine speech using the third person (case law). Now there is a shift to direct address (2nd masc. pl.) along with a personal element ("my tabernacle").

Leviticus 16

16:1-34 To Aaron

The Day of Atonement

16:1 "After the death of the two sons of Aaron . . ." The reference to the death of Nadab and Abihu forms an *inclusio* with chapter 10 which frames the purity laws of chapters 11–15. These have been introduced by the injunction to the priests to separate the holy from the profane (10:10-11; see Fishbane 1980, 439–40).

16:1 The phrase "He shall not come at all times" leads one to expect a designation of *times* when Aaron may enter the holy place, but this is not treated until the end of the chapter, thus forming a framing device. In the meantime, the discussion turns to what is to be brought (v. 3) and what is to be worn (v. 4. See Rodriguez 1996, 273).

16:3-4 A reverse chronological order is employed here. Logically the priest would first bathe, then vest and finally enter the Temple, but these elements are treated from last to first (Damrosch 1987, 73). These verses also form a chiastic pattern with verses 23-25 below:

16:3-4	16:23-25
A bull for sin-offering	C vestments and ritual bath
B ram for burnt-offering	B burnt-offering
C vestments and ritual bath	A sin-offering

(Rodriguez 1996, 281)

16:8 "The other lot for Azazel." The implied reader is expected to know what "Azazel" is. The competence of modern readers is challenged by a certain lack of information as to just what the narrator has in mind. But this lack of clarity may be deliberate, since comparative Ancient Near Eastern material indicates that the biblical Azazel has lost most of his potency (Wright, 1992; Levine, 1989, Excursus 4; Grabbe 1993, 92–93; Janowski).

16:14 Rodriguez (276–77) has pointed out this chiastic arrangement:

a. Some blood of the bull	*wəlāqaḥ middam happār*
b. sprinkle with finger	*wəhizzâ bəʾeṣbāʿô*
c. on the front of the kapporet	*ʿal-pənê hakkappōret qēdmāh*
c' before the kapporet	*wəlipnê hakkappōret*
b' sprinkle seven times	*yazzeh šebaʿ-pəʿāmîm*
a' some of the blood	*min-haddām bəʾeṣbāʿô*

16:29-31 Milgrom (1991a, 39–40, 1057) proposes the following chiastically arranged structuring elements in these verses:

29 A *ḥuqqat ʿôlām* (lasting statute)
B *ʿnh nepeš* (repress appetite)
C *wəkol-məlāʾkâ lôʾ taʿăśû* (you shall do no work)
30 X
31 C' *šabbat šabbātôn hîʾ lākem* (it is a restful sabbath for you)
B' *ʿnh nepeš* (repress appetite)
A' *ḥuqqat ʿôlām* (lasting statute)

16:29 This verse provides us with the first occurrence of a colorful expression the NRSV renders "deny oneself." This expression is made up of the words *ʿinnâ* "to make someone feel his dependence" (Holladay) and *nepeš*, traditionally "soul" but more literally the throat and the sound of breath in the throat. Hence to make the throat feel its dependence, or "to deprive the gullet," the seat of appetite (Schwartz 1991, 41, n. 3), is a way of saying "to fast."

16:33 The verse is framed by the *inclusio wəkipper . . . yəkappēr.*

16:34 "This shall be an everlasting statute." These words repeat those that opened this section (v. 29) and frame this concluding section on the Day of Atonement.

16:34 "And Moses did as the Lord had commanded him." Moses is commanded to speak to Aaron in 16:2 and he fulfills this command in 16:34. The note of fulfillment encloses chapter 16 within a command-fulfillment narrative structure and reinforces the pattern of compliance with the divine will.

Leviticus 17

17:1-16 To Aaron and His Sons and All the Children of Israel

zeh haddābār This is what the Lord has commanded . . .

Proper Slaughtering and the Disposal of Blood

Chapters 17–27 repeat material found in Leviticus 1–6, but this time with stress on the role of the lay person rather than on that of the priest (Grabbe 1993, 77).

17:7 "So that they may no longer offer their sacrifices for goat-demons . . ." The words "no longer" may make the reader wonder when sacrifices to satyrs were performed since this has not been mentioned anywhere in the Torah up until now. This means that this bit of information could be a flashback or a flashforward. Second Chronicles 11:15 accuses Jeroboam of promoting sacrifice to goat demons (see the note on 10:1 above).

17:7 "To whom they prostitute themselves . . ." The expression *znh ʾḥry*, "to whore after," comparing idolatry to a wife's adultery, also occurs in 20:5-6. It would, no doubt, have a strong emotional resonance in a society whose primary value was honor-shame.

17:10-12 The law against eating blood is stated in verse 10, its rationale is given in verse 11, and the law is repeated in verse 12. This forms an *inclusio* that frames and therefore gives special importance to the motive clause (Schwartz 1991, 45).

17:11 "I have given." The "I" here is emphatic. This is because what is being stated is the opposite of what appears. What appears is that people are placing blood on the altar. What YHWH says is that *he* has provided the blood to the people as a means of making atonement (Schwartz 1991, 51).

17:11 "For making atonement." Schwartz (1991, 54 n. 2) claims that the expression *kippēr ʿal hannepeš*, "cover the throat," has the meaning "to act as a ransom for your lives, as payment in place of your lives, which would otherwise be forfeit."

17:12 YHWH quotes himself from verse 10, but not verbatim.

Leviticus 18

18:1-30 Speak to the children of Israel

ʾănî yhwh ʾĕlōhêkem I am the Lord your God

Sexual Morality/Incest

18:3 "You shall not follow their statutes." "Follow" here renders Hebrew *tēlēkû*. The verb *hlk*, "to walk," is often used in Hebrew as a metaphor for the moral aspect of one's way of life.

18:6 "None of you shall approach anyone near of kin to uncover nakedness . . ." The verb *qrb*, "to draw near, approach," in its causative form has occurred several times earlier as a technical term for the offering of sacrifice. Here the same word is now used in reference to sexual morality, thus forming a certain unity between the instructions on sacrifice and those on sexual morality.

18:7 "*You* shall not uncover the nakedness of *your* father, which is the nakedness of *your* mother; she is *your* mother . . ." The repeated use of the second-person singular possessive suffix strengthens the impact of these apodictic laws. This makes the laws more immediate and personal—they are not about someone else's family, but *yours* (Ziskind 1996, 127). This chapter and the one that follows have a very high number of second-person singular forms (seventeen in chapter 18 and fifteen in chapter 19). In Hebrew this verse is framed by the word "nakedness" *(ʿerwâ)*, as are verses 9, 10, 11, and 15.

18:18 Neither the Hittite Laws nor the Code of Hammurabi treat incest as extensively as does Lev 18:1-18, yet they both explicitly mention incest with a daughter, which Leviticus does not. The omission of this category in Leviticus is puzzling and various attempts have been made to explain it (Ziskind; Meacham).

The Cairo Damascus document and 11Q Temple interpret "sister" in this verse as "fellow citizen," seeing here a prohibition against divorce and polygamy in the Jewish community (see Tosato, 1984, who also advocates this interpretation).

18:21 "You shall not give any of your offspring to sacrifice them to Molech . . ." The Hebrew literally says, "From your seed you shall not give to make them cross over to Molech . . ." Just what this consists in is not certain (see Hartley and Dwyer). In other Old Testament references the expression "to cause to pass through fire" is used (Deut 18:10; 2 Kgs 16:3; 17:17; 21:6; 23:10; Ezek 20:31). This is often taken as a reference to child sacrifice. The verb *heʿĕbîr,* "cause to cross," may be used here to avoid the technical term for sacrifice to YHWH *(hiqrîb)*—i.e., to make it clear that the two have absolutely nothing in common.

18:22 "Abomination." This is the first of six occurrences of *tôʿēbâ.* This word contains a certain rhetorical force since the word is "affectively laden" (Gerstenberger 1997, 1429), especially if Zorrell is correct in relating it to Arabic *ʿāfa,* "to feel aversion, disgust." It is the opposite of *rāṣôn,* "[YHWH's] favor." The term *tôʿēbâ* may also imply the death penalty as punishment (Gemser 1953, 58).

18:23 "Perversion." The word *tēbēl* comes from the root *bll* and literally means "mixing." It is the word used for the mixing of languages in the story of the Tower of Babel (Gen 11:7, 9). Such mixing is the antithesis of the separation of the holy and profane enjoined in 10:10.

18:25 "The land became defiled; and I punished it . . ." YHWH, speaking in the first person, explains his motive for driving the Canaanites out of the land. YHWH makes a strong rhetorical appeal by the use of the image of the land vomiting out its inhabitants. This also indicates that the need has been felt for some moral justification for the dispossession of the native population in the story world.

18:26 "But you shall keep . . ." The "you" here is emphatic—*you,* as opposed to those who are being vomited from the land. The implication is, of course, that if *you* do not, *you* will suffer the same fate.

Leviticus 19

19:1-37 To the Whole Congregation of the Children of Israel

qᵊdōšîm tihyû You will be holy

Holiness/Morality

A series of repetitions ties these verses together (Magonet 1983, 151–52):

19:3 You shall keep my Sabbaths
19:30 You shall keep my Sabbaths

19:4 Do not turn (to idols)
19:31 Do not turn (to mediums or wizards)

19:14 You shall fear your God
19:32 You shall fear your God

19:15 You shall not render an unjust judgment
19:35 You shall not render an unjust judgment[5]

19:18 You shall love your neighbor as yourself
19:34 You shall love the alien as yourself

19:19 You shall keep my statutes
19:37 You shall keep all my statutes

19:5 The word "sacrifice" *(zbḥ)* encloses the verse.

wəʾim **"If eaten on the third day . . ." (19:7-8)**

19:11-12 "You shall not steal . . . deal falsely . . . lie . . ." The *Sipra* sees the four forbidden actions as sequential: "The thief in covering up his crime will have to deceive then lie and ultimately take a false oath" (Magonet 1983, 154).

19:11-18 Dealings with one's neighbor. The three words used for "neighbor" pile up as the text goes along (Wenham 1979, 257):

11-12		*ʿāmît*		
13-14				*rēʿa*
15-16		*ʿāmît*	*ʿām*	*rēʿa*
17-18	*ʾaḥ*	*ʿāmît*	*ʿām*	*rēʿa*

[5] The Hebrew is more similar than the NRSV reflects. Both verses begin *lōʾ-taʿăśû ʿāwel bammišpāṭ*.

Each of these units consists in two verses and each unit ends with "I am the Lord." The first two units end with a reference to a person's relationship with God, which is first expressed negatively (v. 12) and then positively (v. 14). The second two deal with one's relationship to one's fellow expressed first negatively (not stand by blood v. 16) and then positively (love, v. 18). The section begins speaking of human relationships in the third person, but from the end of v. 15 the suffix *–kâ* (your) occurs seven times. "There is thus an increasing emphasis on your relatedness to the object of your actions as the passage continues" (Magonet 1983, 154).

19:14 This verse is in chiastic form (Magonet 1983, 155):

do not curse	the deaf	
and before	the blind	do not put a stumbling block

19:15-16 "You shall not be partial to the poor or defer to the great." Pairing "poor" *(dal)* with "great" *(gādôl)* rather than "rich" should catch the reader's attention. The motive for such a combination might be to create assonance. This also happens with *hlk,* "walk," and *rkyl,* "slander," as well as *dam,* "blood," and *ʿmd,* "to stand." The strangeness of these expressions might be due to the play with sounds, but this also has the effect of producing "a dramatic deepening of the meaning of the two verbs employed: your very walking *(hlk)* can be itself a betrayal *(rākîl);* your mere standing *(ʿmd)* can be at the expense of someone's blood (*dam*)" (Magonet 1983, 158).

19:16 "You shall not profit by the blood of your neighbor." A literal translation would be "You shall not stand on (or by) the blood of your neighbor." The NRSV gives one interpretation. Others include "You will not put your neighbor's life in jeopardy" (NJB) and "Nor shall you stand by idly when your neighbor's life is at stake" (NAB). Some understand this to forbid a false accusation that brings the death penalty; others understand it to refer to failing to protect the neighbor in time of danger (Magonet 1983, 157).

19:17 "You shall not hate in your heart . . ." The similarity in thought and vocabulary between Leviticus and Ezekiel has long been noted and various explanations have been suggested. But in this verse we have the first of only three instances of the word "heart" *(lēb, lēbāb)* in Leviticus whereas Ezekiel has forty-seven. Since, in the view of this culture, the heart is the seat of thinking, planning, and willing, what is envisioned here is not inner feelings but plans and actions.

19:18 "You shall love your neighbor . . ." Malamat (1990) suggests that *ʾāhab lᵊ* (found four times in the Old Testament, including the present verse), as opposed to the more common *ʾāhab ʾet,* means "to be of use to, to be beneficial to, to assist or help." Perhaps, on the basis of the other texts cited by Malamat (1 Kgs 5:1 [5:15], 2 Chr 18:28–19:2) it would be better to understand the phrase in terms of covenant relationship (Moran 1963).

19:19 Carmichael sees the "forbidden mixtures" as figurative commentaries on sexual matters narrated in the patriarchal narratives (e.g., Joseph's marriage with Asenath was a mixing of two kinds of seed).

> Presumably, in ordinary life there was nothing untoward about mixing materials in clothing. The idea that there was something wrong about it would occasion surprise. Hence, to prohibit a mixing of two materials is intended to puzzle . . . All three prohibitions are . . . arresting. Not to appreciate this feature is to lose the significance of what they communicate. If the rules had prohibited animals (of the same species) from cross-breeding, a field from being sown with different seeds, and clothing from comprising different materials, they would have prohibited ordinary, sensible usage. To appear to deny standard practice is what is arresting (Carmichael 1995, 447).

If Carmichael is correct, then the competence of the implied reader would require recognition that the prohibitions are not to be taken literally but are here for effect.

Leviticus 20

Sanctions

20:1-27 Speak to the Children of Israel

ʾîš ʾîš mibbᵊnê yiśrāʾēl Anyone of the children of Israel . . .

20:1-5 Child Sacrifice to Molech

20:6-9 Admonition to Holiness Framed by a Prohibition of Mediums and of Cursing One's Parents

20:6 "If any turn to mediums and wizards . . ." Although it may seem that the prohibition against consulting mediums has been haphazardly attached to the prohibition of Molech worship, the repetition of phrases such as "I will set my face against" and "cut him off from the midst of his people" in verses 3 and 6 bind them together (Hartley and Dwyer 1996, 83).

20:6 "If any turn . . . I will set my face against them . . ." There is some word play in this verse on the word "face." "The soul that faces *(tipneh)* ghosts, I will set my face *(pānay)* against her."

20:9 "His blood is on him." Here "blood" is plural in Hebrew, connoting blood shed by violence, in this case presumably when punishment is inflicted. Note the chiastic arrangement:

qll (curse)	*ʾāb wāʾēm* (father and mother)	
	ʾāb wāʾēm (father and mother)	*qll* (curse)

20:10-21 Sanction against Sexual Immorality

20:17 "It is a disgrace." For some reason the narrator (and the author) has selected a word *(ḥesed)* that is a homonym of a very common and theologically important word meaning something like "loving loyalty." But the homonym used here (and only one other time in the Bible in Prov 14:34) means "disgrace." The proscribed act is the antithesis of *ḥesed* or disqualifies one's claim to *ḥesed*.

20:22-26 Separation

20:24 The familiar image of a land flowing not with water but with milk and honey has a strong rhetorical effect.

20:24-26 "I have separated you . . . you shall make a distinction . . ." There is word play between these two verses on the word *hibdîl*, "to separate." YHWH has separated the Israelites from the peoples; the Israelites must separate the clean from the unclean. This is a repetition of a theme first seen in 10:10 and again in 11:47.

20:25 Note the chiastic structure:

clean beast and	unclean		
	unclean bird	and	clean

20:26 Sanction for Turning to a Medium or a Wizard

Leviticus 21

21:1-15 To the Priests, the Sons of Aaron

lᵊnepeš lōʾ yiṭṭammāʾ For the dead one shall not be made unclean

Maintaining the Ritual Purity of the Priests

21:6 Although YHWH is the speaker, he refers to himself in the third person as both YHWH and Elohim. The verse is framed by repetition of the root *qdš*, "holy," as is verse 8.

21:6 "The food of their God." See 3:11.

21:16-24 To Aaron

ʾîš mizzarʿăkâ One from your seed . . .

21:16-24 "Blemishes" that Disqualify Priests from Serving

21:24 The statement of fulfillment rounds off this section.

Leviticus 22

22:1-16 To Aaron and His Sons

Rules for Priests

22:3 Sacred Donations *(qŏdāšîm)*

22:2 "Deal carefully with." The verb used here *(nzr)* has a secondary connotation of separation (see Lev 15:31), so fits in with that theme as it has been used elsewhere in Leviticus (10:10; 11:47; 20:24-26).

22:4-9 Purification of Ritual Contamination

22:10-16 Who in the Priest's Household May Eat the Sacred Donations

22:29 This verse is framed by the word "sacrifice" *(zbḥ)*.

22:32 This verse is framed by the opposites "profane" *(ḥll)* and "holy" *(qdš)*.

22:17-25 To Aaron and His Sons and the Children of Israel

ʾîš ʾîš mibbêt yiśrāʾēl Anyone from the house of Israel . . .

22:17-25 "Blemishes" that Disqualify Animals for Sacrifice

22:26-33

šôr ʾô keśeb ʾô ʿēz Ox or sheep or goat . . .

22:26-30 Rules Concerning Victims

22:26-27 "It shall be acceptable as the Lord's offering by fire." In these verses YHWH is speaking directly to Moses yet refers to himself in the third person as "YHWH." From this it is clear that the other instances in Leviticus where YHWH refers to himself in the third person are not due simply to the fact that these are words to be spoken by Moses. Even when YHWH speaks directly, he refers to himself in the third person.

22:31-33 YHWH's Personal Conclusion

Leviticus 23

23:1-8 Speak to the Children of Israel

môʿădê yhwh The appointed times of the Lord . . .

This chapter has a high incidence of second-person plural forms.

Fixed Times

23:3 The Sabbath

23:4 Festivals

23:4 This verse is framed by *môʿēd* "appointed time."

23:5-8 Passover

23:9-14 First Fruits

23:10 "When you enter the land . . ." YHWH instructs Moses, who will not enter the land, to give instructions to those who will do so in the future.

23:11 The verse is enclosed by the *inclusio wᵊhēnîp . . . yênîpennû.*

23:15-21 Pentecost

23:22 Leave Gleanings for the Poor

23:23-25

23:32 The word "Sabbath" frames the verse.

23:41 The verb *ḥgg* "keep festival" encloses this verse.

23:42 This verse is set off by the *inclusio bassukkôt.*

23:9-22 Speak to the Children of Israel
kî tābōʾû ʾel-hāʾāreṣ When you enter the land . . .

23:23-25 Speak to the Children of Israel
baḥōdeš haššəbîʿî In the seventh month

23:26-32
ʾak beʿāśôr laḥōdeš The tenth of the month . . .

The Day of Atonement

23:33-36 Speak to the Children of Israel
baḥămiššâ ʿāśār yôm laḥōdeš On the fifteenth day of the month . . .

Booths

23:37-38 Conclusion

23:39-43 More Specifics on the Feast of Booths

23:44 Narrator's Conclusion

Leviticus 24

Oil; Bread of Presence; The Mixed-Seed Blasphemer

24:1-12 Command the Children of Israel

24:2-4 Oil

24:5-9 The Bread of Presence

24:6 Gane (1992, 179) holds that, in contrast to the sacrifices offered outside the temple, which are vertical in nature, the inner bread is horizontal, moving in the direction of the divine presence behind the veil. Such a view does not seem to take into account the use of *hiqrîb* (bring near) in the sacrificial vocabulary. Perhaps it would be more accurate to say that, unlike the sacrifices (which are twice referred to as *leḥem ʾiššeh;* 3:11, 16), the bread of presence has no vertical dimension. Gane (1992, 199) also sees in the fact that the bread is offered on a weekly basis, rather than daily, a link to the creation story in Genesis.

24:10-23 The Mixed-Seed Blasphemer

24:10 A new narrative section begins here—the story of the blasphemer. The man is said to be the son of an Israelite mother (who is mentioned first) and an Egyptian father. Thus he is the product of an unlawful mixture. This little drama has more of the features of a narrative. There is an exposition identifying the protagonist and tension is created both by the conflict between the two men but also by the blasphemy. How will YHWH's honor be maintained? There is some delayed exposition in the identification of the man's mother and her lineage. There is new tension in the need to know what to do with the blasphemer. And, finally, there is resolution in the reception of the divine decision and its (and the man's) execution.

24:11 "Blasphemed." Some writers and modern versions hold that *nqb* here implies naming YHWH, i.e., that the blasphemy consisted in pronouncing the divine name (Weingreen; Gabel and Wheeler 1980, 228). So, NJPS "pronounced," NEB "uttered," but SB "reviled."

24:11 "The mother's name was Shelomith . . ." The mother's name has been withheld and is now given. One may wonder whether there is any significance to her name, "Recompense-Daughter-of-My-Word" of the tribe of "[the Deity-]–Has-Judged."

24:12 "They put him in custody, until the decision of the Lord should be made clear to them." Tension arises due to a lack of knowledge of what to do with the blasphemer. This tension will be resolved by the revelation of YHWH's decision in the following verses.

24:17-22 A number of laws have been introduced into YHWH's speech. The foreignness of the blasphemer offers an opportunity to stress that the laws apply to native and foreigner equally and alike.

Leviticus 25

The Sabbatical Year and the Jubilee

25:1–26:46 Speak to the Children of Israel

kî tābōʾû ʾel-hāʾāreṣ When you enter the land . . .

The Sabbatical Year 25:1-7

25:1 The mention of Sinai gives these laws a certain emphasis.

25:1 When you enter The "you" here is singular. This chapter has the highest incidence of second-person singular markers (twenty-three) in Leviticus.

The Jubilee Year 25:8-17

25:14 "You shall not cheat one another." Hebrew: "you shall not cheat your brother." There is a certain rhetorical effect here. The text first speaks of one's neighbor *(ʿāmît),* but ends by referring to the same persons as "brothers" as if to say: "you are not only neighbors but brothers, and brothers would not cheat one another when buying and selling."

25:18-55 Details

25:36 "Do not take interest." "Interest" is literally "a bite"—a colorful and forceful image. One must not take a bite out of kinfolk who borrow money in hard times.

25:42 The repetition of *ʿebed,* "slave," frames the verse.

25:44 Repetition of the word pair "male and female slave" *(ʿebed wᵉʾāmâ)* frames the verse.

wᵉʾim **"If he has not been redeemed . . . (25:54-55)**

Leviticus 26

YHWH's Concluding Speech

YHWH's Promises 26:3-13

This chapter has the highest number of second-person plural forms in Leviticus.

26:3 "If you follow my statutes . . ." This verse begins a final oration in which YHWH, speaking in the first person, promises rewards for fidelity, threatens punishment for infidelity, and speaks of a time of restoration after punishment. In many cases the threatened punishments are simply reversals of the promised rewards (Levine 1987, 20 with additions):

Promise	*Threat*
4 your rains in season	19 your sky like iron
4 land yields produce	20 land will not yield produce
	16 seed sown in vain
	19 earth like copper
4 trees yield fruit	20 trees will not yield fruit
5 threshing overtakes vintage	33 your land shall be a desolation
5 eat bread to satiety	26 break staff of bread / not be satisfied
6 peace	28 fury
6 no one to make you afraid	16 terror
6 remove dangerous animals	22 loose wild animals
6 no sword goes through land	25 I will bring the sword
	33 I will unsheathe the sword
7 chase enemies	17 flee though no one pursues
7 enemies will fall	17 you will be struck down
9 YHWH looks with favor	17 YHWH sets face against
9 YHWH makes fruitful	22 wild animals eat children
9 YHWH multiplies	22 wild animals make you few in number
9 YHWH maintains covenant	25 vengeance for the covenant
10 eat stored grain	29 eat children
13 walk erect	37 stumble

26:8 "You shall give chase to a hundred, and a hundred of you shall give chase to ten thousand . . ." The first two members of this verse have a certain poetic arrangement with the word "pursue" forming an *inclusio* while the words *rdp* and *mēʾâ* are arranged in chiastic order (see Fox 1996, 76):

wᵉrādᵉpû mikkem ḥămiššâ mēʾâ

ûmeʾâ mikkem rᵉbābâ yirdōpû

26:9 "I will . . . make you fruitful and multiply you" echoes the creation story in Genesis (1:28). The blessings promised for those who observe YHWH's instructions continue the blessings of creation, but also recall the possibility of the loss of those blessings.

26:11 "I shall not abhor you." The verb *gʿl* is rare, occurring five times in Leviticus and five times outside of Leviticus. The image involved is that of a person's reaction to spoilage or filth (Levine 1987, 14).

26:13 "I am the Lord your God . . ." This is the conclusion of the promise section and ends with an elaborated version of the formula seen at 11:45; 19:36; 22:33; 23:43; 25:38, 42, 55.

YHWH's Threats 26:14-38

26:14-38 The threat section is longer than the promise section and more clearly structured into five sections each marked off by the words, "If you [still] will not obey me, I will punish you sevenfold . . ." or words to that effect. "The aim seems to have been to create a crescendo effect, so that the longer the Israelites refused to obey, the stronger became the punishment, multiplying sevenfold each time" (Grabbe 1993, 83–84).

26:21 "If you continue hostile to me . . ." The image of the people being punished for walking against YHWH in the threat section contrasts with the image of YHWH habitually walking in the midst of the people in 26:12 (Fox 1996, 79). Perhaps the Hebrew expression *hlk ʿm (b) qry* could be rendered "If you come up against me" or "If you take me on . . ."

26:28 "I will continue hostile to you in fury . . ." The recurrent expression *hlk ʿm (b) qry* is here modified by the addition of *baḥămat-qerî,* "in hot hostility."

26:29 "You shall eat the flesh of your sons . . . and . . . daughters . . ." In the Hebrew this verse features both *inclusio (ʾkl)* and chiastic arrangement (see Fox 1996, 79):

eat flesh-of-sons
flesh-of-daughters eat

26:30 "I will destroy." The use of *hišmîd,* "to exterminate," suggests that the object of destruction will be not only the physical structures of the high places but, more importantly, the persons there.

26:30 Carcasses on carcasses. The idols worshiped by the Israelites are characterized as "corpses." Idols are authoritatively evaluated by YHWH as dead and detestable things and the reader would do well to adopt such an attitude. This image fits in well with the use of the verb *gʿl* (see 26:11), whose subject here is *nepeš* (see 16:29). Levine (1993, 12) tries to convey the appetitive connotation of *nepeš* by the rendering "My feelings will spurn you!" There is also a neat antithesis between *peger* and *nepeš* ("corpse" and "soul," Korpel 1993, 134). Note also the edge in "*your* idols."

26:31 "I will not smell your pleasing odors." This phrase reverses the refrain heard sixteen times previously in Leviticus. It also reverses God's reaction to the sacrifice of Noah (Gen 8:21; see comment on Lev 1:9), which prompted God to promise never to destroy the earth again by flood (Fox 1996, 30–31).

26:32 "I will devastate the land . . . your enemies . . . shall be appalled . . ." There is word play here on two meanings of the verb *šmm*—"to be deserted" and "to be appalled."

26:33 "And as for *you* . . ." The Hebrew has an emphatic "you" plural as the first word in the sentence (Fox 1996, 80).

"I will unsheathe the sword . . ." "Unsheathe" here is *ryq* Hiphil "to empty out" (i.e., empty the scabbard). In Exod 15:9 the Egyptians speak of drawing the sword against the escaping Israelites but are thwarted by God. Here the opposite occurs; it is YHWH who unsheathes the sword against the people. The same image occurs in Ezek 5:2, 12 and 12:14.

26:35 "Your Sabbaths when you dwelt . . ." There is word play here in the Hebrew: *bᵊšabbᵊtōtêkem bᵊšibtᵊkem* (Korpel 1993, 134).

Future Restoration 26:39-45

26:39 "Those who survive shall languish . . ." literally, "fester, rot, putrify."

26:40 "Treachery against me." The use of *bî* here brings out the personal nature of the offence.

26:42 Use of the word "remember" *(zkr)* as the first and last words of the verse forms an *inclusio*. The patriarchs are named in reverse chronological order (Fox 1996, 82).

26:43 "Because they dared to spurn my ordinances . . ." The unusual *yaʿan ûbᵊyaʿan* introduces the reason for the catastrophe as failure to comply with the conditions stipulated in verse 15 above, which are here repeated in reverse order (Fox 1996, 83).

Narrator's Conclusion 26:46

Leviticus 27

27:1-34 Speak to the Children of Israel

27:2 The Lord your God is giving you . . . The second-person forms here are singular. This chapter has a high number of second-person singular forms.

ʾîš kî yaplīʾ neder When one fulfills a vow . . .

Assessments for Redemption of What Has Been Vowed

Commentators have been hard-pressed to find a reason why this seemingly anticlimactic chapter has been added after such a stirring final oration by YHWH. Christopher R. Smith suggests that the act of redemption is here intended to mirror YHWH's saving activity both in the past (Exodus) and in the future (return from exile). Read in this light, chapter 27 would not be a haphazard appendix but represent a deliberate strategy to soften the threats made in the previous chapter. "We are left instead with a picture of a believer making a special, uncoerced vow out of love for and gratitude to God" (Smith 1996, 30).

27:30-32 "All tithes from the land . . ." This is a good example of how Leviticus is not a complete handbook on Israelite cult. The word "tithe" *(maʿăśēr)* occurs only three times in the whole book of Leviticus (as opposed to forty-two times in the whole Old Testament), yet it is much discussed elsewhere in the Old Testament and must have been important to the priests since it was the source of their livelihood (Grabbe 1993, 70–72).

27:34 This is the narrator's conclusion to the book. The last word of the book is "Sinai."

FOR FURTHER READING

Aberbach, M., and L. Smolar. "Aaron, Jeroboam and the Golden Calves." *JBL* 86 (1967) 129–40.

Auld, Graeme. "Leviticus at the Heart of the Pentateuch?" Pages 40–51 in *Reading Leviticus: A Conversation with Mary Douglas.* Edited by John F. A. Sawyer. JSOTSup 227. Sheffield: Sheffield Academic Press, 1996.

Baker, D. W. "Division Markers and the Structure of Leviticus 1–7." Pages 9–15 in *Studia Biblica 1978. I. Papers on Old Testament and Related Themes. Sixth International Congress on Biblical Studies.* Edited by E. A. Livingstone. Sheffield: Sheffield Academic Press, 1979.

Bloom, Harold. "'Before Moses Was, I Am': The Original and Belated Testaments." *Notebooks in Cultural Analysis* 1 (1984) 3–14.

Brettler, Marc Z. "Nadab" *ABD* 4:980–81.

Carmichael, Calum M. "Forbidden Mixtures in Deuteronomy XXII 9-11 and Leviticus XIX 19." *VT* 45 (1995) 433–48.

_____. *Law, Legend, and Incest in the Bible: Leviticus 18–20.* Ithaca, N.Y.: Cornell University Press, 1997.

Chavel, Charles B. *Leviticus: Translated and Annotated.* New York: Shilo, 1974.

Damrosch, David. "Leviticus." Pages 66–77 in *The Literary Guide to the Bible.* Edited by Robert Alter and Frank Kermode. Cambridge, Mass.: Belknap Press, 1987.

Donahue, J. J. "Sin and Sacrifice. Reflections on Leviticus." *AmER* 141 (1959) 6–11.

Douglas, Mary. "The Forbidden Animals in Leviticus." *JSOT* 59 (1993) 3–23.

_____. "Atonement in Leviticus." *Jewish Studies Quarterly* 1 (1993/94) 109–30.

_____. "Poetic Structure in Leviticus." Pages 239–56 in *Pomegranates and Golden Bells. Studies in Biblical, Jewish, and Near Eastern Ritual, Law, and Literature in Honor of Jacob Milgrom.* Edited by David P. Wright,

David Noel Freedman, and Avi Hurvitz. Winona Lake, Ind.: Eisenbrauns, 1995.

Eslinger, Lyle. "The Wooing of the Woman at the Well: Jesus, the Reader and Reader-Response Criticism." *Journal of Literature and Theology* 1 (1987) 167–80.

Fishbane, Michael. "Biblical Colophons, Textual Criticism and Legal Analogies." *CBQ* 42 (1980) 438–49.

Fox, Mary K. Houser. "Leviticus 26: Elevating or Terrifying?" *JOTT* 8 (1996) 73–88.

Gabel, J. B., and C. B. Wheeler. "The Redactor's Hand in the Blasphemy Pericope of Leviticus xxiv." *VT* 30 (1980) 227–29.

Gane, Roy. "'Bread of the Presence' and Creator-in-Residence." *VT* 42 (1992) 179–203.

Gemser, B. "The Importance of the Motive Clause in Old Testament Law." *Congress Volume*. Copenhagen, 1953. VTSup 1. Leiden: Brill, 1953.

Gerstenberger, Erhard, S. *Leviticus: A Commentary*. Old Testament Library. Louisville: Westminster John Knox, 1996.

_____. "תעב *tʿb* pi., to abhor." Pages 1428–31 in *Theological Lexicon of the Old Testament*. Edited by Ernst Jenni and Claus Westermann. Peabody, Mass.: Hendrickson, 1997.

Gnuse, Robert. "Jubilee Legislation in Leviticus: Israel's Vision of Social Reform." *BTB* 15 (1985) 43–48.

Gorman, Frank H. *The Ideology of Ritual: Space, Time and Status in the Priestly Theology*. JSOTSup 91. Sheffield: JSOT Press, 1990.

_____. "Priestly Rituals of Founding: Time, Space, and Status." Pages 47–64 in *History and Interpretation: Essays in Honour of John H. Hayes*. Edited by M. Patrick Graham et al. JSOTSup 173. Sheffield: JSOT, 1993.

Grabbe, Lester L. *Leviticus*. Old Testament Guides. Sheffield: Sheffield Academic Press, 1993.

_____. "The Book of Leviticus." *CR:BS* 5 (1997) 91–110.

Gradwohl, R. "Das 'fremde Feuer' von Nadab und Abihu." *ZAW* 75 (1963) 288–96.

Greenstein, Edward L. "Deconstruction and Biblical Narrative." *Prooftext* 9 (1989) 43–71. Repr. pages 21–54 in Steven Kepnes, ed., *Interpreting Judaism in a Postmodern Age*. New York: NYU Press, 1996.

Harrison, R. K. *Leviticus: An Introduction and Commentary*. Downers Grove, Ill.: InterVarsity Press, 1980.

Hartley, J. E. *Leviticus*. Word Biblical Commentary 4. Dallas: Word Books, 1992.

Hartley, John E., and Timothy Dwyer. "An Investigation into the Location of the Laws on Offerings to Molek in the Book of Leviticus."

Pages 81–93 in *"Go to the Land I Will Show You," Studies in Honor of Dwight W. Young*. Edited by Joseph E. Coleson and Victor H. Matthews. Winona Lake, Ind.: Eisenbrauns, 1996.

Hecht, Richard D. "Patterns of Exegesis in Philo's Interpretation of Leviticus." *Studia Philonica* 6 (1979/80) 77–155.

Hoftijzer, J. "Das sogenannte Feueropfer." *SVT* 16 (1967) 114–34.

Houston, Walter. *Purity and Monotheism: Clean and Unclean Animals in Biblical Law.* JSOTSup 140. Sheffield: JSOT, 1993.

Hutchens, Kenneth D. "Defining the Boundaries: A Cultic Interpretation of Numbers 14:1-12 and Ezechiel 47.13–48.1,28." Pages 215–30 in *History and Interpretation: Essays in Honour of John H. Hayes.* Edited by M. Patrick Graham et al. JSOTSup 173. Sheffield: JSOT, 1993.

Jackson, Bernard S. "Talion and Purity: Some Glosses on Mary Douglas." Pages 107–23 in *Reading Leviticus: A Conversation with Mary Douglas.* Edited by John F. A. Sawyer. JSOTSup 227. Sheffield: Sheffield Academic Press, 1996.

Jagersma, H. "Opbouw en funcie van Leviticus 1:1-9." *Amsterdamse Cahiers voor Exegese en bijbelse Theologie* 13 (1994) 7–13.

Janowski, B. "Azazel." Columns 239–48 in *Dictionary of Deities and Demons in the Bible.* Edited by Karel van der Toorn, Bob Becking, and Pieter W. van der Horst. New York: Brill, 1995.

Johnstone, William. "The Legacy of William Robertson Smith: Reading the Hebrew Bible with Arabic-Sensitized Eyes." Pages 390–97 in *William Robertson Smith: Essays in Reassessment.* Edited by William Johnstone. JSOTSup 189. Sheffield: Sheffield Academic Press, 1995.

Joosten, Jan. "'Tu' et 'vous' dans le code de sainteté (Lev. 17–26)." *Revue des sciences religieuses* 71 (1997) 3–8.

Kirschner, Robert. "The Rabbinic and Philonic Exegesis of the Nadab and Abihu Incident (Lev. 10:1-6)." *JQR* 73, 4 (April, 1983) 375–93.

Klingbeil, Gerald A. "The Syntactic Structure of the Ritual of Ordination (Lev 8)." *Bib* 77 (1996) 509–19.

Korpel, Marjo C. A. "The Epilogue to the Holiness Code." Pages 123–50 in *Verse in Ancient Near Eastern Prose.* Edited by Johannes C. de Moor and Wilfred G. E. Watson. Alter Orient und Altes Testament 43. Neukirchen-Vluyn: Neukirchener Verlag, 1993.

Kselman, J. "The Recovery of Poetic Fragments from the Pentateuchal Priestly Source." *JBL* 97 (1978) 161–73.

Laughlin, J.C.H. "The 'Strange Fire' of Nadab and Abihu." *JBL* 95 (1976) 559–65.

Levine, Baruch. "The Epilogue to the Holiness Code: Priestly Statement on the Destiny of Israel." Pages 9–34 in *Judaic Perspectives on Ancient Israel.* Edited by Jacob Neusner, Baruch A. Levine, and Ernest S. Frerichs. Philadelphia: Fortress, 1987.

_____. *Leviticus: The Traditional Hebrew Text with the New JPS Translation.* JPS Torah Commentary. New York: The Jewish Publication Society, 1989.

_____. "Silence, Sound, and the Phenomenology of Mourning in Biblical Israel." *JANES* 22 (1993) 89–106.

McKane, William. *"qswsy p'h and p'at mdbr."* Pages 131–38 in *Text and Context. Old Testament and Semitic Studies for F. C. Fensham.* Edited by Walter E. Claassen. JSOTSup 48. Sheffield: JSOT, 1988.

McNamara, Martin. *Targum Neofiti 1, Leviticus.* Michael Maher. *Targum Pseudo-Jonathan, Leviticus.* The Aramaic Bible 3. Collegeville: The Liturgical Press, 1994.

Magonet, J. "The Structure and Meaning of Leviticus 19." Pages 151–67 in *Biblical and Other Studies in Honor of Robert Gordis.* Edited by Reuben Ahroni. Hebrew Annual Review 7. Columbus: Ohio State University, 1983.

Malamat, Abraham. "Love Your Neighbor as Yourself: What It Really Means." *BAR* 16, 4 (1990) 50–51.

Mann, Thomas, W. *The Book of the Torah: The Narrative Integrity of the Pentateuch.* Atlanta: John Knox, 1988.

Meacham, Tirzah. "The Missing Daughter: Leviticus 18 and 20." *ZAW* 109 (1997) 254–59.

Milgrom, Jacob. (1991a) *Leviticus 1–16.* AB 3. Garden City, N.Y.: Doubleday, 1991.

_____. (1991b) "The Consecration of the Priests. A Literary Comparison of Leviticus 8 and Exodus 29." Pages 273–86 in *Ernten, was man sät: Festschrift für Klaus Koch zu seinem 65 Geburtstag.* Edited by Dwight R. Daniels et al. Neukirchen-Vluyn: Neukirchener Verlag, 1991.

_____. (1991c) "The Composition of Leviticus, Chapter 11." Pages 182–91 in *Priesthood and Cult in Ancient Israel.* Edited by Gary A. Anderson and Saul Olyan. JSOTSup 125. Sheffield: JSOT, 1991.

_____. (1993a) "The Priestly Consecration (Leviticus 8): a Rite of Passage." Pages 57–61 in *Bits of Honey: Essays for Samson H. Levey.* Edited by Stanley Chyet and David Ellenson. Atlanta: Scholars, 1993.

_____. (1993b) "Sweet Land and Liberty." *BRev* 9 (4, 1993) 8, 54.

_____. "The Land Redeemer and the Jubilee." Pages 66–69 in *Fortunate the Eyes That See: Essays in Honor of David Noel Freedman in Celebration of His Seventieth Birthday.* Edited by Astrid B. Beck et al. Grand Rapids: Eerdmans, 1995.

_____. (1997a) "The Firstfruits Festivals of Grain and the Composition of Leviticus 23:9-21." Pages 81–89 in *Tehilla le-Moshe: Biblical and Judaic Studies in Honor of Moshe Greenberg.* Edited by Mordechai Cogan, Barry L. Eichler, and Jeffrey H. Tigay. Winona Lake, Ind.: Eisenbrauns, 1997.

_____. (1997b) "Jubilee; A Rallying Cry for Today's Oppressed." *BRev* 13 (2, 1997) 16, 48.

Moran, William L. "Ancient Near Eastern Background of the Love of God in Deuteronomy." *CBQ* 25 (1963) 77–87.

Morgenstern, Julian. *The Fire upon the Altar.* Chicago: Quadrangle, 1963.

Munk, Elie. *The Call of the Torah: An Anthology of Interpretation and Commentary on the Five Books of Moses. Vol. 3 Vayikra.* Edited by Yitzchok Kirzner. Translated by E. S. Mazer. Brooklyn: Mesorah, 1992.

Neudecker, Reinhard. "'And You Shall Love Your Neighbor as Yourself—I Am the Lord' (Lev 19:18) in Jewish Interpretation." *Bib* 73 (1992) 496–517.

Péter-Contesse, René. *Lévitique 1–16.* CAT IIIA. Geneva: Labor et Fides, 1993.

Rendsburg, Gary A. "The Inclusio in Leviticus xi." *VT* 43 (1993) 418–21.

Rendtorff, Rolf. "Another Prolegomenon to Leviticus 17:11." Pages 23–28 in *Pomegranates and Golden Bells. Studies in Biblical, Jewish, and Near Eastern Ritual, Law, and Literature in Honor of Jacob Milgrom.* Edited by David P. Wright, David Noel Freedman, and Avi Hurvitz. Winona Lake, Ind.: Eisenbrauns, 1995.

_____. "Is It Possible to Read Leviticus as a Separate Book?" Pages 22–39 in *Reading Leviticus: A Conversation with Mary Douglas.* Edited by John F. A. Sawyer. JSOTSup 227. Sheffield: Sheffield Academic Press, 1996.

Rodriguez, Angel Manuel. "Leviticus 16: Its Literary Structure." *AUSS* 34 (1996) 269–86.

Rosenbaum, M., and A. M. Silbermann. *Pentateuch: with Targum Onkelos, Haphtaroth, and Prayers for Sabbath and Rashi's Commentary.* London: Shapiro, Vallentine, 1946.

Sawyer, John F. A. "The Language of Leviticus." Pages 15–20 in *Reading Leviticus: A Conversation with Mary Douglas.* Edited by John F. A. Sawyer. JSOTSup 227. Sheffield: Sheffield Academic Press, 1996.

Schwartz, Baruch J. "The Prohibitions Concerning the 'Eating' of Blood in Leviticus 17." Pages 34–66 in *Priesthood and Cult in Ancient Israel.* Edited by Gary A. Anderson and Saul Olyan. JSOTSup 125. Sheffield: JSOT, 1991.

Segal, Peretz. "The Divine Verdict of Leviticus 10:3." *VT* 39 (1989) 91–95.

Sherwood, Stephen K. *"Had God Not Been on My Side": An Examination of the Narrative Technique of the Story of Jacob and Laban. Genesis 29,1–32,2.* European University Studies XXIII/400. Frankfurt am Main: Peter Lang, 1990.

Smith, Christopher R. "The Literary Structure of Leviticus." *JSOT* 70 (1996) 17–32.

Sullivan, K. "The Book of Leviticus." *Worship* 31 (1975) 465–75.

Tosato, Angelo. "The Law of Leviticus 18:18: A Reexamination." *CBQ* 46 (1984) 199–214.

Van der Ploeg, J.M.P. "Lév. IX,23–X,2 dans un texte de Qumran." Pages 153–55 in *Bibel und Qumran: Beiträge zur Erforschung der Beziehungen zwischen Bibel- und Qumranwissenschaft, Hans Bardkte zum 22. 9. 1966.* Edited by S. Wagner. Berlin: Evang. Haupt-Bibelgesellschaft, 1968.

Wegner, J. R. "Leviticus." Pages 36–44 in *The Women's Bible Commentary.* Edited by Carol Newsom and Sharon Ringe. Louisville: Westminster John Knox, 1992.

Wenham, Gordon J. *The Book of Leviticus.* New International Commentary. Grand Rapids: Eerdmans, 1979.

_____. "The Theology of Unclean Food." *EvQ* 53 (1981) 6–15.

Whitekettle, Richard. "Leviticus 15.18 Reconsidered: Chiasm, Spatial Structure and the Body." *JSOT* 49 (1991) 31–45.

_____. "Leviticus 12 and the Israelite Woman: Ritual Process, Liminality and the Womb." *ZAW* 107 (1995) 393–408.

Wieseltier, Leon. "Leviticus." Pages 27–38 in *Congregation: Contemporary Writers Read the Jewish Bible.* Edited by David Rosenberg. San Diego, Calif.: Harcourt Brace Jovanovich, 1987.

Wilkinson, John. "Leprosy and Leviticus: A Problem of Semantics and Translation." *SJT* 31 (1978) 153–66.

Wright, David P. "Azazel." Pages 1:536–37 in *Anchor Bible Dictionary.* Edited by David Noel Freedman et al. New York: Doubleday, 1992.

Wright, David P., David Noel Freedman, and Avi Hurvitz, eds. *Pomegranates and Golden Bells. Studies in Biblical, Jewish, and Near Eastern Ritual, Law, and Literature in Honor of Jacob Milgrom.* Winona Lake, Ind.: Eisenbrauns, 1995.

Ziskind, Jonathan R. "The Missing Daughter in Leviticus xviii." *VT* 46 (1996) 125–30.

Zohar, Noam. "Repentance and Purification: The Significance and Semantics of חטאת in the Pentateuch." *JBL* 107 (1988) 609–18.

NUMBERS

INTRODUCTION

Name

The English title given to this book, "Numbers," translates the name by which it is known in Latin, *Numeri*, and Greek, *Arithmoi*. In Hebrew the book is known as *Bammidbar*, which means "In the Wilderness." This difference in titles reveals a difference in conception as to the real subject of the book. Is it about the two censuses with which the book begins and ends or is it about the forty years of wandering in the wilderness? Or is it about the transition from the old generation to the new (Olson 1997, 230)? Certainly the first and second censuses, the census of the Levites, and the enumeration of the gifts of the princes are important moments in Numbers, but so are the departure from Mount Sinai, the journey, the conflicts, and the provisions made for the distribution of the land.

Interest

Numbers in the Roman Catholic Lectionary

Of the 156 Sundays of the three-year lectionary cycle used by Roman Catholics, Numbers is read four times or 2.56% of Sundays. The number of verses read on Sundays is eleven, or 0.85% of the book's 1288 verses. On weekdays Numbers is read eight times (1.28% of the pericopes read at these liturgies), covering seventy (5.43%) verses.

Numbers in the New Testament

Some New Testament texts that have the Book of Numbers as their background:

Num 5:6-7 In Luke 19:8 Zacchaeus offers to pay back four times what he has gained wrongfully. This exceeds the demand of full restitution plus a fifth found in Numbers.

Num 5:11-31 The ordeal of the suspected adulteress prescribed in this text forms the background of the story of the adulteress found in John 8:3.

Num 6:1-21 In Acts 21:24, 26 Paul sponsors four Nazirites. The meaning of this act of dedication is found in Numbers.

Num 6:3 According to Numbers, Nazirites are not to drink wine or strong drink. In Luke 1:15 John the Baptist is forbidden to drink wine or strong drink.

Num 6:18 Just as the nazirites shave their heads, Paul shaves his head in fulfillment of a vow in Acts 18:18.

Num 9:12 In John 19:36 the reader learns that Jesus' bones are not broken in fulfillment of scripture. This is a reference to Num 9:12.

Num 11:16 Moses is told to gather seventy elders. In Luke 10:1 Jesus appoints and sends out seventy apostles.

Num 11:25 Spirit rested on the seventy elders in Numbers and, in Acts 2:3, tongues of fire rested on the believers.

Num 11:34 This text describes what the Septuagint calls the "graves of craving" (LXX: *mnēmata tēs epithymias*). 1 Corinthians 10:6 says "These things happened so that we might not desire evil (*eis to mē einai hēmas epithymētas kakōn, kathōs kakeinoi epethymēsan*)."

Num 15:17-21 The people of Israel are instructed to offer the first batch of dough to YHWH. Romans 11:16 teaches that if the part of the dough offered as first fruits is holy, then the whole batch is holy.

Num 15:35 Then the LORD said to Moses, "The man shall be put to death; all the congregation shall stone him outside the camp." Hebrews 13:13 alludes to this text when it says, "Let us then go to him outside the camp and bear the abuse he endured."

Num 15:35-36 The death of the blasphemer by stoning is alluded to a number of times in the New Testament. Matthew 23:37 and Luke 13:34 say that Jerusalem stones those sent to it. In John 8:59; 10:31-33 the crowd attempts to stone Jesus, and in Acts 7:58 Stephen is stoned.

Num 15:38-39 The Israelites are commanded to wear fringes on their garments. In Matt 9:20 a hemorrhaging woman touches the fringe of Jesus' garment. Similarly, in Mark 6:56 people asked to touch the fringe of Jesus' cloak, while in Matt 23:5 the Pharisees are described as having enlarged their fringes.

Numbers 16 Jude 11 refers to Korah's rebellion.

Num 16:28 Just as Moses was sent by the Lord and does not act of his own accord, John 5:30 says that Jesus does not do his own will but the will of him who sent him and, in John 7:17, is not speaking on his own.

Num 18:8 YHWH assigns portions of the sacrifices to the priests. In 1 Cor 9:13 readers are reminded that those employed in temple service got their food from the temple.

Num 20:7-11 Water flowed from the rock, which, according to 1 Cor 10:4, was Christ.

Num 21:8-9 The bronze serpent was lifted up to save the people. John 3:14 recalls this and applies it to Jesus when it says, "And just as Moses lifted up the serpent in the wilderness, so must the Son of Man be lifted up . . ."

Num 24:17 According to Balaam's oracle, "A star shall come out of Jacob . . ." Matthew 2:2 says that ". . . We observed his star at its rising . . ." and in Rev 22:16 Jesus says, "I am . . . the bright morning star."

Num 25:1-2 The people of Israel have sex with Moabite women and bow down to their gods. Revelation 2:14 alludes to this when it accuses some in Pergamum of following the teaching of Balaam.

Num 27:17 Moses asks YHWH to appoint a leader who will lead the people out and bring them in. In John 10:9 Jesus says, "I am the gate. Whoever enters by me will be saved, and will come in and go out and find pasture."

Language

It is often said that biblical narrative is short on description. In Numbers this is reflected in the paucity of adjectives. The total number of adjectives in Numbers is about 1,347, spread over 561 of the 1,289 verses of the book. Most of these adjectives are numbers or demonstrative adjectives. If these (and the word *zāqēn,* "elder") are discounted, the total number of individual words used as descriptive adjectives in the book of Numbers comes to some forty-three.[1] Of these, eighteen occur only

[1] This statistical information is based on Accordance, which counts *qᵊlōqēl* as an adjective, but which I, following Holladay (s.v.), am treating as a noun, "a specific

once in the book, nine occur twice, and three occur three times.[2] The most common adjective is "full" *(mlʾ)*, used twenty-five times in chapter 7 in reference to vessels brought by the princes containing fine flour or incense. "Whole" *(tāmîm)* occurs nineteen times, "much/many" *(rb)* seventeen times, "few" *(mᵊʿaṭ)* eleven times, "unclean" *(ṭmʾ)* also eleven times, "big" *(gdwl)* eight times, "clean" *(ṭhwr)* seven times, "holy" *(qdš)* seven times, "bitter" *(mr)* six times, "living" *(ḥy)* six times, "near" *(qrb)* five times, "good" *(ṭwb)* four times, and "other" *(ʾḥr)* four times.

Many of these words are so common that they scarcely jump out at the reader.

Numeruswechsel

Only four verses in Numbers exhibit *Numeruswechsel:*

Num 13:2 Send *thou* men, that they may search the land of Canaan, which I give unto the children of Israel: of every tribe of their fathers shall *ye* send a man, every one a ruler among them.

Num 31:29 Take *[ye]* it of their half, and give *[thou]* it unto Eleazar the priest, for an heave offering of the LORD. (In this case, since YHWH is speaking to Moses, the plural form can be explained by dittography of the following *waw*. The Samaritan and Syriac have the singular here.)

Num 33:54 And *ye* shall divide the land by lot for an inheritance among *your* families: and to the more *ye* [some Hebrew Mss: sg] shall give the more inheritance, and to the fewer *ye* shall [Heb: *thou shalt*] give the less inheritance: every man's inheritance shall be in the place where his lot falleth; according to the tribes of *your* fathers *ye* shall inherit.

Num 35:34 Defile [Heb: *thou*, but some Hebrew Mss and most versions read plural] not therefore the land which *ye* shall inhabit, wherein I dwell: for I the LORD dwell among the children of Israel.

(unappetizing) leguminous plant." There is also some question as to whether the word *mārîm* in the expression *mê mārîm* is actually an adjective rather than a noun meaning "bitterness." See Bach, 33, note 8; McKane renders the word as "poisonous."

[2] Adjectives occurring once: blue *(kᵊ lîl)*, swollen *(ṣābâ)*, moist *(lḥ)*, distant *(rḥwq)*, on foot *(rgly)*, meek *(ʿnw)*, slack *(rph)*, fat *(šâmēn)*, lean *(rāzâ)*, long *(ʾerek)*, blood-colored *(ʾādōm)*, willing *(nādîb)*, small *(qṭn)*, upright *(yšr)*, ever-flowing *(ʾêtān)*, beaten *(kātît)*, new *(ḥdš)*, free of obligation *(nāqî)*. Two times: dried *(ybš)*, heavy *(kbd)*, strong *(ḥzq)*, strong *(ʿz)*, numerous *(ʿāṣûm)*, wicked *(ršʿ)*, sinful *(ḥṭʾ)*, *šᵊ tûm* (reading disputed), firm *(kēn)*. Three times: bad *(rʿ)*, summoned *(qārîʾ)*, constricting *(ṣr)*.

Rhetorical Questions

Numbers features a large number of rhetorical questions:

Num 11:11 So Moses said to the LORD, "Why have you treated your servant so badly? Why have I not found favor in your sight, that you lay the burden of all this people on me?"

Num 11:12 "Did I conceive all this people? Did I give birth to them, that you should say to me, 'Carry them in your bosom, as a nurse carries a sucking child,' to the land that you promised on oath to their ancestors?"

Num 11:13 "Where am I to get meat to give to all this people?"

Num 11:20 . . . "'Why did we ever leave Egypt?'"

Num 11:22 "Are there enough flocks and herds to slaughter for them? Are there enough fish in the sea to catch for them?"

Num 11:23 . . . "Is the LORD's power limited?

Num 11:29 . . . "Are you jealous for my sake?"

Num 12:2 . . . "Has the LORD spoken only through Moses? Has he not spoken through us also?"

Num 12:8 "Why then were you not afraid to speak against my servant Moses?"

Num 12:14 . . . "If her father had but spit in her face, would she not bear her shame for seven days?"

Num 14:3 "Why is the LORD bringing us into this land to fall by the sword? . . . would it not be better for us to go back to Egypt?"

Num 14:11 And the LORD said to Moses, "How long will this people despise me? And how long will they refuse to believe in me, in spite of all the signs that I have done among them?"

Num 14:27 "How long shall this wicked congregation complain against me?"

Num 14:41 . . . "Why do you continue to transgress the command of the LORD?"

Num 16:3 . . . "So why then do you exalt yourselves above the assembly of the LORD?"

Num 16:9 "Is it too little for you that the God of Israel has separated you from the congregation of Israel, to allow you to approach him in order to perform the duties of the LORD 's tabernacle, and to stand before the congregation and serve them?"

Num 16:11 . . . "What is Aaron that you rail against him?"

Num 16:13 "Is it too little that you have brought us up out of a land flowing with milk and honey to kill us in the wilderness, that you must also lord it over us?"

Num 16:14 . . . "Would you put out the eyes of these men?"

Num 16:22 . . . "O God, the God of the spirits of all flesh, shall one person sin and you become angry with the whole congregation?"

Num 17:28 [NRSV 17:13] . . . "Are we all to perish?"

Num 20:4 "Why have you brought the assembly of the LORD into this wilderness for us and our livestock to die here?"

Num 20:5 "Why have you brought us up out of Egypt, to bring us to this wretched place?"

Num 20:10 . . . "Listen, you rebels, shall we bring water for you out of this rock?"

Num 21:5 . . . "Why have you brought us up out of Egypt to die in the wilderness?"

Num 22:28 . . . "What have I done to you, that you have struck me these three times?"

Num 22:30 . . . "Am I not your donkey, which you have ridden all your life to this day? Have I been in the habit of treating you this way?"

Num 22:32 . . . "Why have you struck your donkey these three times?"

Num 22:37 . . . "Did I not send to summon you? Why did you not come to me? Am I not able to honor you?"

Num 22:38 . . . "do I have power to say just anything?"

Num 23:8 "How can I curse whom God has not cursed? How can I denounce those whom the LORD has not denounced?"

Num 23:10 "Who can count the dust of Jacob, or number the dust-cloud of Israel?"

Num 23:11 . . . "What have you done to me?"

Num 23:12 . . . "Must I not take care to say what the LORD puts into my mouth?"

Num 23:19 . . . "Has he promised, and will he not do it? Has he spoken, and will he not fulfill it?"

Num 24:9 "He crouched, he lay down like a lion, and like a lioness; who will rouse him up?"

Num 24:12-13 And Balaam said to Balak, "Did I not tell your messengers whom you sent to me, 'If Balak should give me his house full of silver and gold, I would not be able to go beyond the word of the LORD, to do either good or bad of my own will; what the LORD says, that is what I will say'?"

Num 24:22 "How long shall Asshur take you away captive?"

Num 24:23 . . . "Alas, who shall live when God does this?"

Num 27:4 "Why should the name of our father be taken away from his clan because he had no son?"

Num 32:6 . . . "Shall your brothers go to war while you sit here?"

Num 32:7 "Why will you discourage the hearts of the Israelites from going over into the land that the LORD has given them?"

The total number of such questions is fifty-three, distributed among the following characters:

Moses: 17
Balaam: 11
The Rebels: 10
YHWH: 6
Balak: 4
The Donkey: 3
The Angel: 1
The Daughters of Zelophehad: 1

Theological Passive

The following are examples of the theological passive in Numbers:

Qal Passive Participle

Num 5:2 . . . everyone who is *leprous* [i.e., struck with leprosy]

Num 24:4, 16 with eyes *uncovered*

Num 24:9 . . . *Blessed* is everyone who blesses you, and *cursed* is everyone who curses you.

Num 24:21 . . . your nest is *set* in the rock . . .

Num 26:9 . . . *chosen* from the congregation . . .

Niphal

Num 1:17 . . . men who had been *designated* by name.

Num 5:19 . . . be *immune* to this water of bitterness that brings the curse (also 5:31).

Num 9:13 But anyone who is clean and is not on a journey, and yet refrains from keeping the Passover, *shall be cut off* from the people. . . .

Num 10:9 . . . so that you may *be remembered* before the Lord your God and *be saved* from your enemies.

Num 12:7 Not so with my servant Moses; he is *entrusted* with all my house.

Num 14:10 . . . Then the glory of the Lord *appeared* at the tent of meeting to all the Israelites.

Num 14:14 . . . You, O Lord, *are seen* face to face, . . .

Num 14:21 . . . all the earth shall *be filled* with the glory of the LORD—

Num 15:25, 26, 28 The priest shall make atonement for all the congregation of the Israelites, and *they shall be forgiven* . . .

Num 15:30 But whoever acts high-handedly . . . *shall be cut off* from among the people.

Num 15:31 Because of having despised the word of the LORD and broken his commandment, such a person *shall be utterly cut off* and bear the guilt.

Num 16:19 . . . the glory of the LORD *appeared* to the whole congregation.

Num 16:26 He said to the congregation, "Turn away from the tents of these wicked men, and touch nothing of theirs, or you *will be swept away* for all their sins."

Num 16:29 If these people die a natural death or if a natural fate *comes* [is visited] on them, then the LORD has not sent me.

Num 16:48 . . . the plague *was stopped*.

Num 18:27 It *shall be reckoned* to you as your gift . . .

Num 18:30 . . . the rest *shall be reckoned* to the Levites . . .

Num 19:13 . . . such persons *shall be cut off* from Israel . . .

Num 19:20 . . . those persons *shall be cut off* from the assembly . . .

Num 20:6 . . . the glory of the LORD *appeared* to them.

Pual

Num 3:16 So Moses enrolled them according to the word of the LORD, as he *was commanded.*

Num 12:10 When the cloud went away from over the tent, Miriam *had become leprous,* [i.e., struck with leprosy] as white as snow. And Aaron turned towards Miriam and saw that she *was leprous.*

Num 15:34 They put him in custody, because *it was not clear* [i.e., it had not been made clear—by YHWH] what should be done to him.

Num 22:6 . . . whomever you bless *is blessed* . . .

Hophal

Num 22:6 . . . whomever you curse *is cursed (yûʾār).*

Plot

Between the beginning of Numbers and its end some important changes take place in the overall plot of the Torah: The number of men who are of fighting age is established. The arrangement of the camp and the order of march are set. This leads up to the important moment when the people leave Mount Sinai and begin their journey to the Promised Land (Mann 1988, 126). But it turns out that there is an obstacle in their way. That obstacle is the people themselves (or, rather, their lack of faith in YHWH). This is manifested in a series of conflicts between the people, on the one hand, and Moses, Aaron, and YHWH, on the other. The completion of the journey has to be delayed until the rebellious generation dies out. After this happens, a second census is taken, a successor to Moses is named, and the method for distributing the land is established.

Tension

Numbers features many more instances of narrative tension than does Leviticus. Most of the plot tension in Numbers comes from a series of rebellions against Moses (and Aaron) and YHWH that begin in chapter 11.

Foreshadowings of Future Tension

There are a couple of foreshadowings of future tension before chapter 11. First, the repeated (12x) statement that the purpose of the census was to establish the number of men able to bear arms. This notice prepares for the future battles in the story. Second, there is the notice in 1:53 that the Levites should camp around the Tabernacle "that there may be no wrath on the congregation of the Israelites." This is followed in 3:4 by a flashback to the story of Nadab and Abihu and the notice that any outsider who encroaches on the sacred precinct is to be put to death (3:10) and that any Kohathite who comes in contact with the holy things will die (4:15, 18-20). All of this prepares the way for the conflict stories that begin in chapter 11 which have to do with who is to approach the holy. Milgrom (1997, 243–44) thinks that the key word to understanding Numbers is the verb *qārēb,* "which should be rendered 'encroach' in prohibitive contexts and 'qualify' in permissive contexts." With reference to the prohibitions, he continues, "Illicit contact with the sacred produces divine wrath or plague . . . which is liable to strike down not only the sinner but the entire community."

There is a certain amount of suspense also in the ritual prescribed for a woman suspected of adultery (the *sotah*). However, the dramatic tension is much lessened by the fact that the legislation is given in abstract—i.e., it is not the narration of an actual case involving a real person—so there is no denouement to the story. Nevertheless, the reader may well be wondering what happens in an actual case when a woman drinks the prescribed potion and everyone waits to see what will happen to her. It should be noted that no punishment is prescribed if she is found guilty.

Another minor point of tension arises with the case of those who could not celebrate the Passover at the proper time (9:6). There is some delay in the resolution of this problem while Moses consults YHWH (9:8), but soon the solution of an alternative celebration is forthcoming (9:10-11).

The reader will naturally wonder what the final outcome was when Moses invited Hobab to accompany the people as guide (10:29). Hobab declined, but Moses continued with an offer of land. The incident ends at that point with no indication of the outcome.

The Revolts

Much more tension-filled are the stories of the various revolts, running from chapters 11–20.

Numbers 11:1-3 is a miniature conflict story in three verses, which functions to set the tone and act as a preview of what is to come:

> The people complain.
> YHWH hears, becomes angry, and sends fire.
> The people cry out to Moses.
> Moses prays and the fire is abated.
> The place is given a name that reflects the story.

A much longer and more complicated story begins in 11:4 when riffraff among the people complain about food and Moses complains about the complainers (11:11-15). YHWH proposes to put some of Moses' spirit on seventy elders and to give the people meat, but Moses questions whether even YHWH can provide enough to satisfy so many people. When the spirit falls on Eldad and Medad outside the camp, Joshua sees this as a crisis but is calmed by Moses. The promised meat comes in the form of quail but the people are struck with plague while the meat is still between their teeth (11:33). Unlike other conflict stories, there is no indication of the number of people who died from the plague, of intercession for the people by Moses, or of the end of the plague. The narrative arc that began with the craving of the riffraff ends with the naming of the place "graves of craving." The reader can connect the dots.

Immediately following the rebellion of the riffraff comes the rebellion of Moses' own kin (12:1-16). This story is set off from what precedes and follows by change of characters and of place:

> Miriam and Aaron speak against Moses.
> YHWH hears it.
> YHWH comes down to the tent and summons them.
> YHWH rebukes Miriam and Aaron and strikes Miriam with "leprosy."
> Aaron asks Moses for forgiveness and intercession.
> Moses asks God to heal Miriam.
> YHWH replies with a rhetorical question.
> Miriam is shut out of the camp for seven days and then readmitted.

The next crisis comes in chapter 14 when the people refuse to enter the Promised Land after the spies bring back a report that giants inhabit the land. The Israelites are ready to stone Joshua and Caleb, who advocate entering the land (14:10). YHWH is ready to disown all the people and start over again with Moses (14:12). This is clearly the highest point of tension in this episode. Moses persuades YHWH not to kill the people, but YHWH condemns them to die in the desert (14:20-23). Only a new generation will be allowed to enter the land. This is not the end of the story. Once the people hear their sentence, they decide to take matters into their own hands. They have changed their minds and are now ready to take possession of the land, but it is too late. Their attempt to go up without the ark and without Moses is doomed to failure.

A drama on a smaller scale begins in 15:32 with the story of the Sabbath breaker. Some suspense is built with the delay caused by the need to consult YHWH about what to do. But once the order for execution comes, it is carried out swiftly.

A much more serious crisis arises with the revolt of Korah, Dathan, Abiram, On (only mentioned in 16:1), and the two hundred fifty leaders (16:1-35). Tension is heightened by personal confrontation (16:3) or refusal to answer Moses' summons (16:12). A contest involving fire pans is proposed for Korah and the leaders (16:6, 16) and Moses appeals to YHWH not to heed the prayers of his opponents (16:15). Once again, YHWH threatens to wipe out the whole people (16:20) but is dissuaded by the intercession of Moses and Aaron (16:22). The crisis ends with Korah, Dathan, and Abiran being swallowed up by the earth, along with all their families (16:31-33), and the two hundred fifty leaders being incinerated by fire from YHWH (16:35).

But this is not enough to convince the people and the very next day they accuse Moses and Aaron of causing the deaths (17:6). Once again YHWH threatens to wipe them all out and Moses and Aaron must act swiftly to halt the plague that has broken out (17:11-15). The legitimacy of Aaron's authority is confirmed by the contest with the staves (17:16-28).

The earlier warnings against encroachment are repeated in 18:3, 5, and 7.

Chapter 20 features the famous conflict over lack of water and its resultant twist—Moses and Aaron are excluded from the land.

Hostile Encounters with the Local Population

The story of water from the rock is followed immediately by a different kind of plot tension. Moses asks Edom for permission to pass through and is threatened by a huge military force even after an assurance that the Israelites will not use the resources of the country and will not deviate from their path. The tension is resolved by Israel's circumvention of Edom.

Another encounter is told in the first three verses of chapter 21:

> The king of Arad hears about Israel.
> He takes some of them captive.
> The Israelites vow a ban if they are successful.
> YHWH heeds them and they carry out the ban.

But another crisis arises immediately when the people again speak against Moses and YHWH sends fiery serpents to punish them. The people plead for Moses' intercession and are cured by looking at the bronze serpent (21:4-9).

Chapter 21 narrates the challenge posed by Sihon and Og and their defeat. This is followed by a much more extended and suspenseful narrative—the story of Balaam.

The main cause of tension in the Balaam story is, of course, the question whether Balak will succeed in his attempt to curse Israel. In addition to this over-arching tension, tension is also created by Balaam's need to wait a day before answering Balak's delegation (22:8), God's anger at Balaam's going (22:22), the threefold threat from the angel, and the threefold attempt to curse Israel.

The foiling of Balak's attempt to curse the people is followed immediately by the notorious incident at Baal-peor. However, this incident is not told with much dramatic tension. It is only at the end of the story that the reader is informed that the actions that have been portrayed resulted in halting the outbreak of another plague.

The story of the daughters of Zelophehad in chapter 27 contains a little tension in the wait for an answer, and there is even less tension in the story of Joshua's appointment as Moses' successor (27:15-23).

YHWH's command in 31:2 to avenge the Israelites on the Midianites raises the reader's interest as to whether this will succeed, and the story contains within it another small drama when Moses is angered by the failure of the military leaders to kill the Midianite women and children (31:14-15). But this tension is soon resolved by the execution of Moses' orders to kill off male children and non-virgin girls.

A different kind of tension arises with the request of the Reubenites and Gadites to remain in Transjordan. Moses reacts to their proposal as a betrayal, comparing it with the refusal of the first generation to enter the land after the unfavorable report of the spies. But the two tribes stand their ground (32:16) and Moses must back down and compromise—they can leave their wives and children behind but must accompany the other tribes and even act as vanguard (32:17).

Finally, there is a slight element of tension in the revisiting of the case of Zelophehad's daughters, with which the book closes in chapter 36.

Structure

Douglas (1993a, 103) sees six law sections alternating with seven narrative sections. I find Douglas' working out of the proposal somewhat forced. On page 107, for example, she states, "There is no way in which Num 8:1-4 should count as a legal section jutting up in the middle of the narrative." And, again, on the same page, speaking of 15:32-36 she says, "If [these five verses] were counted as narrative they would add a new section." The forced nature of her analysis leads me to question the need to make such a strict distinction between narrative and law. Would it not be preferable simply to view the instruction as part of the narrative?

Apart from an outline of the book, I have not found any proposed structure convincing.

Characterization

Numbers features a large cast of characters. As in most biblical narrative, characterization comes about mostly through showing rather than telling. The reader must construe the character from what he, she, or they do and say. There is very little description.

In the following treatment I have tried to avoid "job description" as an indicator of character since such a description does not tell what a character has actually done or said. It is not, however entirely possible to avoid some of the "job description" material in outlining the words and deeds of the cast of Numbers since giving a job to a person supposes (rightly or wrongly) that that person is capable of doing the job.

YHWH

What YHWH Says about YHWH

The following is a summary of all the statements that YHWH makes about himself in Numbers:

Num 3:12 I hereby accept the Levites . . . The Levites shall be mine,

Num 3:13 for all the firstborn are mine; I killed all the firstborn in the land of Egypt, I consecrated for my own all the firstborn in Israel, they shall be mine. I am the LORD.

Num 3:41 But you shall accept the Levites for me—I am the LORD

Num 3:45 the Levites shall be mine. I am the LORD.

Num 5:3 . . . they must not defile their camp, where I dwell among them.

Num 6:27 So they shall put my name on the Israelites, and I will bless them

Num 8:14 the Levites shall be mine.

Num 8:16 For they are unreservedly given to me from among the Israelites; I have taken them for myself . . .

Num 8:17 For all the firstborn among the Israelites are mine. . . . On the day that I struck down all the firstborn in the land of Egypt I consecrated them for myself,

Num 8:18 but I have taken the Levites in place of all the firstborn among the Israelites.

Num 8:19 Moreover, I have given the Levites as a gift to Aaron and his sons . . .

Num 10:10 . . . I am the LORD your God.

Num 10:29 . . . the place of which the LORD said, 'I will give it to you'

Num 11:16 "Gather for me seventy of the elders of Israel . . .

Num 11:17 I will come down and talk with you there; I will take some of the spirit that is on you and put it on them . . .

Num 11:23 . . . you shall see whether my word will come true for you or not."

Num 12:6 . . . "Hear my words:
When there are prophets among you,
I the LORD make myself known to them in visions;
I speak to them in dreams.

Num 12:7 Not so with my servant Moses;
he is entrusted with all my house.

Num 12:8 With him I speak face to face . . . Why then were you not afraid to speak against my servant Moses?"

Num 13:2 "Send men to spy out the land of Canaan, which I am giving to the Israelites . . ."

Num 14:11 . . . "How long will this people despise me? And how long will they refuse to believe in me, in spite of all the signs that I have done among them?

Num 14:12 I will strike them with pestilence and disinherit them, and I will make of you a nation greater and mightier than they."

Num 14:20 "I do forgive, just as you have asked;

Num 14:21 nevertheless—as I live . . .

Num 14:22 none of the people who have seen my glory and the signs that I did in Egypt and in the wilderness, and yet have tested me these ten times and have not obeyed my voice,

Num 14:23 shall see the land that I swore to give to their ancestors; none of those who despised me shall see it.

Num 14:24 But my servant Caleb . . . I will bring into the . . .

Num 14:27 How long shall this wicked congregation complain against me? I have heard the complaints of the Israelites, which they complain against me."

Num 14:28 . . . "As I live . . . I will do to you the very things I heard you say:

Num 14:29 . . . who have complained against me,

Num 14:30 not one of you shall come into the land in which I swore to settle you . . .

Num 14:31 But your little ones . . . I will bring in. . . .

Num 14:34 . . . you shall know my displeasure."

Num 14:35 I the LORD have spoken; surely I will do thus to all this wicked congregation gathered together against me . . .

Num 15:2 . . . the land . . . which I am giving you,

Num 15:18 . . . the land to which I am bringing you,

Num 15:40 So you shall remember and do all my commandments. . . .

Num 15:41 I am the LORD your God, who brought you out of the land of Egypt, to be your God: I am the LORD your God.

Num 16:21 . . . so that I may consume them in a moment.

Num 17:10 (NRSV: 16:45) . . . so that I may consume them in a moment.

Num 17:19 (NRSV: 17:4) . . . I meet with you.

Num 17:20 (NRSV: 17:5) And the staff of the man whom I choose shall sprout; thus I will put a stop to the complaints of the Israelites . . .

Num 17:25 (NRSV: 17:10) . . . complaints against me . . .

Num 18:6 It is I who now take your brother Levites from among the Israelites. . . .

Num 18:7 . . . I give your priesthood as a gift . . .

Num 18:8 . . . I have given you charge of the offerings made to me . . .

Num 18:9 . . . every offering of theirs that they render to me . . .

Num 18:11 . . . I have given to you . . .

Num 18:12 All the best of the oil and all the best of the wine and of the grain, the choice produce that they give to the LORD, I have given to you.

Num 18:19 All the holy offerings that the Israelites present to the LORD I have given to you . . .

Num 18:20 . . . I am your share and your possession among the Israelites.

Num 18:21 To the Levites I have given every tithe . . .

Num 18:24 because I have given to the Levites as their portion the tithe of the Israelites. . . . Therefore I have said of them that they shall have no allotment among the Israelites.

Num 18:26 . . . the tithe that I have given you . . .

Num 20:12 . . . "Because you did not trust in me, to show my holiness before the eyes of the Israelites, therefore you shall not bring this assembly into the land that I have given them."

Num 20:24 Aaron . . . shall not enter the land that I have given to the Israelites, because you rebelled against my command at the waters of Meribah.

Num 21:16 . . . I will give them water.

Num 21:34 . . . I have given him into your hand . . .

Num 22:20 . . . do only what I tell you to do.

Num 25:11 Phinehas . . . has turned back my wrath from the Israelites by manifesting such zeal among them on my behalf that in my jealousy I did not consume the Israelites.

Num 25:12 . . . I hereby grant him my covenant of peace.

Num 27:12 . . . Go up . . . and see the land that I have given to the Israelites.

Num 27:14 because you rebelled against my word in the wilderness of Zin when the congregation quarreled with me. You did not show my holiness before their eyes at the waters . . .

Num 28:2 . . . My offering, the food for my offerings by fire, my pleasing odor, you shall take care to offer to me at its appointed time.

Num 32:8 . . . I sent them from Kadesh-barnea to see the land.

Num 32:11 Surely none of the people who came up out of . . . shall see the land that I swore to give to Abraham, to Isaac, and to Jacob, because they have not unreservedly followed me—

Num 33:53 . . . I have given you the land to possess.

Num 33:56 And I will do to you as I thought to do to them.

Num 35:34 You shall not defile the land in which you live, in which I also dwell; for I the LORD dwell among the Israelites.

In assessing the character of YHWH, the most authoritative statements are, naturally, those made by YHWH about YHWH. Of these, no doubt, the key saying is Num 15:41:

> I am the LORD your God,
> who brought you out of the land of Egypt,
> to be your God:
> I am the LORD your God.

Two other important self designations would be "I am YHWH" (3:13, 41, 45; 10:10; 15:41) and "I am your share and your possession" (18:20). YHWH sometimes refers to himself as "the Lord" even though speaking in the first person (as in 18:12). YHWH also swears by his own life, *ḥay ʾānî* (14:21, 28).

What YHWH Does

YHWH describes himself as performing a number of actions. Of these the most common, by far, is giving (19x). Most often YHWH speaks of giving the land to the Israelites or of giving the offerings and tithes to the priests and Levites.[3] YHWH has also taken *(lqḥ)* the Levites as a substitute for the firstborn Israelites (3:12; 8:16, 18; 18:6) and given them as a gift to Aaron and his sons (8:19). YHWH gives the priesthood of Aaron and his sons as a gift (18:7), he will give the people water (21:16), he will give King Og into the hand of Moses (21:34), he gives a covenant of peace to Phinehas (25:12).

Two other activities that YHWH describes himself as engaging in (about six times each) are speaking (*dbr* 11:17; 12:6, 8; 14:35; 22:20; *ʾmr* 18:24) and acting *(ʿśh)*. The latter includes performing signs (14:11, 22), threatening to make Moses a nation greater than Israel (14:12), actually carrying out what the complaining people accused him of doing, i.e., bringing them to the desert to kill them (14:28, 35), or threatening to do to the Israelites what he had once intended to do to the Canaanites (33:56).

Finally, some other activities that are mentioned between one and three times each include removing *(ʾṣl)* spirit from Moses and putting it *(śym)* on the seventy elders (11:17), striking down *(nkh)* the Egyptian firstborn (3:13; 8:17) and threatening to do the same to Israel with pestilence (14:12), consecrating (*qdš* Hiphil) the Israelite firstborn (3:13; 8:17), dwelling *(škn)* among Israel (5:3; 35:34 bis), blessing *(brk)* Israel (6:27), coming down (*yrd* 11:17), making himself known (*ydʿ* Hithpael) to prophets (12:6), forgiving *(slḥ)* the people (14:20), swearing (*šbʿ* Niphal 14:23, 30; 32:11), bringing the people out of Egypt (*yṣʾ* 15:41) and into the land (*bwʾ* Hiphil 14:24, 31; 15:18), hearing *(šmʿ)* the Israelites' complaints (14:27), consuming *(ʾkl)* the wicked (16:21; 17:10 [NRSV: 16:45]), not finishing off (*klh* Piel) the Israelites (25:11), meeting with (*yʿd* Niphal) the people (17:19 [NRSV: 17:4]), putting a stop (*škk* Hiphil; literally: drain off) to the people's complaints against Moses and Aaron (17:20 [NRSV 17:5]),[4] and sending *(šlḥ)* the spies (32:8).

What YHWH Says People Do to Him

YHWH also speaks of himself as the recipient of the (mostly negative) actions of others: "How long will this people despise me?" (14:11, 23), "they refuse to believe in me" (14:11), "why have they tested me

[3] Land: 10:29; 13:2; 15:2; 20:12, 24; 27:12; 33:53.
Offerings: 18:8, 11, 12, 19, 21, 24, 26.

[4] Whether Aaron is to be included here depends on how one solves a problem of textual criticism in 17:19. The Leningrad Codex, on which BHS is based, has "you" plural at this verse, but other Hebrew manuscripts, the Samaritan version, the Septuagint, and the Vulgate all read "you" singular.

these ten times?" (14:22), "[they] have not obeyed my voice" (14:22), "complain against me" (14:27, 2x). Moses and Aaron "did not trust me to show my holiness before the eyes of the Israelites" (20:12; 27:14), the people "rebelled against my command at the waters of Meriba" (20:24), "rebelled against my word" (27:14), "the congregation quarreled with me" (27:14), and the first generation "have not followed me unreservedly" (32:11). On the other hand, "Phinehas has turned back my wrath by manifesting zeal on my behalf" (25:11).

Other self-references are made by possessive suffixes (excluding those that have already been mentioned): "my word(s)" (11:23; 12:6), "my house" (12:7), "my servant Moses" (12:8), "my servant Caleb" (14:24), "my glory" (14:22), "my displeasure" (*tᵊnûʾātî* 14:34), "my commandments" (15:40), "my offering" (*qorbān* and *ʾiššeh* 28:2), "my pleasing odor" (28:2). YHWH also claims the firstborn Israelites as his own (3:13 bis; 8:17) as well as the Levites (3:41, 45; 8:14, 16).

Characterization of YHWH by Others

The character "YHWH" in Numbers is a person who is very specific about what he wants. He makes his will known by giving detailed instructions.

The Cult

In the area of worship (which is the worship of YHWH himself) he sets the Levites apart, ordering that they not be counted in the general census (1:48). He assigns them specific tasks (3:6-10) and establishes their work rules (8:23-26). He then orders a separate census of the Levites (3:15) and of each levitical clan separately (4:2, 22, 29).

The Levites are to act as a buffer between YHWH and the people. This is necessary because if the people encroach on YHWH's holiness he will react by striking them with plague (8:19). But even the Levites, whose dedication ceremony YHWH prescribes (8:8-22) and who are purified according to YHWH's instructions (8:6-7) so that they can function in sacred space, must be careful to avoid going beyond the limits set for them. YHWH orders that the Kohathites (whose job it was to carry the sanctuary and its vessels) not witness the dismantling of the sanctuary lest they die (4:17-20). Of course, this notice prepares the way for the later crisis of the rebellion of Levites (16:7-11).

YHWH orders the expulsion of unclean persons from the camp (5:2-3). He instructs the priests on the formula to be used in blessing Israel (6:22-27). He orders the presentation of the chieftains' gifts (7:11) and instructs on the setting up of the lamps (8:2).

YHWH gives instructions on the celebration of Passover on an alternative date by those who could not celebrate at the regular time (9:1-14).

YHWH orders the making of two silver trumpets to be blown by the sons of Aaron and specifies their use in summoning the leaders, the whole assembly, in warfare, and on festival days (10:1-10).

Perhaps under the category of worship we might also include YHWH's order of the stoning of the Sabbath-breaker (15:35).

YHWH outlines the preparation of the ashes of the red heifer (19:1-13) and their use (19:14-22). He also specifies the offerings of food to be made to him (28:1–29:39) and demands victims without physical defects (28:31).

The Land

YHWH orders the census so as to prepare an army that will conquer the land (1:2).

YHWH also makes provision for the entrance into and possession of the land. He orders Moses to send spies to reconnoiter the land (13:2) but when these spies give an unfavorable report YHWH wills their death (14:37).

YHWH orders the apportionment of the land by lot (26:55) according to the size of each group (26:56). He declares the pleas of Zelophehad's daughters to be just and tells Moses to give them a stake (27:7) and also gives general principles for similar cases (27:8-11). He specifies the boundaries of the land as a whole (34:1-12) and appoints those who are to apportion the land among the tribes (34:17-29). YHWH also orders the apportionment of levitical cities and provides for cities of refuge (35:1-29).

YHWH tells Moses to view the land (27:12) and tells him that after seeing the land he will die because of his disobedience (27:13-14).

YHWH commands the Israelites to dispossess the inhabitants of Canaan (33:52)

The Journey

YHWH determines the layout of the camp (2:1-34). By means of the cloud, YHWH indicates when to break camp and when to pitch camp (9:15-23).

The Rebellion

The reader is reminded that YHWH had willed the deaths of Nadab and Abihu (3:4).

When the people complain, YHWH hears them and becomes angry, causing fire to break out (11:1), but when the people pray to YHWH, the fires dies down (11:2). YHWH's anger at this incident is again told in 11:10 and becomes evident in the words "until it comes out your nostrils" in reference to the quail (11:20). YHWH once again strikes the people with plague (11:33).

Again, YHWH's anger is initiated by his hearing. This time, it is the complaint of Miriam and Aaron against Moses (12:2). YHWH rebukes Aaron and Miriam and strikes her with "leprosy" and departs in anger (12:6-15).

The people are condemned to wander in the wilderness so that they will learn what it means to thwart YHWH (NJPS: 14:34).

YHWH also orders the death by stoning of the man caught gathering wood on the Sabbath (15:35). YHWH has the earth open and swallow Korah and his followers (16:32) and sends fire to consume the two hundred fifty rebel chieftains (16:35). This death is to be memorialized in the bronze altar cover made from the censers of the deceased rebels to serve as a warning to others (17:3 [NRSV: 16:38]).

YHWH sends another plague in 17:11 (NRSV: 16:46).

When the authority of Aaron is challenged, YHWH orders the test of the staves (17:17). He has Aaron's (flowering) staff kept as a sign (17:25).

When Moses and Aaron fail to manifest YHWH's holiness to the people, YHWH forbids them to enter the land (20:13).

YHWH heeds the plea of the people for deliverance from the king of Arad (21:3), but then the people once more complain (21:5), and YHWH sends fiery serpents to bite them so that they die (21:6). But when the people confess their sin, YHWH provides a remedy (21:8).

YHWH is again angered by the incident at Baal-peor (25:3). He orders Moses to impale the ringleaders of the idolaters in front of him so that his wrath may turn away from Israel (25:4). YHWH later orders an assault against the Midianties in revenge for Baal-peor (Cozbi being the daughter of a Midianite chieftain; 25:17-18; 31:2).

Other

YHWH orders the restitution of wrongs (5:6-10) and the ordeal of a suspected adulteress (5:11-31) and institutes the Nazirites (6:1-21).

YHWH opens the ass's mouth (22:28), uncovers Balaam's eyes (22:31), and puts a word in Balaam's mouth (23:5). He also appears to Balaam (23:16).

YHWH designates Joshua as Moses' successor (27:18).

YHWH does not allow execution on the testimony of only one witness (35:30), and a murderer cannot be ransomed (35:31).

Elohim

Elohim is identified with YHWH in 16:22, where Moses and Aaron address YHWH as *ʾēl ʾĕlōhê hārûḥōt lᵊkol-bāśār,* "El, the God of the spirits of all flesh." All other occurrences of Elohim in Numbers come in the Balaam story, where Elohim has several speaking parts. When Balak's emissaries arrive, Elohim comes to Balaam and asks, "Who are these men with you?" (22:9). Elohim then tells Balaam not to go with them and not to curse the people (22:12). Later, Elohim tells Balaam to go with the delegation but only to say what Elohim tells him (22:20). Balaam says that it is Elohim who puts words in his mouth (22:38) and the spirit of Elohim comes upon Balaam in 24:2.

El

That Moses addresses YHWH as El in 12:13 and 16:22 establishes the identity of YHWH and El. As with Elohim, most of the references to El come in the Balaam story, with the difference that El does not speak at all but is only spoken of by others. However, it is known that there are utterances of El to be heard (24:4). El has not cursed Israel (23:8). El is not a human that he should lie. He does not change his mind, but does what he promises and fulfills what he says (23:19). El brings Israel out of Egypt. For Israel, El is like the horns of a wild ox (23:22). Jacob and Israel can only exclaim, "What El has done!" (*mah-pāʿal ʾēl,* 23:23). El will devour the nations that are his foes and break their bones. He will strike with his arrows (24:8). The following verse goes on to compare El to a lion.

The statement made about El in 24:23 is difficult to interpret. The Hebrew *mî yiḥyeh miśśumô ʾēl* has been variously rendered or emended in modern Bible translations.

The Angel of YHWH

YHWH's angel, who only appears in the Balaam story (but see 20:16), is characterized both by actions and by speech. The angel takes his stand in the road as Balaam's adversary (*lᵊśāṭān lô,* 22:22, 24, 26) with a drawn sword in his hand (22:23). The angel gives a speech of two verses demanding to know why Balaam has struck his donkey. The angel speaks in the first person, saying that he has come out as Balaam's adversary and that if the donkey had not turned away the angel would have killed Balaam (22:32-33). Finally, the angel tells Balaam to go with Balak's delegation but to speak only what the angel tells him (22:35; compare 22:20).

Moses

The most authoritative characterization of Moses comes from YHWH, who says that Moses has spirit on him—a spirit that can be drawn off for others (11:17). In 12:7 YHWH makes a series of statements about Moses: that Moses is not like other prophets, that he is YHWH's servant to whom YHWH entrusts his household, that he is someone to whom YHWH speaks "mouth to mouth," plainly and not in riddles, and that Moses beholds the likeness of YHWH. But YHWH also tells Moses that Moses did not trust YHWH enough to affirm his holiness before the people (20:12). Later YHWH will say that Moses disobeyed his command (27:14).

The narrator tells us that Moses was the most *ʿānāw* of all people (12:3; for discussion of the term, see the notes). He also represents Aaron as addressing his brother as "my lord" (12:11).

Moses is frequently said to carry out YHWH's command (1:17, 19; 3:16, 42, 49-51; 4:34-37; 8:20; 17:26; 20:9, 27; 27:22-23; 30:1; 31:3-4, 31; 36:5). All of these notices of Moses' obedience make his exclusion from the land for disobedience all the more remarkable.

Much of Moses' activity in Numbers is as an intermediary and intercessor between YHWH and the people.

As intermediary, Moses is someone to whom YHWH speaks throughout the book. He used to enter the meeting tent and speak with YHWH; he would hear a voice speaking to him from the cover of the ark (7:89). In 14:39 Moses repeats to the people the words he has heard from YHWH in 14:20-38 and relays YHWH's order to deposit a staff from each tribe in the meeting tent (17:21). Moses consults with YHWH about specific cases, such as the men who missed the Passover (9:4) and the daughters of Zelophehad (27:5; 36:5). He conveys YHWH's instructions about vows, particularly those made by women (30:2-17).

Moses' intermediary role is also exhibited in his intercession on behalf of the people. At his intercession a fire from YHWH that had broken out in the outskirts of the camp subsides (11:2). He cries out to YHWH to heal Miriam of her "leprosy" (12:13). When the people rail against Moses and Aaron the two of them fall on their faces—a gesture of intercession. Moses does the same when he is accused by Korah of putting himself above the rest of the congregation (16:4) and Moses and Aaron both fall face-down when YHWH once again threatens to annihilate the community (16:22; 17:10). Moses asks YHWH to punish only the guilty (16:22). When YHWH proposes to wipe out the community and begin anew with Moses, Moses counters that this will harm YHWH's reputation among the Egyptians and Canaanites (14:13-19). Moses and Aaron fall on their faces again in 20:6. Moses intercedes for the people when seraph serpents (21:7) bite them. He asks YHWH to appoint someone to succeed him over the community (27:15-17). Although, on several occasions, Moses intercedes to get YHWH to change his mind, he does not attempt to do so when he is told that he will not enter the land—in fact, he does not seem to react at all.

Moses also acts. He is charged with taking the census (1:2). He sets up the Tabernacle and anoints and consecrates it along with its furnishings (7:1). He receives the ox carts from the princes and gives them to the Levites (7:6). He gathers the seventy elders and stations them around the tent (11:24), he sends the spies (13:3) and changes Hoshea's name to Joshua (13:16). He orders Aaron to make expiation with incense to end a plague that has broken out (17:11). He deposits the twelve staves before YHWH and later retrieves them (17:22-23). He summons the people, calls them rebels, and then strikes the rock twice with a staff (20:10-11). He sends messengers to the king of Edom asking for permission for the people to pass through the land (20:14). He makes a copper snake and mounts it on a standard (21:9). He sends spies to Jazer (21:32).

Moses' speech is often characterized by the use of sarcastic rhetorical questions (see the list above). He protests to YHWH that the people are too much of a burden to him (11:11) and asks YHWH just to kill him if he intends to continue treating him the way he has (11:15). He questions YHWH's assertion that he will give the people meat (even Moses does not think it possible) in 11:21-22. He responds to YHWH's threat to wipe out the people by quoting back to YHWH his own self-description from the Sinai theophany (14:18). He castigates Korah and his companions for not being satisfied with their status as Levites and for desiring the priesthood as well, which is, in effect, a conspiracy against YHWH (16:8-11). He is angry with the military leaders of the campaign against the Midianites for not killing Midianite women and orders the killing of boys and non-virgins (31:14, 17). He is also angered at the rebuke of Dathan and Abiram (16:15). Moses tells the people that the way Dathan and Abiram die will show that what Moses does is of the Lord and not his own devising. He replies to the request of the Reubenites and Gadites to settle in Transjordan by comparing them with those who had refused to enter the land because of the bad report of the scouts and suggests that their actions would have the same consequence—wandering in the wilderness (32:6-16). But then he backs down and agrees to a counter-proposal (32:20) and assigns towns to them (32:28). He also recorded the starting points of the people's marches (33:2). He sets the boundaries of the territory to be divided among the nine and a half Cisjordan tribes (34:13).

The reader may wonder what it says about the narrator's characterization of Moses that he has Moses ask Hobab to act as guide *after* informing the reader that the people were being guided by the cloud (10:29-32)—is Moses the kind of person who likes to hedge his bets?

On the other hand, the fact that Moses shows no jealousy for his own prerogatives (unlike his assistant) in his response to the report that Eldad and Medad are prophesying in the camp indicates that he is not a person who acted simply in his own self-interest, as is alleged by those who challenge his authority.

Aaron

Aaron is most often associated with Moses or with the leaders. He is a person to whom YHWH speaks (18:1). His assigned campsite is in front of the meeting tent (a privileged position 3:38). The Levites are subordinate to him and his sons (3:6, 9; 8:19, 22), he oversees their enrollment (3:39; 4:34, 37, 41, 45), assigns tasks to the Kohathites (4:19), and directs the service of the Gershonites (4:27). He presents the Levites to YHWH as an elevation offering (8:11, 13).

Aaron is the object of the complaints of "all the children of Israel" (14:2), but is defended by Moses ("what is Aaron that you rail against him?" 16:11). He is accused by the whole congregation of killing YHWH's people (17:6 [NRSV: 16:41]). The fact that those who challenged Aaron's claim to the priesthood were swallowed by the earth (16:32) or incinerated by fire from YHWH (16:35) and the fact that his staff alone produced almonds when put in the sanctuary (16:23 [NRSV: 17:8]) indicate the wrongfulness of his challengers' assertions.

Yet the characterization of Aaron is not entirely positive. He joins with Miriam in speaking against Moses (12:1), complaining that God has spoken to him as well and not only to Moses (12:2). Because of his failure to believe YHWH, he will not bring the assembly *(qāhāl)* into the land (20:12). He rebelled against YHWH's command (20:24).

By going up a mountain and dying there he becomes a forerunner of his brother, Moses (20:28).

The People

Various words are used to refer to the people as a whole.

Qāhāl

The word connotes a company of people who have come together in response to a summons. Words derived from the root *qhl* occur about twenty-one times in Numbers. The only characterization of the *qāhāl* comes from "Moab," who refers to Israel as a *qāhāl* that will lick up all around it the way an ox licks up all the grass in a field.

ʿēdâ

The people are referred to eighty-three times as the *ʿēdâ*. Silver trumpets are used to summon them (10:2). They make an offering for unintentional offenses (15:24). The person caught gathering wood on the Sabbath is brought before them (15:33) and they take him outside the camp and stone him to death (15:36). At Moses' warning, they move away from the dwellings of Korah, Dathan, and Abiram (16:27). They and their livestock drink water from the rock (20:11). They witness Moses' and Aaron's ascent of Mt. Hor (20:27) and perceive that Aaron has died (20:29). They also witness the installation of Joshua (27:22). The trial of a manslayer is to be held before the *ʿēdâ* of a city of refuge (35:12) and the *ʿēdâ* is to judge between the manslayer and the avenger of blood (35:24). If the manslaughter was involuntary, the *ʿēdâ* is to rescue the manslayer from the avenger of blood (35:25).

Negative Characterization

Often, the actions of the *ʿēdâ* are represented as reprehensible. They raise a loud cry at the report of the spies (14:1) and YHWH himself calls them "an evil assembly" who have gathered against YHWH and will die in the wilderness (14:35) as a result. Nevertheless, the whole congregation complained against Moses (14:36). In the story of the rebellion of Korah, those who follow him are referred to as his *ʿēdâ* (16:5, 6) who have gathered against YHWH (16:11) and against Moses (16:19) and Aaron (17:1 [NRSV: 16:42]; 20:2). YHWH would consume the *ʿēdâ* were it not for the intercession of Moses (16:21) and the atonement made by Aaron (17:10-11 [NRSV: 16:45-46]). In 26:9-10, the narrator flashes back to Dathan and Abiram whom he says were of the *ʿēdâ* of Korah who died. In 27:16-17 there is another flashback to events in the wilderness of Zin where the *ʿēdâ* had quarreled with YHWH.

The *ʿēdâ* needs someone over them so that they will not be like sheep without a shepherd (27:16-17).

ʿam

The word *ʿam* means "people" or "kin" but may also refer to a military force. A few of the people's actions are neutral or positive in characterizing them: they gather manna (11:8) and quail (11:32); they number 600,000 (11:21); they did not set out until Miriam had been brought back into the camp (after her "leprosy"); they set out on their journey (11:35; 12:16). Probably the most positively characterizing action of the *ʿam* is to admit to Moses that they have sinned and ask him to pray YHWH to take away the serpents (21:7). Some of the most positive characterization of the people comes from an enemy—Balak. The king of Moab says that his country is in great dread of the *ʿam* on account of their vast numbers (22:3). An observer from a high place could only see a part of them (22:41). The *ʿam* have come out of Egypt and spread over the face of the earth (22:5). They are stronger than Balak (22:6). They live apart and do not reckon themselves among the nations (23:9). They rise up like a lioness and do not lie down until they have eaten prey and drunk the blood of the slain (23:24).

Negative Characterization

Such is the perception of an outsider, but the narrator often puts the *ʿam* in a bad light both in their actions and in their speech. They complain in YHWH's hearing (11:1); they weep at the entrance of their tents because they have no meat and miss the food they used to eat in Egypt (11:5, 10) and even go so far as to say that they were better off in Egypt (11:18). This makes them a burden to Moses (11:11, 14). They panic at the report of the spies and, although Caleb attempts to quiet them (13:30), they weep that night (14:1). YHWH himself says that the people despise *(nʾṣ)* him and refuse to believe in him despite all the signs he has performed among them (14:11). They decide to attempt to take the land by their own efforts after they have been told that they will not enter (14:40). Moses says that they continue to transgress (14:41) and that YHWH is not with them (14:42) because they have presumed *(wayyaʿpīlû)* to go up without the ark or Moses. So they are defeated by the Amalekites (14:45).

Later, in chapter 20, the *ʿam* again quarrel with Moses, saying that they wish they had died (20:3-5). In 21 they become impatient and speak against God and Moses. As a result YHWH sends serpents to bite them so that they die (21:4-6). Their worst behavior takes place at Baal-peor, where they cavort with Midianite women and bow down to their gods (25:1-2).

The Israelites (*bᵊnê yiśrāʾēl* and *yiśrāʾēl*)

Much of what has been said about the above-listed terms applies to the "children of Israel" who are, of course, to be identified with these terms and are frequently in apposition to them. That is, the "people" or "the assembly" are not distinct from the Israelites, but simply different ways of referring to the same group (however, in 31:12 the "children of Israel" bring booty to the *ʿēdâ,* thus allowing for the possibility of a distinction between the two terms).

The Israelites are said to encamp by companies (1:52) facing the tent on all sides (2:2). They carry out YHWH's orders (2:34) and YHWH's name is put on them and YHWH blesses them (6:27). The narrator takes up seven verses to describe, both positively and negatively, with much repetition of detail, how the Israelites would set out whenever the cloud lifted, and camp where it settled (9:17-23).

But the term "children of Israel" is also found together with the terms *ʿēdâ* and *ʿam* in the stories about rebellion against God and Moses (11:4; 14:2, 27; 17:6 [NRSV: 16:41], 27 [NRSV: 17:12]; 20:13; 25:6; 31:16). In 14:2 they make a long and bitter speech in which they propose to return to Egypt. In 17:14 [NRSV: 16:49], 14,700 die of plague and in 25:8-9 another 24,000 are killed by plague.

Besides the phrase "children of Israel," the word "Israel" is used alone beginning in chapter 16.

Many of the words and deeds of "Israel" are neutral as far as a moral characterization goes. They vow a ban if YHWH will deliver up their enemies (21:2), sing the song of the well (21:17-18), send messengers to Sihon (21:21) asking to pass through the land and promising not to veer off the road to take crops or water (21:22); they put Sihon to the sword and take land from the Arnon to the Jabbok rivers (21:24).

But much of what is said of "Israel" is positive: YHWH (21:3) listens to Israel's voice. No one can number their dust (23:10). YHWH is with them (23:21). No divination is effective against them (23:23). Blessing Israel pleases YHWH (24:1). Israel's encampments are fair (24:5-9). They do valiantly (24:18). They defeat the Midianites (31:4, 7).

But there is also the negative. Israel died from the bites of the serpents (21:6) and yoked itself to the Baal of Peor (25:3).

The Men

Another word that is used to refer to the people is "the men." All but one of these references is negative. The men who had spied the land said, "We are not able to go up against these people, for they are stronger than we" (13:31). The men who saw YHWH's glory nevertheless did not obey his voice (14:22-23). The men sent to spy out the land die of plague (14:36). The two hundred and fifty rebels were "men of name" (16:2). The men who came up out of Egypt above the age of twenty will not see the Promised Land (32:11).

Leaders

Aside from Moses and Aaron/Eleazar, the leaders of the people are referred to as "leaders" (sg. *nāśîʾ*) and "heads" (sg. *rōʾš*). Others in leadership positions are the elders *(zᵊqēnîm)*, judges *(šōpᵊṭîm)*, and commanders of the army *(pᵊqūdîm)*.

YHWH appoints by name a *nāśîʾ* from each tribe to assist Moses in taking the census of the people (1:5-16) and of the Kohathites (4:34 *[nᵊśîʾê hāʿēdâ]*, 46 *[nᵊśîʾê yiśrāʾēl]*). These same people are designated by YHWH as *nāśîʾ* of their respective tribes when YHWH assigns the camping places to each of the tribes (2:2-31). YHWH also appoints a *nāśîʾ* over the Levitical clans of the Gershonites, Kohathites, and Merarites (3:24, 30, 35). In chapter seven these leaders bring offerings of wagons, oxen, vessels, and food for the cult (all of which would characterize them as men of considerable means). A single trumpet blast is used to summon the leaders to assemble before Moses (10:4). The *nāśîʾ* of each tribe is to give a staff to Moses with the tribe's name written on it (Aaron's name will be on the staff of Levi: 16:17 [NRSV: 18:3]).

Negative Characterization

In some instances the characterization of the leaders is unfavorable. Those sent to spy out the land are called *nᵊśîʾîm* (although they are not the same persons so designated in chapters 1, 2, and 7). These persons, with the exception of Joshua and Caleb, spread a report about the land and its inhabitants that discourages the people from entering the land (13:31-33). In 16:2-3 two hundred and fifty leaders assemble against Moses and Aaron. They accuse them of exalting themselves over the assembly. The narrator adds to the negative characterization of these leaders by associating them with Korah, Dathan, Abiram, and On in their rebellion against Moses. Eventually the whole two hundred and fifty are consumed by fire from YHWH (16:35). The unnamed Israelite who was killed along with a Midianite woman (by Phinehas) is identified as a *nāśîʾ* of the tribe of Simeon. (The woman, Cozbi, is said to be the daughter of a Midianite *nāśîʾ* in 25:14, 18.)

As pointed out in the Notes that follow this Introduction, the fact that the new generation of leaders appointed in chapter 34 is not descended from the leaders of the lost generation would seem to imply an indictment on the latter—i.e., they are not succeeded in office by their sons.

Heads

The heads are mentioned several times in the book, and identified with the leaders (1:16; 7:2; 10:4; 13:3; 36:1). Moses addresses them on the subject of vows (30:2 [NRSV: 30:1]). They assist Eleazar in making a head count of the booty taken from the Midianites (31:26) and are among those to whom Moses gives instructions regarding the Gadites and Reubenites (32:28).

The only significant negative characterization comes in 25:4 where Moses orders all the heads of the people *(roʾšê hāʾām)* to be impaled as a result of the Baal-peor affair. This leads to the question of how many "heads" there were. When Moses asks for staves in 17:18 [NRSV: 17:3], he says that there is to be one staff for each "head of their households." Since twelve staves are given, one might get the impression that there are only twelve households, but this cannot be the case.

The father of the notorious Cozbi is identified as "the head of a clan, an ancestral house in Midian" (*rōʾš ʾummôt bêt-ʾāb bᵊmidyān,* 25:15).

Elders

When Moses complains to YHWH about his workload, YHWH takes some of Moses' spirit and puts it on seventy elders, who proceed to prophesy (11:25). But they do not appear again in the story except in 16:25 where they follow Moses as he goes to confront Dathan and Abiram.

Judges

The "Judges of Israel" appear only in 25:5, where Moses tells them to kill "each of his men" who yoked themselves to Baal-peor.

Commanders

Moses became angry with the commanders when they failed to kill the Midianite women and children that they took as booty (31:14). Later, after they had ascertained that none of their men had been lost in the battle, they approached Moses with offerings to make atonement before YHWH (31:48-50).

The Rebels

Korah

Korah's name, which could be understood to mean "baldy," might be an ill omen. His genealogy is traced back four generations (16:1), which would be an indication that he was a person of some importance and hence makes his rebellion all the more dangerous and treacherous *(corruptio optimi pessima).* The Levite Korah assembles *(qhl)* the whole congregation against Moses and Aaron (16:19). Moses accuses Korah's followers of wanting the priesthood (16:10) and characterizes them as wicked *(rᵊšāʿîm).* The fate of Korah and his co-conspirators vindicates

Moses' negative assessment of them (16:31-33). The fact that it is YHWH who orders the thuribles of the two hundred fifty leaders (with whom Korah is associated) to be made into a sign that would serve as a warning indicates that YHWH shares Moses' estimation of the rebels.

Dathan and Abiram

Perhaps the most damning thing that characterizes them is their statement that Moses has brought the people *out of* the land flowing with milk and honey (i.e., Egypt! 16:13). Moses calls them wicked (16:26), and their fate confirms this (16:31-33).

Outside Enemies

The cast of characters in Numbers includes a host of outside enemies of Israel.

śārîm

The officials whom Balak sends on embassy to Balaam are characterized by their not taking Balaam's response (that YHWH has refused to let him go) seriously when they report to Balak that Balaam refused to go with them (22:14).

Amalek (13:29; 14:25, 43, 45; 24:20)

Kain (Kenite) (24:21-22)

The People Who Live in the Land ***(hāʿām hayyōšēb bāʾāreṣ)***

They are described as strong (13:28) and of great size (13:32 *ʾanšê middôt)*. Those not driven out will become a barb in the eyes and a thorn in the side and will trouble *(ṣrr)* Israel (33:55).

The Canaanite

This term always occurs in the singular in the Hebrew of Numbers, but is translated variously according to its apparent referent. A character called "The Canaanite, the King of Arad" appears in chapter 21 (see also 33:40). He fights against Israel and takes some captives. But when the Israelites promise to put his towns under the ban, YHWH hands him over into the power of the Israelites, who utterly destroy his forces (21:3).

As for the Canaanites (plural), they are said in 13:29 to live by the sea and along the Jordan *(yōšēb ʿal-hayyām wᵊʿal-yad hayyardēn)*. This pairing of sea/river is seen both in the Bible and in Ugaritic poetry in connection with chaotic forces overcome by the deity. The association of the Canaanites with these mythic forces may be both an indication that they are to be counted among the forces opposed to YHWH and a foreboding of their defeat. The Canaanites are associated with the Amalekites in 14:43, 45.

Egypt (*miṣrayim* in all cases in Numbers)

If YHWH were to disinherit the people, Egypt would hear of it and tell the people of Canaan (14:13-14). Egypt oppressed Israel and their ancestors (20:15). The Israelites had gone out in the sight of all Egypt while they were burying their dead (33:3-4).

Edom

A personified Edom speaks in Numbers: in 20:18, "You shall not pass through or we will come out with the sword against you," and in 20:20, "You shall not pass through." They proceed to come out against Israel with a large, heavily armed force.

Moab

A personified "Moab" is said to be overcome by fear of Israel (22:3-4).

Sihon

Sihon is characterized both by his actions within the time of the story and before. He had captured the land of the king of Moab (21:26) and when Israel asked to pass through he refused and led his army out to fight Israel, who proceeded to defeat him and seize his territory. The despoiler was despoiled.

Balak

Much of the characterization of Balak is done by speech. In fact, Balak's speeches are given a great deal of space (22:5, 16, 37; 23:11, 13, 17, 25, 27; 24:10).

Balaam

Balaam's most consistent trait seems to be that he can neither say nor do anything except what YHWH tells him to (22:8, 13, 18, 38; 23:12,

26). For discussion on the difficulty of construing Balaam's character, see the Notes.

Minor Characters

Joshua

Joshua is first introduced as a *mᵊšārēt* ("assistant") of Moses in 11:28. The meaning of *mibbᵊḥûrāyw* in this verse is disputed. It can be interpreted to mean either "one of his [Moses'] picked men" (so the Greek and Latin versions, NRSV) or "from his youth" (Luther, NAB, NJB, NJPS). Joshua had been called Hoshea, but Moses changed his name to Joshua (13:16). He is one of the spies sent to reconnoiter the land (13:8). Only he and Caleb think that the land can be taken. Joshua makes an impassioned speech (he and Caleb tear their clothes 14:6), in which he expresses the faith that if YHWH is pleased with the people, YHWH will bring them into the land (14:7-9). YHWH then says that, of the Exodus generation, only Joshua and Caleb will be allowed to enter the land (14:30). YHWH says of Joshua that the spirit is in him (27:18), and that he and Caleb have unreservedly followed YHWH (*milʾû ʾaḥărê yhwh,* 32:12). Joshua is entrusted with the implementation of Moses' decision regarding the Gadites and Reubenites (32:28) and is one of those who will apportion the land (34:17).

Caleb

Caleb was also one of the spies (13:6) and he tried to calm the people after the bad report given by ten of the spies by saying, "Let us go up at once and occupy it, for we are well able to overcome it" (13:30). YHWH calls him "my servant," who has a different spirit and has followed YHWH with a whole heart (14:24). Only Caleb and Joshua remained alive after a plague killed the other spies (14:38).

Miriam

Miriam, together with Aaron, spoke against Moses because of the Cushite woman he had married, claiming that YHWH had spoken to her and Aaron as well as to Moses (12:1-2). How the reader is to evaluate these allegations can be seen from the fact that she was struck with "leprosy" (12:10).

Eleazar

Eleazar served as priest during the lifetime of his father Aaron (3:4). He was chief of the leaders of the Levites (*nᵊśîʾ nᵊśîʾê hallēwî* 3:32) and was given charge of the oil for the light, the incense, the regular grain offering, the anointing oil, the tabernacle and its contents and utensils (4:16). He is in charge of the slaughter and blood manipulation of the red heifer (19:3). He goes up to Mt. Hor with Moses and Aaron, and the vestments stripped from Aaron are put on him (20:25-28). Joshua is to stand before him while Eleazar inquires of the Urim for him. It is at Eleazar's word that the Israelites are to go out and come in (27:21). He receives a portion of the booty given to YHWH (31:29, 41, 51, 54). He is among those charged with apportioning the land (34:17).

Phinehas

Phinehas (whose name is Egyptian) is the son of Eleazar and grandson of Aaron. His claim to fame is that when he saw an Israelite man bringing a Midianite woman into his family *(ʾel-ʾeḥāyw)* he got up, left the assembly, took a spear in his hand, and went after the man into the *qubba*, where he pierced the two of them through the belly (25:7). This expression of zeal had the effect of stopping a plague that had broken out. Phinehas' action turned back YHWH's wrath. Phinehas is granted a covenant of peace (25:12) and perpetual priesthood (25:13). Later in the story Phinehas accompanies the expedition to wreak vengeance on the Midianites. He has the vessels of the sanctuary and the trumpets in his hand (31:6).

The Levites

The Levites are separated *(bdl)* from the other Israelites and belong to YHWH (8:14, 16). They are not numbered with the rest of the tribes (1:47, 49; 2:33), but are counted separately and by different criteria of age (3:15). YHWH accepts them as a substitute for the firstborn (3:12, 41, 45; 8:16, 18). They are presented as an elevation offering (8:11, 13-15) and are given to Aaron and his sons (3:9; 8:19; 18:4, 6) to assist him (3:6). They are appointed to the tent and its gear. They camp and march immediately around the tent as a buffer against the divine wrath (1:50-53) and make atonement for Israel thereby protecting them from plague (8:19).

In chapter 16 Moses reproaches the Levites (and their leader, Korah) for not being content with their role but seeking the priesthood illegitimately (16:7, 9-10) and for gathering against YHWH (16:11).

They are given wagons with which to carry the tent and its equipment (7:5-6; except the Kohathites, who carried the holy things on their shoulders) but they are to have no part in the dismantling of the sanctuary since this is reserved to the sons of Aaron (4:1-15; 18:3). They receive tithes from the people (18:21), from which they, in turn, give a tithe to Aaron (18:28).

Numbers 18:23-24 states that the Levites are to have no allotment *(naḥălâ)* because their *naḥălâ* ("portion") is the tithe, but 35:2-8 has the Israelites giving from their inheritance *(minnaḥălat ʾăḥuzzātām)* towns for the Levites to live in and pasture land around the towns.

The Reubenites and Gadites

The Reubenites and Gadites are said to own large numbers of cattle and to have spotted ideal pastureland in Transjordan. They are quoted as saying to Moses, "Do not make us cross the Jordan." Moses responds by comparing them to the lost generation, which refused to enter the land (implying a similar fate). But they stand up to Moses (if such is the nuance of *ngš* in 32:16 as suggested by the NJPS "they stepped up to him"; NAB: "they were insistent") and made a counter-proposal (32:16-19). Moses agrees, and the two tribes affirm their obedience to Moses and to YHWH, "Your servants will do as my lord commands" (32:25); "As the Lord has spoken to your servants, so we will do" (32:31-32).

Imagery

For all of its lists of census records, Numbers is not without its engaging images, among which we may list the following:

4 packing up the tent and its equipment for transport

5 the ordeal of the suspected adulteress

6 the long-haired Nazirites who, at the end of the period of their vow, shave off their hair and burn it on the altar

7 the princes bringing offerings of carts and oxen, silver bowls and basins, gold ladles, bulls, rams, and goats. The Tent of Meeting, the Ark of the Covenant, the Cherubim, and the lamps

8:10, 12 the Israelites laying their hands on the Levites and the Levites laying their hands on the bulls to be sacrificed

9:15-16 the cloud that covers the Tent and leads Israel

10 silver trumpets used for signaling

10:12 Israel setting out from Sinai

11:1 a fire ravaging the outskirts of the camp

11:5 the cucumbers, melons, leeks, onions, and garlic that the complainers remember eating in Egypt

11:12 a nurse carrying an infant

11:20 quail coming out of people's nostrils

11:25 the seventy elders prophesying

11:31 quail strewn on the ground two cubits deep

12:10-11 Miriam struck with "leprosy"—like a stillborn child whose flesh is half eaten away

12:14 a father spitting in the face of his daughter

13:17 spies scouting out the land

13:23 a cluster of grapes carried by two men

13:27 a land flowing with milk and honey

13:28 large, fortified cities

13:30 Caleb calming the people, who were alarmed by the report of the scouts

13:32 a land that devours its inhabitants

13:32 giants and grasshoppers

14:1 the people wailing through the night (after the report of the scouts)

14:3 wives and children carried off by enemies

14:3 returning to Egypt

14:6 Moses and Aaron fall on their faces

14:6 Joshua and Caleb tear their clothes

14:10 the people threaten to stone Joshua and Caleb

14:10 the glory of YHWH appears in the Tent

14:32 "your dead bodies shall fall in the wilderness"

15:3 an odor pleasing to YHWH

15:32-36 the story of the Sabbath breaker: finding him gathering wood on the Sabbath, bringing him before the community, stoning him to death

15:38 fringes and blue cord

16:6-7, 17, 35; 17:3 the contest with the fire pans: two hundred fifty elders bringing fire pans with coals and incense; a fire from YHWH consuming the men; an altar covering made from the fire pans

16:14 gouging out eyes

16:15 taking an ass

16:27 the people distancing themselves from the tents of Korah, Dathan and Abiram

16:32 the earth opening its mouth and swallowing the rebels

17:12 [NRSV: 16:47] Aaron running

17:13 [NRSV: 16:48] Aaron standing between the dead and the living

17:16-26 [NRSV: 17:1-11] the contest with the staves (Aaron's produced almonds)

18:17 dashing blood on the altar and turning fat to smoke

18:19 a covenant of salt

18:27 grain from the threshing floor or fullness from the winepress

19:2 the ashes of the red heifer

20:11 Moses striking the rock twice with his rod; the rock producing abundant water

20:20 Edom sending out a large, heavily-armed force against Israel

20:26 stripping Aaron of his vestments and putting them on Eleazar

20:29 the people weeping for Aaron thirty days

21 the seraph serpents and the bronze serpent

21:18 rulers digging a well with their scepters

22:4 an ox that licks up all the grass in a field

22:5 a people so numerous that they hide the earth from view

22:18 a house full of silver and gold

22:23, 25, 28 an ass sees an angel with drawn sword, pushes Balaam's feet against a wall, and speaks

22:31 eyes are uncovered

23:5 YHWH put a sword in Balaam's mouth

23:10 the horns of a wild ox (also 24:8)

23:24 a pouncing lion (24:9 crouching lion)

24:17 a scepter smashing a brow [NRSV: borderlands]

25:1 the people whoring with Moabite women and sacrificing to their gods

25:4 leaders publicly impaled

25:6 the people weeping at the entrance of the Tent

25:7-8 Phinehas following a whoring Israelite and his Moabite accomplice into a tent and running them through with a spear

26:55 apportioning the land by lot

27:17 sheep without a shepherd

27:23 Moses laying hands on Joshua

28:3 a burnt offering

28:7 a libation

29:1 sounding a horn

31:2 being gathered to one's kin

31:7 slaying every male Midianite

31:8 putting Balaam to the sword

31:9 taking Midianite women and children captive, seizing animals as booty, burning towns

31:12 bringing captives and spoils before the leaders of the community

31:17 killing boys and non-virgin girls

32:13 wandering in the wilderness

32:42 capturing "daughters" (dependent villages) of a town

33:4 the Egyptians burying those who had been struck down (by the angel of death)

33:8 passing through the sea

33:9 twelve springs; seventy palm trees

33:52 destroying images and cult places

33:55 stings in the eyes and thorns in the side

35:2 pasture land around towns

35:16-18 killing a person with an iron, stone, or wooden tool

35:19 the avenger of blood putting a murderer to death

35:20, 23 striking with the hand, pushing a person, throwing an object at a person, dropping a lethal object on a person

Knowledge

Some instances in which manipulation of knowledge plays a role in Numbers are:

Reader Elevation

The reader hears YHWH inform Moses that Israel's enemies will be defeated. Therefore this is something that the reader and some characters in the story know but that Israel's enemies, presumably, do not. The fact that the reader shares this knowledge with some characters in the story also creates empathy with those characters.

Israel's enemies do not know that Israel will be saved from them (10:9), nor that they are consumable ("bread") by Israel (14:9). Similarly, the Canaanites did not know that YHWH had responded favorably to Israel's vow to put their cities under the ban (21:3). Og does not know (as Moses and the reader do) that YHWH has handed him over to Moses and Israel (21:34). Edom does not know that it will be Israel's possession (24:18), nor does Amalek know that it will be destroyed (24:20). The Kenites do not know that they will be carried off as captives of Assyria (24:21-22) and Assyria does not know that it will be oppressed by the Greeks (*kittîm,* 24:24).

But Israel, likewise, does not know when it is in danger. They do not know that YHWH proposes to destroy them and begin anew with Moses (14:12). They do not know when they are in danger of being consumed by fire (16:20) or destroyed (17:10). They do not know that at Baal-peor YHWH would have consumed them were it not for the action taken by Phinehas (25:11).

In the story of Balaam the irony comes about from the fact that neither Moses nor the Israelites know anything about what is happening. They are oblivious of the danger or of the drama that is unfolding; unaware that YHWH is foiling all attempts to destroy them by means of divination. The reader alone is witness to these events.

The reader and the ass know (and Balaam does not) that an angel holding a drawn sword is blocking his way (three times! 22:22-23). The reader is able to recognize the irony in Balaam's wish that he had a sword in his hand with which to kill the ass (22:29). The reader is able to recognize that Balak's first delegation to Balaam withheld from the king the key information that it was YHWH who would not allow Balaam to accompany them (22:14).

There are some things that the reader does not know: Whether or not Hobab accepted Moses' offer of land in exchange for his services as guide (10:31), or why God became angry with Balaam for going with Balak's delegation after giving leave (22:20, 22).

The narrator has to explain to the reader what manna was and how it was gathered and prepared (11:7-9).

The narrator sometimes delays giving information to the reader: that Moses had married a Cushite woman (12:1), that the anger of YHWH against Israel had taken the form of a plague (17:11, but Moses knows what to do to stop the plague from spreading). In 1:48-49 the narrator has withheld from the reader the fact that the Levites were excluded from the census (although the reader may have wondered why no one was appointed from the tribe of Levi to participate in the numbering). The narrator then flashes back in time to fill in knowledge that the Levites were not to be counted with the general population.

In the story of the water from the rock, the reader knows that Moses has been commanded to speak to the rock (20:8) but that instead he speaks to the people. Moses was not told to strike the rock. Thus it appears that Moses either did not do as he was told, or knew more than the reader about what he was supposed to do (character elevation). The latter is unlikely since Moses is punished, but the reader does not know exactly why.

5:11-31 Knowledge plays a role in the ordeal of the suspected adulteress. Only she and her accomplice know whether or not she is guilty. The outcome of the ordeal is both punishment and knowledge. If the woman suffers ill effects from drinking the curse, then all will know that she is guilty. But, strangely, nothing is made of this knowledge—the adulteress is not put to death as the law requires (unless this is implied in the closing verse 5:31, *nśʾ ʿwn*).

9:18-23 The people did not know when the cloud would move (when they would break camp and set out on their journey) or when it would remain in one place, or how long they would stay.

12:6-8 YHWH says that Moses' way of knowing YHWH is qualitatively different from the way other prophets know YHWH (something that Aaron and Miriam learn when they challenge Moses' authority).

The Israelites are supposed to *know* (16:28) from the punishment of Dathan, Abiram, Korah, and the two hundred fifty elders (16:31-35) that YHWH has sent Moses, but in 17:6 they do not seem to have learned.

17:23 The Israelites learn from the budding of Aaron's rod that he has been chosen as priest. This new knowledge leads them to fear the divine wrath as punishment for encroachment (17:27 [NRSV: 17:12]).

Point of View/Focalization

Almost all the focalization in Numbers is external, although characters sometimes report their perceptions.

Examples of Shift of Viewpoint

Shifts in viewpoint in biblical narrative are frequently signaled by the Hebrew word *hinnēh*. This word used to be translated "behold" but now goes unrepresented in modern translations.

In 12:10, with the first *hinnēh,* the narrator calls the reader's attention to Miriam's leprous condition, while the second *hinnēh* shifts the viewpoint from that of the narrator to that of the character Aaron (Ska 1990, 78).

17:7 [NRSV: 16:42] Use of *hinnēh* here shifts the focus from that of the narrator to that of Moses and Aaron (and the congregation?) to whom the glory of YHWH appears.

17:23 [NRSV: 17:8] Use of *hinnēh* here shifts the focus to Moses, who sees that Aaron's rod has blossomed and produced ripe almonds.

23:6, 17 Use of *hinnēh* shifts the focal point to Balaam's perception of the forlorn Balak standing with his officials beside his futile offerings.

32:1 Use of *hinnēh* shifts the focus to the Reubenites' and Gadites' perception of what a great place Gilead would be for cattle ranching.

First-Person Reports of Perception

11:6 "there is nothing at all but manna to look at"

11:15 "do not let me see my misery"

13:28 "we saw the descendants of Anak there"

13:32 "all the people that we saw in it [the land] are of great size"

14:28 "I will do to you the very things I heard you say"

Examples of Indirect Perception

Seeing

Num 12:8 YHWH says that Moses beholds the form of YHWH

Num 13:33 The people think that they must have seemed like grasshoppers to the Nephilim

Num 14:10 The glory of YHWH appeared to the Israelites

Num 14:22 Some people have seen YHWH's glory and the signs he did in Egypt

Num 20:12 Moses failed to show YHWH's holiness before the eyes of the Israelites

Num 20:27 Moses and Aaron went up Mount Hor in the sight of the whole congregation

Num 20:29 The congregation saw that Aaron had died

Num 22:2 Balak son of Zippor saw what Israel did to the Amorites

Num 22:23, 25, 27 The donkey saw the angel of the LORD standing in the road . . .

Num 22:31 "Then the LORD opened the eyes of Balaam, and he saw the angel of the LORD standing in the road, with his drawn sword in his hand . . ."

Num 22:41 Balak took Balaam up to where he could see part of the people

Num 24:2 Balaam saw Israel encamped tribe by tribe

Num 24:4, 16 Balaam sees the vision of the Almighty

Num 25:6-7 Moses, Phinehas, and the whole congregation saw an Israelite bring a Midianite woman into his family

Num 33:3 The Israelites set out from Rameses in the sight of the Egyptians

Hearing

Num 7:89 Moses used to hear the voice speaking from above the mercy seat in the tent

Num 11:1 the people complained in the hearing of YHWH

Num 11:10 Moses heard the people weeping

Num 11:18 the people wailed in the hearing of YHWH

Num 12:2 "and they said, 'Has the LORD spoken only through Moses? Has he not spoken through us also?' And the LORD heard it."

Num 16:34 All Israel heard the voices of those swallowed by the earth

Num 21:1 The Canaanite, the king of Arad, heard that Israel was coming

Num 24:4 Balaam hears the words of God

An important use of point of view or perception in Numbers is the contrast between Israel's perception of itself and that of its enemies. Whereas Israel fears the great size of it s potential opponents, Balak and his allies fear Israel's great numbers. The Israelites think that they must appear to the Canaanites as mere grasshoppers, but Balak sees the people as an ox that licks up all the grass in the pasture.

Verse Numbering

In the following verses there is a difference between the verse numbers of the NRSV and the MT:

MT	NRSV
17:1-15	16:36-50
17:16-28	17:1-13
25:19	added to 26:1
30:1	29:40
30:2-17	30:1-16

In other chapters the numbering of the verses is the same in the two versions.

NOTES

Numbers 1

The Census

This chapter has a unity of place, time, characters, and formal structure (command-fulfillment). There is some exposition in the specification of the names of those who assist in the census. Since the census is for the purpose of conscription, there is an implied tension that looks to future conflict.

1:2 "Take a census." YHWH orders Moses (and others—plural imperative) to take a head count *(nśʾ rʾš)* of all young men to register for the draft (Mann 127), but the fact that what is to be numbered is the *ʿêdâ* may connote that the group thus numbered constitutes not only a potential army but also a worshiping assembly.

1:2 "Individually." Literally "by their skulls." The expression has occurred in Exod 16:16 (an omer of manna per person).

1:3 "Able to go to war." The note that the men counted are conscriptable prepares for the irony in chapter 13 that they refuse to go to war.

1:46 "Their whole number was six hundred three thousand five hundred fifty." Harrelson (28) suggests that the incredibly high number would not have missed the notice of the implied author or implied reader but is deliberately exaggerated for effect. What effect? To demonstrate the fulfillment of the patriarchal promises of numerous progeny, to prepare for the theme of the dread of other nations, and to demonstrate the groundlessness of Israel's fear of the other nations.

1:54 "The Israelites did . . . just as the Lord commanded Moses." The chapter ends with a fulfillment statement, which is framed by the repetition of *ʿśh*, "to do."

Numbers 2

This chapter enjoys unity of place, time, characters, formal structure, and subject. The hierarchical arrangement of the camp, in which Moses gives himself the privileged place in front of the tent, prepares the way for the conflict over Moses' authority that will come later in the book.

The Arrangement of the Camp

2:1-16 One might have expected the arrangement of the camp to follow the geographical disposition of later Israel, but that is not the case. Reuben and Gad, who live in the east, camp on the south side where one might expect to see Judah, who camps on the east side along with Issachar and Zebulun, who live in the north. Benjamin, whose name means "southerner," camps on the west side. But Dan, Asher, and Naphtali, who all live in the north, also camp on the north side. If we look at the inner ring of Levitical encampments we can see that the privileged place is on the east, in front of the door of the tent. This is where Moses and Aaron camp. The Levites who camp on the south are the Kohathites, among whom is Korah, the leader of the revolt in chapter 16. This suggests that encampment on the south side is a sign of disfavor or disgrace. If encampment in the south is a sign of disfavor, why would Reuben, Gad, and Simeon be there? Reuben is cursed by his father (Gen 49:4) for having sexual relations with Jacob's concubine, Bilhah (Gen 35:22), Simeon is rebuked for his excessive violence in avenging the rape of Dinah (Gen 34:30), and Gad ends up on the south side simply because of his low status as the son of Leah's concubine, Zilpah (Douglas 1993a, 175–79). This means that the arrangement of the camp is a literary device aimed at projecting both the past narrative and also future plot developments in Numbers.

2:34 "The Israelites did just as the Lord had commanded Moses . . ." The fulfillment formula helps to establish a pattern of the people's obedience to divine instruction.

Numbers 3

The Levites: Duties, Census, Encampment (3:1-39)

3:6 "Set [the tribe of Levi] before Aaron." More literally, "cause them to stand before Aaron." To "stand before" a person here means to serve that person (1 Sam 16:21 [where NRSV renders Hebrew "he stood before him" as "he entered his service"]; 1 Kgs 1:2; 10:8; 12:8; 17:1; 18:15; 2 Kgs 3:14; 5:16; Jer 52:12; Ezek 44:11, 15; Esth 4:5; Dan 1:5, 19; 2 Chr 29:11).

3:12-13 "I hereby accept the Levites . . ." YHWH speaks in the first person, indicating a more personal investment in this action. The word "mine" in 13 is emphasized in the Hebrew.

3:14-37 When this list is compared with the general census in chapter 1 the impression is conveyed that the Levites are given more importance by being named in more detail.

3:15 "Enroll the Levites . . ." The command is framed by the verb *pqd*, "enroll."

3:15 "From a month old and upward." The other tribes are numbered from twenty years and upward (1:3), but for the Levites (except the Kohathites, 4:3) the same criterion is used as will be applied to the firstborn (3:40) whom the Levites will replace.

3:21 "To Gershon belonged . . ." This first verse on the assignment of the Gershonites is included within a chiastic repetition: *gēršôn mišpaḥat . . . mišpᵊḥōt haggēršunnî.*

3:27 "To Kohath belonged . . ." As with the Gershonites, the first verse on the Kohathites begins and ends with a chiastic arrangement of the name of the clan and the word for "clan": *qᵊhāt mišpaḥat . . . mišpᵊḥōt qehātî.*

3:30 "Elzaphan son of Uzziel . . . head of the . . . Kohathites." An ancient reader conscious of genealogy may have noticed that the assignment of the son of Uzziel as head of the clan passes over Korah, who is senior to him. This may foreshadow the revolt of Korah to come in chapter 16 (Douglas 1993a, 180).

3:33 "To Merari belonged . . ." The section on the Merarites is framed by the same kind of structure that was used for the Gershonites and Kohathites: *mᵊrārî mišpaḥat . . . mišpᵊḥōt mᵊrārî.*

3:38 "Those who were to camp in front of the tabernacle . . ." Here the order followed in the census is altered to emphasize the privileged position of those who encamped in front of the sanctuary. This position is emphasized by the double expression

lipnê hamiškān qēdmâ	in front of the dwelling toward the east
lipnê ʾōhel môʿēd mizrāḥâ	in front of the tent of meeting toward the orient

Enrollment of the Firstborn (3:40-43)

Levites Accepted in Place of Firstborn; Redemption of Surplus

Numbers 4

Kohathites, Gershonites, Merarites: Census, Duties

Dismantling the Sanctuary (4:5-20)

4:15 certainly gives one the impression that what the Kohathites carry is the *qōdeš* and its gear, but 10:21 has the *miškān* set up before they arrive at a new camp.

4:18 "You must not let the tribe of the clans of the Kohathites be destroyed from among the Levites" foreshadows the destruction of Korah and his adherents, who will be destroyed precisely because they refuse to accept their subordination to the Aaronic priests, which is here represented as being established for their protection from encroachment on YHWH's potentially lethal holiness.

4:20 "Even for a moment" renders Hebrew *kəbillaʿ*. The word has to do with swallowing. Some treat it as referring to the dismantling of the sanctuary (NJPS "dismantling," VG *priusquam involvantur*). Others think that it refers to a short time (the time it takes to swallow—see Job 7:19). Such is the understanding of LXX and 11QTemple 46:9 (Milgrom 1990, 301, note 25). I wonder if the unusual word is not chosen to foreshadow 16:32 where the earth swallows up Korah (a Kohathite) and his followers.

Gershonites: Census, Duties (4:21-28)

4:27 "And you shall assign." "You" here is plural (LXX: singular) even though the introduction (v. 21) has YHWH speaking only to Moses. A plural comes again in v. 32.

Merarites: Census, Duties (4:29-33)

The Results of the Census of the Levites (4:34-49)

Numbers 5

Expulsion of the "Lepers" from the Camp (5:1-3)

5:2-3 The order to put "lepers" out of the camp prepares the way for the exclusion of leprous Miriam in 12:3 (Budd 53). YHWH's holiness cannot tolerate unclean persons living in the camp in which YHWH is dwelling. The modern reader may wonder what became of the unfortunates who were expelled from the camp, but the emphasis of the text is on the dwelling of the all-holy God in the camp.

Instruction on Restitution (5:4-10)

5:4 This verse has a poetic quality, and serves to close the section on the expulsion of the "lepers."

wayyaʿăśû-kēn bᵊnê yiśrāʾēl

wayyišlᵊḥû ʾôtām ʾel miḥûṣ lammaḥăneh

kaʾăšer dibber yhwh ʾel-mōšeh

kēn ʿāśû bᵊnê yiśrāʾēl

they did thus, the children of Israel

they sent them outside the camp

as spoke YHWH to Moses

thus did the children of Israel

The *Sotah* (5:11-31)

5:11 "The Lord spoke to Moses . . ." The fact that the instruction on how to treat the suspected wife comes straight from YHWH indicates that the narrator wanted to represent the rite as coming from God rather than from the community (Bach 39).

5:12 "If a man's wife goes astray." The verb *śṭh* connotes a turning aside, a "breaking out of her proper place 'underneath her husband" (*taḥat ʾîšēk* [5:19], "with possible sexual connotation," Bach 37).

5:14 "If a spirit of jealousy comes on him." It seems that verses 12-13 deal with the case of a wife who has committed adultery but has not been caught whereas verse 14 deals simply with suspicion. Such a reading is supported by the *ʾô*, "or," separating the two cases in verse 30 (Fishbane 1980, 439; Frymer-Kensky 17, n. 11, citing Fishbane 1974).

5:18 Just what the priest does to the woman's hair is not clear. The verb *prʿ* is variously interpreted in modern versions:

He uncovers or bares the woman's head (NAB, NJPS).

He loosens, unbinds, unbraids her hair (ASV, NJB, SB, Holladay).

He dishevels her hair (NRSV).

The word "hair" does not appear in the Hebrew and is supplied as understood. The verb *prʿ* also has a connotation of letting someone go out of control or run wild (so used of the people in the Golden Calf incident, Exod 32:25). For a married woman to have to stand in public with her head uncovered and have her hair unbound by a man who is not her husband would act out the shame of the suspected adultery and make her appear as she would have if caught *in flagrante delicto*. Once she has appeared publicly in such a state it would be difficult for her to regain respect in the community (Bach 30, 34, 40). But it would also deprive the husband of honor. One would expect that a husband would think long and hard before exposing himself to such a loss of honor. In fact, this seems to be the kind of law that would never actually be put into practice.

5:18 "The water of bitterness." McKane (475–76) thinks that *mārîm* here means "poisonous."

5:19-20 "The priest shall make her take an oath saying . . ." One might expect the woman to recite some kind of self-curse, but this is not the case (Bach 30). The way the curse is worded does not leave much room for the possibility that the woman might be innocent (Bach 41).

5:21-22 These verses are united by a double reverse of both individual words and phrases:

21:	*yrk*	*npl*	thigh	fall
	bṭn	*ṣbh*	belly	swell
22:	*ṣbh*	*bṭn*	swell	belly
	npl	*yrk*	fall	thigh

5:24b, 27 "The water that brings the curse." The word order *hamʾʾārʾrîm . . . lʾmārîm* is the reverse of that used in 18 and 19 and 24a, giving unity to the description of the ordeal. Another change in order, compared with verse 21, comes from putting the words "she will become a curse in the midst of her people" after the belly/thigh phrases.

5:27-28 (If the woman is guilty, the water will have harmful effects.) The text seems to presuppose some kind of divine intervention. ("This is the only case in biblical law where the outcome depends on a miracle" [Milgrom 1997, 246].) That any punishment that may or may not come is left to divine intervention is also indicated by the phrase *tiśśāʾ ʾet-ʿăwōnāh* in verse 31 (the first of seven occurrences in Numbers). Zimmerli (8–11) holds that this expression connotes the expectation of divine rather than human punishment.

5:28 "Able to conceive." Hebrew *wᵊnizrᵊʿâ zāraʿ*, "she will be seeded with seed," forms an inclusion with the *zeraʿ* (seed) of verse 13.

Numbers 6

Nazirites (6:1-21)

6:7 "Not even for his father or mother . . ." The *nāzîr* must observe the same degree of purity as that demanded of the High Priest (Lev 21:11; Budd 71).

6:9b This verse has a certain poetic form, featuring inclusio:

wᵊgillaḥ rōʾšô	*beyôm ṭohŏrātô*	
	bayyôm haššᵊbîʿî	*yᵊgallᵊḥennû*
He will shave his head	on the day of his purification	
	on the seventh day	he will shave it.

6:12 "Separate themselves . . . consecrated head." The concluding verse of this sidebar on what to do in case the nazir is defiled is included within the repetition of the verb *nzr*.

6:21 "This is the law for the Nazirites . . ." The Torah colophon of the section on Nazirite vows is framed by the repetition *tôrat hannāzîr . . . tôrat nizrô*.

The Priestly Blessing (6:22-27)

Only Aaron and his sons can bless the people. The role of Aaron and his sons will become a source of conflict later in the book.

Numbers 7

The Offering of the Princes

Though for the modern reader this narrative is numbingly repetitious, it might work as a hypnotically repetitious chant.

7:1 "On the day Moses finished erecting the dwelling . . ." This day is presumably that narrated in Exodus 40. Therefore temporally our present narrative ought to follow Exodus 40. There has obviously been a displacement in the order of the narration (Budd 81, citing Dillmann).

7:3 "Six covered wagons and twelve oxen . . ." The mention of the wagons looks forward to the key moment of departure from Sinai coming up in 10:11-12 (Budd 84).

7:4 "Then the Lord said to Moses." Hebrew: "Said the Lord to Moses, saying . . ." This is the first of seven verses in Numbers that are framed by the repetition of some form of the verb *ʾmr,* "to speak."[1]

7:88 "This was the dedication offering . . ." The narrative of the offerings of the princes certainly illustrates an extraordinary prosperity. Is this to be understood as the result of despoiling the Egyptians (Exod 3:22; 11:2; 12:35)?

7:89 (YHWH used to speak to Moses in the tent.) This notice seems out of place at the end of the long narrative about the offering of the princes. It could conceivably be the beginning of the next section (the notice of the circumstances of Moses' communication with God coming before the communication itself). In any case, it is an important plot development since it prepares for the challenges that will come to Moses' authority (from the very princes who have just presented their offerings) as the narrative progresses (16:2).

Numbers 8

Setting up the Lamps (8:1-5)

8:4 The description of the lampstand and its manufacture is included within the repetition of the root *ʿśh,* "to make:" *wᵊzeh maʿăśeh hammᵊnōrâ . . . kēn ʿāśâ ʾet-hammᵊnōrâ.*

[1] The others are 15:37; 20:23; 24:12; 26:1; 27:6; and 31:25. There are, in all, fifteen verses that have the *ʾâmar . . . lēʾmōr* combination and more of these would be *inclusios* if the verses were divided differently.

Dedication of the Levites (8:6-26)

8:12 In the Hebrew this verse begins and ends with the word "Levites."

8:5-22 Milgrom (1987a, 205–206) proposes the following chiastic structure for these verses (which I have modified as explained below):

A. Introduction (5-7a)

B. Prescription (7b-13)

1. The Levites (7)

a. lustral water

b. shaving

c. laundering

2. The Sacrificial Procedure (8-12)

a. Handlaying by Israel on Levites [10]

b. *tᵊnûpâ* of Levites [11]

c. Hands laid by Levites on bulls [12]

3. Levites subordinated to priests (13) [stand before]

C. The Rationale (14-19)

1. Separate Levites to God (14)

2. Qualify Levites for sanctuary labor (15)

3. Replace firstborn with Levites (16-18)

4. [Ward off plague for encroachment] (19)

B' Description (20-22a)

1. The Levites

a. lustral water [no shaving] [21]

b. laundering [21]

2. The Sacrificial Procedure

tᵊnûpâ of the Levites [21]

3. Levites subordinated to priests [21 *lipnê ʾahărōn wᵊlipnē bānāyw*]

A' Conclusion (22b) [YHWH's command fulfilled]

In B.1 Milgrom has "d. bathing," but this is not in the text. At C.2 there is another mention of the *tᵊnûpâ*, which Milgrom does not mention, but which upsets the balance somewhat. Also, the length and poetic structure of C.3 give it more importance than is represented in this proposed structure. Subordination of the Levites is also a part of C.4 but is not reflected in the outline.

8:11-12 There is a strong parallel between the ritual of sacrifice and the ritual of dedication of the Levites. The Levites are, as it were, a sacrifice offered by Israel for the redemption of the firstborn. Just as the bull upon which the Levites lay their hands makes atonement for them, so the Levites, upon whom the Israelites lay their hands, make atonement for the Israelites (Milgrom 1987a, 207).

8:16-19 YHWH speaks personally. The fact that verse 17 begins and ends with *lî*, "to me," stresses YHWH's claim to the firstborn.

Numbers 9

The Passover (9:1-14)

9:1 This section has a somewhat more elaborate introduction, specifying place and time.

9:5 The statement of fulfillment closely follows the command, giving the impression of prompt obedience.

Second Date for Those Who Miss Passover (9:6-14)

9:6-14 This section has a problem-solution narrative structure.

9:10 Another circumstance is foreseen by YHWH that was not included in the original request: those away on a journey. The mention of descendants not only applies the solution to the present situation but looks forward to the future.

9:13 The force of this verse is enhanced by its similar beginning and ending: *wᵊhāʾîš ʾăšer hûʾ . . . hāʾîš hahûʾ*.

The Cloud that Led the People (9:15-23)

9:15-23 "On the day when the Dwelling was erected . . ." Here, as in 7:1, we seem to have a flashback to Exodus 40. We are now informed about the cloud (Eerdmans 89). This section on the cloud prepares for the beginning of the march (Budd 103).

9:18 The connection between the cloud and YHWH is made explicit. In following the cloud, the people are being directed by YHWH. How can a people who are being led by YHWH go wrong?

9:23 This verse has a certain poetic quality:

ʿal-pî yhwh yaḥănû	at the command (mouth) of YHWH they encamped
wəʿal-pî yhwh yissāʿû	and at the command of YHWH they set out
ʾet-mišmeret yhwh šāmārû	the charge of YHWH they observed
ʿal-pî yhwh	at the command of YHWH
bəyad-mōšeh	by the hand of Moses

Numbers 10

Two Silver Trumpets (10:1-10)

10:9 "In your land" looks forward to a time in the future when the land will be theirs.

10:9 *haṣṣar haṣṣōrēr.* A poetic repetition of the same root—"the squeezer squeezing."

10:10 The section ends with a somewhat formal conclusion and personal speech by YHWH.

Departure from Sinai, Order of March (10:11-36)

10:11-28 The ordered tribes marching in the divinely determined formation (echoing chapter 2) project an image of the people advancing confidently with the Lord in their midst and in conformity to YHWH's will. This prepares for the contrasting stories of rebellion that will follow, beginning in the next chapter (Budd 111).

Moses Asks Hobab to Guide the People (10:29-32)

10:29-32 The reader can only wonder why Moses would ask Hobab to come along as guide when we have been told with great emphasis and detail (9:17-22, and as recently as 10:11-12) that the people are following YHWH in the cloud, that when the cloud moves, they move; that when the cloud stays put, they stay put; and that they go wherever the cloud goes (and don't go where the cloud doesn't go). Are we to see Moses portrayed as hedging his bets and therefore showing a lack of confidence in YHWH? (Ackerman 80).

10:30 "I will go back to my own land and to my kindred." Is Hobab being portrayed as an anti-Abraham (Gen 12:1)? anti-Jacob (Gen 31:3, 13; 32:9)? anti-Ruth (Ruth 2:11)? Hobab's words are framed by the verb *hlk* and arranged in chiastic order:

I will not go	rather, to my land		
	and to my birthplace		I will go
lōʾ ʾēlēk		*kî ʾim-ʾel-ʾarṣî*	
	wᵊ	*ʾel-môladtî*	*ʾēlēk*

10:33-34 The expressions "the mountain of YHWH" (only one other time in the Pentateuch) and "the cloud of YHWH" (only one other time in the Bible) might have struck the ancient reader by their rarity.

10:35 "Arise, O Lord, let your enemies be scattered . . ." points to potential conflict with YHWH's enemies.

Numbers 11

Murmurings:
The Seventy Elders, Eldad and Medad, Quail, Plague

No sooner have the people begun to move than there is trouble. The image of the people all marching together at YHWH's command is now shattered by dissension (Olson 1997, 230), a theme that will be played out from now until the death of the old generation in chapter 25. These episodes of rebellion will involve not only the general populace but also the Levites and even Moses and Aaron! (Olson 1997, 231).

The complaining has not been prepared for by the narrator and so comes as a surprise to the reader.

The Murmuring Pattern Established

11:1-3 The first little drama is like a miniature of the rebellions that will follow and serves as a kind of paradigm (Mann 129). It is told so succinctly that it is evident that the narrator wants the reader to focus on the pattern rather than on the event (Culley 1990, 28–29).

11:1 "The people complained." A rare word is used here and an unusual construction. *ʾnn* occurs only twice in the whole Hebrew Bible (here and Lam 3:39 [BDB relates it to an Assyrian word meaning "to sigh"]). The use of the Hithpael may connote habitual or continuous action—the people kept complaining. The participial form is preceded by the preposition *kᵊ*, which can be interpreted temporally (so NRSV "when") or adverbially (so SB "Now the people were like those-who-grieve [over] ill-fortune"). In any case, it seems that the words were deliberately chosen by the writer to create an effect in the reader.

11:1 "The Lord heard it." YHWH did not hear them praying to him but *overheard* them complaining without trying to communicate with him (Jobling 1986, 29).

11:3 The name Taberah is taken to derive from a root meaning "to burn" and so the place name memorializes, in the mind of the narrator, the divine punishment for the people's murmuring.

The Quails and the Elders

Num 11:4-35 Many commentators see here a weaving together of two different stories: one about the people's craving meat, and the other about the seventy elders. Source critics (e.g., Noth) will say that the stories have not been joined very well whereas literary critics will ask what meaning could have been intended by the joining. The two stories have as a common element *rûaḥ*, "wind/spirit." The wind brings the quail; some of Moses' spirit is taken from him and placed on the elders (Milgrom 1987, 53; see also the proposed structure on pages 51–52).

11:4 (The rabble had a craving.) The root *ʾwh*, "to crave," frames the whole story, which begins with the rabble craving meat and ends with the naming of the place Kibroth-hattaavah—"Graves of Craving" (11:34-35).

11:4 How are we to construe the characterization of the rabble? What does their craving for meat mean? Are they demanding a necessity or a luxury (Culley 1990, 29)? And what about all the cattle that are supposed to be with them (Exod 12:38)? The word *ʾăsapsup* suggests some kind of gathering. But it is neither the *ʿēdâ*, "assembly," nor the *qāhāl*, "congregation," and its presence here clashes with the well-ordered arrangements of the tribes narrated in the first part of the book.

11:5 "We remember the fish we ate in Egypt for free . . ." Note the irony—what had been food given to slaves is now recalled as free *(ḥinnām),* as if the Israelite slaves were totally free of obligation.

11:6-7 (Nothing but manna to look at . . . its color was like the color of . . .) There is a curious word play on *ʿayin,* which can mean "eye" or "appearance" (NRSV: "color").

11:10 "Throughout their families" Hebrew: *lᵊmišpᵊḥôtāyw.* This expression has been used above in reference to the numbering of the people and in the description of the order of their encampment and of their march, so its use here to describe their weeping has a certain irony to it.

11:11 "Why have you treated your servant so badly?" In this first of the "murmuring" stories Moses behaves differently than in the rest. In the latter he stands between YHWH and the people as their intercessor (Milgrom 1987, 50), but here he is so frustrated with the burden that he asks for death (v. 15). One may wonder, in light of this incident, whether Moses' later interventions represent a change in character.

11:11-13 The march has barely begun and Moses is exasperated. His reaction comes in the form of a series of rhetorical questions that boil down to "Why me?" He pictures the people as a burdensome child that *he* has not conceived and is not willing to carry or play nurse *(ʾōmēn)* to.[2] The burden of feeding such clamorous children is more than he can bear. He distances himself from them by referring to *their* ancestors (not "our") in verse 12.

11:15 Moses ends with the dramatic and ironic, "If I find favor in your sight, just kill me."

11:18 "Surely it was better for us in Egypt." 10:29 and 32 had spoken of the good that YHWH has in store for the people in the land. In contrast with this good, the people complain about the evil that has befallen them (11:1) and even go so far as to call Egypt "good" (Milgrom 1987, 54).

11:20 "For a whole month—until it comes out your nostrils . . ." This puts the previous verses in a new light. The provision of meat for such a long time is now seen as a sign of YHWH's disgust with the people rather than as a sign of compassion. As a result they will eat meat until it comes out their nostrils!

[2] Some modern translations understand the masculine singular form *ʾōmēn* as referring to a female wet nurse (for which the feminine form *ʾōmenet* occurs in 2 Sam 4:4 and Ruth 4:16); others render "foster father" or the like.

11:25 "The Lord came down in the cloud and spoke to him . . ." There is spatial symbolism here. Despite the fact that Moses has been conversing with him, YHWH is somewhere from whence he must come down.

11:30 "Returned," literally "were gathered." The use of *ʾsp* here forms an inclusion with verse 24, thus framing this section.

11:33 "While the meat was still between their teeth . . . the Lord struck them . . ." The people crave a taste of Egypt and that is what they get—a plague! (Ackerman 81).

Numbers 12

Miriam and Aaron Challenge Moses' Authority

12:1 Miriam is mentioned before Aaron—but in a negative light. The reason why Miriam and Aaron would object to Moses' Cushite wife is not given. Since the only thing we know about her is that she was a Cushite, this is often taken to be the reason. Many see racism as the motive, but is this a projection of modern problems on the past? The tension in the story does not center on the race of Moses' wife but on the uniqueness of his authority. Is his taking a foreign wife a sign of his authority to choose freely?

12:2 "Is it through Moses alone . . ." In the Hebrew, the combination *hăraq ʾak* makes it clear that what is at stake is Moses' uniqueness (Budd 136). What is the reader to make of Miriam and Aaron's claim that the Lord has spoken with them? In fact, YHWH has spoken to Aaron in Lev 10:8 and will again in Num 18:1, 8, 20. There is no text in which YHWH speaks to Miriam, but she is identified as a prophet in Exod 15:20. However, the rhetorical question overstates the case. The issue is not whether or not YHWH speaks only to Moses but the nature of Moses' authority.

12:3 "The meekest man on the face of the earth." Such direct characterization is rare in biblical narrative, but is necessary here for the development of the plot. Is Moses inventing a religion in which he gives himself exaggerated authority? The Hebrew word rendered "meek" is *ʿānāw*. This word is usually explained as deriving from a root (II *ʿnh*) that has to do with a stronger person using force against a weaker in order to show dominance. Coats (1982a, 100–102) wants to derive it from I *ʿnh,* "to answer," hence "honorable" in the sense of responsible, rather than "humble." Moses demonstrates this quality by interceding for those who challenge him. This ability to intercede is the result of his face-to-face relationship with YHWH (Coats 104). The fact that the narrator felt it necessary to address this question indicates that someone was asking it with sufficient credibility to require a response.

12:6-8 "And he said, 'Hear my words . . .'" Ironically, Miriam and Aaron's claim that YHWH speaks to them is now vindicated in their being rebuked. YHWH speaks personally and with divine authority upholds the unique authority of Moses. J. S. Kselman (501) emends the MT and proposes a chiastic structure for these verses as follows:

A	*ʾm yhyh nbyʾ bkm*	If there be a prophet among you,
B	*bmrʾh lw ʾtwdʿ*	I make myself known to him in a vision;
C	*bḥlwm ʾdbr bw*	In a dream I speak with him.
D	*lʾ kn ʿbdy mšh*	Not so (with) my servant Moses;
D'	*bkl byty nʾmn hwʾ*	In all my household he (alone) is faithful.
C'	*ph ʾl ph ʾdbr bw*	Mouth to mouth I speak with him,
B'	*bmrʾh wlʾ ḥydt*	In clarity and not riddles;
A'	*tmnt yhwh ybyṭ*	The form of Yahweh he beholds.

Kselman also points out (footnote 3) a chiasmus between B and C: *lw ʾtwdʿ*||*ʾdbr bw.*

12:8 YHWH answers Miriam and Aaron's rhetorical question (2) with one of his own: "Why aren't you afraid . . .?"

12:10 "Miriam had become leprous." What conclusion is one to draw from the fact that Miriam is punished but not Aaron? Those who see racism behind Miriam and Aaron's complaint (1) point out the contrast between the dark-skinned Cushite and Miriam's snow-like "leprosy." The narrator uses *wᵉhinneh* to focus the reader's perception through that of the characters. Miriam is seen to be *mᵉṣōraʿat* "struck with 'leprosy,'" i.e., by YHWH—theological passive.

12:13 "Moses does not show his obedience to God by a meek acceptance of Miriam's punishment as the obvious will of God. To the contrary, his obedience emerges only when he stands face to face with God and defends his own" (Coats 105–106). Once YHWH had punished Miriam,

"Moses showed how little of an intolerant tyrant he really was by pleading for Miriam. . . . The unique role of Moses, which he discharged without its turning his head, was thus clearly vindicated by his reaction to Miriam's spiteful and devious attack on him" (Robinson 432).

12:15 "So Miriam was shut out of the camp . . ." The command-fulfillment narrative structure is now restored as the episode comes to an end.

Numbers 13

The Spies

This story is an important turning point in the plot of Numbers. It explains the reason for the forty years in the wilderness.

13:2 There is some suspense involved in sending men to reconnoiter Canaan. Will they be caught? Will they return safely? What will they find?

13:4-15 Is there any characterization in the names of the spies?

šammûaʿ	unexplained (root = hear)
šāpāṭ	x has judged
kālēb	Dog (connotation: faithful; Fretz and Panitz *ABD* s.v.)
yigʾāl	may x redeem
hôšēaʿ	x has saved
palṭî	[YHWH?] is deliverance
gaddîʾēl	El is good fortune
gaddî	[YHWH?] is good fortune (Hobbs *ABD* s.v.)
ʿammîʾēl	El is kinsman
sᵉtûr	hidden by x (Noth; *IDB*)
naḥbî	fearful, timid (Paulien, *ABD* s.v.; Noth 229) [YHWH is fearsome?]
gᵉʾûʾēl	majesty of El

Most of the names of the spies are hypochoristic, i.e., consisting in a verb or noun form without a divine name as subject/predicate. There are no YHWH names and only three El names. Hobbs wants to read the final *yod* in the name Gaddi as Yah. If this is accepted, then the same could be done for Palti and Nahbi. In verse 16 Moses changes Hoshea's name by specifying the deity who saves as YHWH.

13:16 "These were the names . . ." forms an *inclusio* with 13:4, framing the list.

13:16 The change of Hoshea's (הושע) name to Joshua (יהושע) insures that YHWH (יהו *yᵊhô*) will be "with" him (Sonnet 1997, 133).

13:17 "Go up . . ." This is the first instance in Numbers of the verb *ʿlh* in reference to going up into the land. The Hebrew Bible consistently uses this expression with regard to the land. Movement to the land is characterized as "going up" while departure is "going down." This expression is not just geographical, but theological as well (Wehmeier *TLOT* s.v.).

13:20 "Be bold." The fact that Moses has to exhort the spies to courage indicates that there is some risk involved and thus adds tension to the narrative. One might not think that "be brave" would have to accompany "bring back some fruit."

13:25 Pace: Narration time is shorter than narrative time. A period of forty days is covered by a phrase.

13:27 "And they told him [Moses] . . ." In verse 26 we are told twice that the report was made to the whole congregation, but here the spies are represented as speaking to Moses. This may be preparing the way for the tension between Moses and the people that will be the result of the report.

13:28 The use of *wᵊgām* plus the word order puts emphasis on the Anakites as being the object of their (horrified) vision. "And besides, it was descendants of Anak that we saw!"

13:29 "The Amalekites live in the land of the Negeb." Fear of the Amalekites may seem unreasonable in view of their defeat by Joshua in Exodus 17 and the command of YHWH to Moses in Exod 17:14 to write in a book and recite to Joshua, "I will utterly blot out *(māḥōh ʾemḥeh)* the remembrance of Amalek from under heaven." But the fact that other peoples inhabit the land was not reported in the narration of the expedition, so the revelation of this information now impacts the reader as it would the first hearers.

13:30 The narrator does not report the people's reaction but skips to Caleb's attempt to calm them down—the reader's imagination can supply the people's reaction to the report. Caleb's exhortation uses two infinitive absolutes, *ʿālōh naʿăleh* and *yākôl nûkal,* stressing his belief in the people's ability to take possession of the land.

13:32 "The land that we explored is a country that consumes its inhabitants." The land that YHWH wants to give his people is said to be like the underworld, which swallows up the living (McEvenue 135–36).[3] But in fact it is vomiting them out (Lev 18:25, 28; 20:22). The narrator orients the reader's perception of the spies by labeling the report as a calumny *(dibbâ).*

13:33 The ten scouts perceived not only themselves but the 600,000 warriors as mere grasshoppers in comparison with the giants they saw in the land. They even project their perception of themselves onto their potential opponents ("So we seemed to them"). In doing so they attribute to their enemies a point of view that is really God's (Isa 40:22 "It is he [YHWH] who sits above the circle of the earth, and its inhabitants are like grasshoppers . . ."). Aren't grasshoppers capable of devouring the land because of their numbers? (2 Chr 7:13 "When I [YHWH] . . . command the locust to devour the land . . ."). Had humans (or giants, for that matter) ever defeated a swarm of locusts? Yet, as we see in the next verse, the mere report is enough to cow the whole force (Harrelson 28; Mann 128–29).

Numbers 14

People Revolt, and are Condemned to Wander. Defeat at Hormah

Word repetitions bind the units of this chapter together internally and with each other. They sometimes also indicate the core idea of a section (Newing).

[3] Hab 2:5: "He who opens wide his throat like the nether world, and is insatiable as death, Who gathers to himself all the nations, and rallies to himself all the peoples." Isa 5:14: "Therefore the nether world enlarges its throat and opens its maw without limit; Down go their nobility and their masses, their throngs and their revelry." Prov 1:12: "Let us swallow them up, as the nether world does, alive, in the prime of life, like those who go down to the pit!"

14:2a The reaction of the people was skipped over between 13:29 and 30. Here it is given and with stress on the fact that it was the whole people who complained: *kôl bᵊnê yiśrāʾēl . . . kōl-hāʿēdâ,* all the children of Israel . . . the whole congregation.

14:2b The second half of the verse is laid out in chiastic form (McEvenue 464; Douglas 1993a, 106; Milgrom 1990, xxii):

A If only we had died

  B in the land of Egypt

  B' or in this wilderness

A if only we had died

lû-matnû *bᵊʾereṣ miṣrayim*

  ʾô bammidbār *lû-mātnû*

This is not just whining. It is a denial of YHWH's oft-repeated self-identification as "Your God who brought you out of Egypt" (Mann 132; Exod 6:7; 20:2; 29:46; Lev 22:33; 23:43; 25:38, 55; 26:13, 45). Numbers began with a head-count draft registration, but now the warriors refuse to fight.

14:5 "Then Moses and Aaron fell on their faces . . ." Falling on their faces is something that Moses and Aaron will be doing a lot of in this section of Numbers (16:4, 22, 45; 20:6). Budd (156) interprets the gesture as "intercessory, aimed at averting divine wrath . . ." Such an interpretation is possible in Gen 44:14 where Joseph's brothers fall on their faces before him after Joseph's cup has been found in Benjamin's sack, and also in Josh 7:6 where Joshua fell on his face before the ark after being routed by the men of Ai. In Judg 13:20, 22 Manoah and his wife fall on their faces when they see the angel ascend in the flame of their sacrifice, and Manoah expresses his fear of divine punishment. In 1 Sam 25:23 Abigail falls on her face before David, who has threatened to wipe out all of Nabal's male descendants. In 1 Chr 21:16 David and the elders fall on their faces when David sees the angel of the Lord holding a drawn sword stretched out over Jerusalem.

14:5 ". . . before all the assembly of the congregation of the Israelites." This expression combines "the whole assembly" of vv. 1 and 2 with "the children of Israel" of v. 2, adding the word "congregation." The force of this is to stress that it was the whole people that were involved in receiving the report and reacting to it (McEvenue 111).

14:9 "They are no more than bread for us," *laḥmēnû hēm.* Or, in modern parlance, "We eat Canaanites for breakfast."

14:10 It is at the highest point of tension in the story that the glory of YHWH appears in the tent—a *deus ex machina*? But instead of resolving the tension, YHWH's appearance heightens it since he proposes to wipe out the whole people (12).

14:12 "I will make you a nation greater and stronger than him" *(wᵊʾeʿĕśeh ʾōtᵊkā lᵊgôy-gādôl wᵊʿāṣûm mimmennû).* The wording recalls God's promises to the patriarchs (Gen 12:2; 18:18; 46:3), but also Exod 32:10 where YHWH proposes to wipe out the Israelites and start all over with Moses after the incident of the golden calf. This may mean that our narrator is comparing the peoples' unwillingness to capture the land with the unfaithfulness shown in the worship of the golden calf. Moses did not accept the offer when it was made the first time, but he has recently expressed his exasperation with the burdensome people. Will he take the offer this time?

14:13-19 Moses' prayer is framed by the word "Egypt" in verses 13 and 19 (*inclusio*; Newing 217). The parallel with the golden calf episode continues. The same argument is used in both stories: the Egyptians will hear of it. But here another element is added; the Egyptians will tell the inhabitants of the land and YHWH's reputation as a patron will be ruined.

14:14 "Face to face." More literally, "eyeball to eyeball."

14:15 "The nations who have heard about you" *(šāmᵊʿû ʾet-šimʿăkâ).* Moses seems to be trying to get YHWH to calm down and think about what impact killing off his people would have on his reputation in the region—what will the Egyptians *say* (not think, but say)? Is the reader to construe YHWH as petulant or as cleverly bringing out the best in a leader? Since Moses has already asked to die because he has experienced the people as such a burden, we might well have expected him to take up YHWH's offer to make him the new Abraham. (But then what becomes of the promises made to the first Abraham?) What is Moses' motive for interceding for the people?

14:18 "The Lord is slow to anger . . ." Moses quotes YHWH's own revelatory self-description (Exod 34:6-7) against him!

14:23 "None . . . shall see the land." The Hebrew uses an oath formula here. The verse is framed by the repetition of "to see:" *ʾim-yirʾû . . . lōʾ yirʾûhā.*

14:28 YHWH uses the prophetic *nᵊʾum yhwh,* "utterance of YHWH," and an oath formula, speaking personally. Ironically, YHWH will now do the very thing that the people had unjustly said he had done (bringing them out to the wilderness to die).

14:29 "Your dead bodies shall fall . . . and [the bodies] of all your number, included in the census . . ." The census had originally been for the purpose of military organization in view of the conquest of the land. Now it becomes a list of those condemned to perish in the wilderness.

14:33 "Faithlessness" (Hebrew *zᵊnût,* adultery). The people's lack of faith is like the unfaithfulness of adultery.

14:36-38 This subunit is held together by the structure (McEvenue 11):

lātûr ʾet-hāʾāreṣ	*lᵊhôṣîʾ dibbâ ʿal-hāʾāreṣ*	
	môṣîʾê dibbat-hāʾāreṣ	*lātûr ʾet-hāʾāreṣ*
to spy out the land	bring back bad report	
	bring back bad report	to spy out the land

The People Attempt to Take the Land without YHWH's Help

14:39-45 Douglas (1993a, 110) points out the use of *ʿlh* (go up) and *yrd* (go down) as framing devices of this narrative. The Israelites went up (v. 39) to take the land; the Amalekites and Canaanites came down and defeated them (v. 45).

14:40 "We will go up to the place that the Lord has promised . . ." The people seem to pay no attention to the oracle that has just been given. They admit that they have sinned by not being willing to go up into the land.

Numbers 15

Instruction on Grain and Wine Offerings Accompanying Sacrifices (15:1-16)

First Fruits (15:17-26)

Atonement for Unintentional Faults (15:27-31)

15:2 "When you come into the land . . ." A ray of hope and of grace appears. Immediately after the people are told that they will not enter the land and fail to do so on their own, YHWH makes provisions for the time when the new generation will enter the land (Mann 133).

15:12 "According to the number . . ." This verse features a chiastic structure:

kammispār	*ʾăšer*	*taʿăśû*		
	kākâ	*taʿăśû lāʾeḥād*	*kᵊmispārām*	
according to the number	that	you prepare		
	thus	you prepare	according to their number	

15:30 "Whoever acts high-handedly . . . affronts the Lord." In the Hebrew of this verse the divine name YHWH is put in emphatic position. This makes it clear that it is YHWH himself who is affronted by such treatment of one's fellow citizens (Budd 174).

The Sabbath Breaker 15:32-36

The story is told with just a few brush strokes, as it were. For example, the man is brought to Moses but nothing is said about the accusation that presumably was made against him. However, its plot-line and language make it a parallel to the story of the mixed-seed blasphemer in Lev 24:10-14, 23:

Lev 24:12 *wayyannîḥūhû bammišmār liproš*

they put him in custody to make clear . . .

Num 15:34 *wayyannîḥû ʾōtô bammišmār kî lōʾ pōraš*

they put him in custody since it was not clear . . .

Lev 24:14 *(hôṣēʾ) . . . ʾel-miḥûṣ lammaḥăneh . . . wᵊrāgᵊmû ʾōtô kol-hāʿēdâ*

(bring out) . . . to outside the camp . . . and stone him—the whole assembly

Num 15:35 *rāgôm ʾōtô . . . kol-hāʿēdâ miḥûṣ lammaḥăneh*

stone him . . the whole assembly outside the camp

Lev 24:23 *wayyôṣîʾû . . . ʾel-miḥûṣ lammaḥăneh wayyirgᵊmû ʾōtô . . . kaʾăšer ṣiwwâ yhwh ʾet-mōšeh* they brought out . . . to outside the camp and stoned him . . . as YHWH commanded Moses

Num 15:36 *wayyôṣîʾû . . . ʾel-miḥûṣ lammaḥăneh wayyirgᵊmû ʾōtô . . . kaʾăšer ṣiwwâ yhwh ʾet-mōšeh*

they brought out . . . to outside the camp and stoned him . . . as YHWH commanded Moses

Tassels and Blue Cords 15:37-41

Is there any connection between the story of the Sabbath breaker and the tassels? The only apparent connection is the commandments—the Sabbath breaker broke a commandment; the fringes remind one to keep all the commandments.

15:41 "I am the Lord your God . . ." The instruction ends with a solemn covenant formula that begins and ends with *ʾănî yhwh ʾĕlōhêkem.*

Numbers 16

Revolt of Korah, Dathan, Abiram, Two Hundred Fifty Leaders

16:3 "They assembled . . . the assembly of the Lord." The verse is framed by the root *qhl.*

16:4 Two hundred fifty leaders get in Moses' face *(wayyāqūmû lipnê mōšeh* [16:2]) and he falls on his face *(wayyippōl ʿal-pānāyw).*

16:5 "Korah and all his company." "Company" here is *ʿēdâ,* which usually refers to the worship assembly of the Israelites. There may be a note of sarcasm in the use of *ʿēdâ* here, and *qhl* in verse 3, which will indicate to the reader how one is to evaluate Korah's initiative. Korah is attempting to set up a rival "Israel" (Magonet 17; Budd 186–87).

16:7 "You Levites have gone too far!" Moses makes the same accusation against the Levites that the rebels make against him in verse 3. It is not Moses who is exalting himself, but the Levites who are not contented with being separated for holy service but seek the priesthood as well.

16:10 In the Hebrew, the "you" switches between plural and singular: "He has allowed thee to approach him, and all thy brother Levites with thee; yet you (all) seek the priesthood as well!"

16:12, 14 "We will not come." Literally, "We will not go up." There is irony in these twice-spoken words that frame their response to Moses' summons. Not only will they not go up (to Moses or to the land), they will, in fact, soon go down into the earth (Magonet 18).

16:13 "Is it too little . . ." The rebels mockingly repeat Moses' words to them in verse 9 (Magonet 18).

16:13-14 The irony of the speech is heightened yet further by the accusation that Moses has brought the people *out of* a land flowing with milk and honey (Egypt) but not into such a land. They are using the words that YHWH himself has used to describe the land he intends to give to the people (Exod 3:8, 17; 33:3; Lev 20:24; Mann 133). Dathan and Abiram seem to treat the promise as if it came from Moses and he has not kept it, but the reader knows that it is God's promise.

16:13 The accusation that Moses has been lording it over the people is proved false both by the integrity Moses has displayed in the case of Miriam and Aaron (Numbers 12) and by the divine punishment that will follow in this chapter. The divine intervention makes clear that Moses' leadership position is not the result of his own scheming, and his care for Miriam illustrates that he exercises his role with integrity (Magonet 15).

16:14 "Would you put out the eyes of these men?" NJB "Do you think you can hoodwink these people?" Certainly, a forceful rhetorical question. The combination *nqr ʿyn* occurs only three other times in the Hebrew Bible (Judg 16:21; 1 Sam 11:2; Prov 30:17) and in each of those it is not figurative but literal. Budd (187) takes it to be figurative in the sense of misleading.

16:15 "I have not taken one donkey from them." What is the logic of Moses' statement here? Samuel makes a similar statement in 1 Sam 12:3-5. It seems to be a disavowal of self-interest.

16:17 This verse is framed by the repetition of *ʾîš maḥtātô,* "each his censer."

16:19 "YHWH's glory appeared" just at the highest point of tension, as in 14:10.

16:21 Once again YHWH threatens to make an end of the whole assembly and once again Moses falls on his face.

16:26 "Swept away." The same word *(sph)* is used of the destruction of Sodom (Gen 18:23, 24; 19:15, 19). YHWH will not sweep away the good with the bad, but eventually the good must get out of the way lest they be swept up with the wicked.

16:27 The narrators notice that the wives, sons, and little ones also stood at the entrance of the tent to prepare for what is to come (v. 32).

16:28 "It has not been of my own accord." Hebrew "from my heart"—the heart being seen as the seat of thought. The narrative seems to be addressing the criticism that the law serves the interests of those who write (and interpret) it, in which case there must have been a felt need for such an *apologia.*

16:30 "But if the LORD does something entirely new . . ." Hebrew: "creates a creation." It may seem strange that something as positive as creation would be associated with making the earth swallow up living people, unless these rebels are to be somehow tied to the forces of chaos that are overcome in the act of creation.

16:30 "These men have despised YHWH." In a culture where honor and shame are the driving force it would be unimaginable that anyone could despise (dishonor) YHWH and not suffer the consequences (otherwise YHWH would lose honor). Challenging Moses' authority amounts to dishonoring YHWH.

16:32 "The earth opened its mouth and swallowed them up . . ." What the spies had feared would be true of the land (that it eats its inhabitants, 13:32) has proved true of the wilderness for those who rebel against Moses' authority—even their property *(rᵊkûš)* is swallowed.

The narrator's description of the event in words identical to Moses' prediction gives him great credibility.

16:35 "A fire came out from the Lord . . ." This verse seems to come as an afterthought tying up loose ends. One may note that the instantaneous cremation of the two hundred fifty leaders is reported rather matter-of-factly. One cannot help but be reminded of Lev 10:3 (though the wording here is a little different).

Numbers 17

A Metal Altar Cover Is Made from the Rebels' Censers as a Sign (17:1-4 [NRSV: 16:37-40])

17:3 [NRSV: 16:38] "They shall be a sign." The hammered metal cover for the altar made out of the firepans of the two hundred fifty leaders who had been consumed by fire from YHWH would be a sign to the Israelites. There is some implication here of future time; the meaning of the "sign" will be spelled out in verse 5.

17:4 [NRSV: 16:39] "Eleazar took the bronze censers . . . of those who were burned . . ." The two hundred fifty leaders are now (somewhat off-handedly) referred to as "those who were burned" *(haśśᵊrūpîm)*.

17:5 [NRSV: 16:40] "No outsider." In Leviticus 10, Nadab and Abihu had been burned by fire from YHWH because they brought unauthorized fire *(ʾēš zārâ)*. Here the prohibition is against the similar sounding *ʾîš zār* which is specified to be one who is not of the seed *(zeraʿ)* of Aaron.

Rebellion Against Moses and Aaron (17:6-28 [NRSV: 16:41–17:13])

17:6 [NRSV: 16:41] "On the next day." It is not just that some people begin to complain again later, but the whole assembly complains the very next morning. There is something comic in this. They don't appear to have gotten the message in the death of the two hundred fifty leaders or in the making of the altar cover as a sign and reminder. They blame the deaths on Moses and Aaron and refer to those whom the narrator has characterized as "the burned" (4) as "YHWH's people."

17:7 [NRSV: 16:42] "When the congregation had assembled against them . . ." Once again, at the height of the tension the glory of YHWH appears (14:10; 16:19).

17:10 [NRSV: 16:45] "Get away . . . that I may consume . . ." Once again YHWH proposes to finish off (*klh* 16:21) the congregation in a moment (*kᵊrāgaʿ* as in 16:21) and again Moses and Aaron fall on their faces (14:5; 16:4, 22).

17:11 [NRSV: 16:46] "Make atonement for them. For wrath has gone forth from the Lord." Numbers 1:53 had set up the Levites as a buffer around the dwelling so that God's wrath *(qeṣep)* would not strike the people. Numbers 8:19 depicts this same arrangement as protection from plague *(negep)*. The buffer prevents anyone who is not a descendant of Aaron from entering the sanctuary. If such a thing should happen and the divine wrath would be provoked in the form of plague (as the reader now learns), Aaron must make atonement for the people and this is exactly what we see happening here (Magonet 21).

17:12 [NRSV: 16:47] Moses told Aaron to act quickly; now Aaron runs. Running is not something that one would normally expect to see the High Priest doing. Imagine reading, "The pope ran to the altar . . ."

17:13 [NRSV: 16:48] In chapter 16 persons who were not priests offered incense and died; here Aaron the priest offers incense and saves the people (Wenham 1981a, 280). The reader can conjure up the image of Aaron standing between the living and the dead.

The Test with the Rods (17:16-28 [NRSV: 17:1-13])

This narrative plays on the fact that the word *maṭṭeh* means both "rod" and "tribe."

17:20 [NRSV: 17:5] "Thus I will put a stop to the complaints . . ." Here "put a stop" is *škk* which means to drain off or cause to abate—a word that occurs only three times in the Hebrew Bible. The previous instance was in Gen 8:1 in reference to the receding flood waters. This raises the possibility that the complaints of the people are somehow being compared to the chaos waters—a force opposed to God's will and rule but overcome in battle.

17:25 [NRSV: 17:10] "A warning to rebels." YHWH himself authoritatively characterizes the murmurers as "children of rebellion" (an expression that only occurs here in the Bible).

17:26 [NRSV: 17:11] The verb "to do" *(ʿśh)* forms an *inclusio* (first and last word of the verse).

17:27-28 [NRSV: 17:12-13] The people's cry has a poetic quality, framed by inclusio:

hēn gāwaʿnû	we are perishing
ʾābadnû kulānû ʾābadnû	we are lost, all of us, we are lost
kōl haqqārēb	everyone who is near
haqqārēb ʾel-miškan yhwh	who is near the dwelling of YHWH
yāmût	will die
haʾim tamnû ligwōaʿ	are we all to perish?

17:27-28 "We are perishing . . ." The people fear that they will die because they have been symbolically brought into God's presence by the rods (remember that *maṭṭeh* also means "tribe"). But only Aaron's sons can be in God's presence and not die. The test of the rods ritually reenacts the rebellion narrated in chapter 16. The flowering of Aaron's rod indicates that Aaron and his sons can enter the sanctuary and continue living whereas the lifelessness of the other rods means that others will die if they enter (Wenham 1981b, 280–81). This would seem to indicate that the people have finally gotten the message that only the sons of Aaron can enter the sanctuary (Magonet 22). If so, is this a turning point in the story?

Numbers 18

The Role of the Levites (18:1-7)

18:2, 4 "That they may be joined." The Hebrew *wᵉyillāwû* plays on the name "Levi." This same word play occurs in Gen 29:34 where Leah, the unloved wife, expresses the hope that because she had born Jacob three sons he will become attached to her.

18:4 "Outsider," *zār,* the same word used of Nadab and Abihu's illegal fire (Lev 10:1; Num 3:4). Such a person who comes near the tent shall be put to death (Num 1:51; 3:10, 38). No such person shall offer incense (17:5 [15:40]). But here it may be noteworthy that what is forbidden is not that the *zār* should enter the sanctuary or offer incense but that he should not approach "you," i.e., the priests, presumably while they are in the tent.

18:5 "You yourselves shall perform the duties . . ." Here the speech shifts from third to second person. YHWH now speaks directly to the priests.

18:6 "It is I who now take . . ." YHWH speaks personally and with some emphasis: *wᵊʾănî hinnēh lāqaḥtî . . .*

Aaron Put in Charge of Offerings (18:8-20)

18:8 "I have given you charge . . ." An expression similar to that in verse 6 is used: *wᵊʾănî hinnēh nātattî . . .*

18:9 This verse is held together by a chiastic structure:

zeh- yihyeh *lᵊkā* *miqōdeš haqqŏdāsîm*

qōdeš qŏdāšîm *lᵊkā hûʾ ûlᵊbānệkā*

This will be for you from the most holy things

a most holy thing for you it is and for your sons

Here the *zeh-yihyeh,* "this will be," is matched by *hûʾ,* "it." The last word (*ûlᵉbānệkā,* "and to your sons") falls outside the chiasmus or can be regarded as an addition to it—perhaps for emphasis.

18:12 "All the best." Hebrew: "All the fat" (see note on Lev 3:3). The last four words of the verse are arranged chiastically: they give to YHWH/to you I give. Note also how YHWH refers to himself in the third person and then speaks in the first person.

18:15 "But the firstborn of human beings you shall redeem . . ." The end of the verse has a chiastic arrangement:

ʾak pādōh tipdeh	*ʾēt bᵊkôr hāʾādām*	
	wᵊʾēt bᵊkôr habbᵊhēmâ haṭṭᵊmēʾâ	*tipdeh*
you shall redeem	the firstborn of a human	
	and the firstborn of an unclean animal	
		you shall redeem

18:17 "You shall dash their blood on the altar, and shall turn their fat into smoke as an offering by fire for a pleasing odor to the Lord." The language here is redolent of Leviticus.

Levites Given Tithes (18:21-32)

18:21, 31 The section on the tithe given to the Levites is framed by the word *ḥēlep,* "payment."

Numbers 19

The Ashes of the Red Heifer and Lustral Water

19:5 "Then the heifer shall be burned . . ." *(wᵊśārap . . . yiśrōp).* This verse is included within the repetition of the verb "to burn."

19:12 "They shall purify themselves . . . but if they do not purify themselves . . ." The first part of the verse gives the instruction positively, the second half negatively. This makes for balance and emphasis.

Numbers 20

Water from the Rock (20:1-13)

20:2 "They held a council." The use of the verb *qhl* here may be ironic, as in 16:3 (q.v.).

20:3 "Would that we had perished" echoes "We are perishing" in 17:11. It seems to be the narrator's intention to link the two episodes together (Mann 134).

20:3-5 The people's complaint moves in reverse chronological order: Korah, desert, exodus. As it does, the lack of water grows ever more acute: no water for people (2), for cattle (4), for plants (5) concluding with "there was no water to drink" (Propp 21, note 15).

20:6 Once again, at the height of tension, Moses and Aaron fall on their faces and the glory of YHWH appears (14:10; 16:19; 17:7).

20:10 "Are we to bring water . . . ?" Doob Sakenfeld (1985, 148) explores the possible ways of understanding Moses' question. It could indicate a straightforward question: "shall we (or shall we not) give you water," expecting a positive reply. It could express or elicit disbelief that water will actually come out of the rock, or it could mean a refusal on the part of Moses and Aaron to provide water.

20:11 "Water came out abundantly . . ." The expression *mayim rabbîm* ("many waters") can simply refer to an abundance of water (Num 24:7; Ezek 17:5, 8; 31:5, 7; 2 Chr 32:4) or it can conjure up the image of the waters of chaos (2 Sam 22:17 = Psa 18:16; Isa 17:13; Ezek 27:26; 31:15; Hab 3:15; Psa 77:19). Ackerman (84) wants to see here a possible reference to forces hostile to YHWH.

20:12 "You shall not bring the assembly into the land . . ." The irony is almost unbearable. "Moses, the faithful leader who bore the burden alone until given help, received constant abuse, advised Yahweh wisely, bore a special spirit, and who alone spoke to Yahweh face to face is the one punished" (Culley 1990, 30–31). But what did Moses do wrong? S. D. Luzzato has wryly remarked, "Moses our Teacher committed one sin, but the exegetes have loaded upon him thirteen sins and more, since each of them has invented a new sin" (quoted in Propp 19). It is not necessary here to review all the proposals for what constitutes the sin of Moses (and Aaron). The fact that there are so many is a clear indication of the ambiguity of the text. More important is the observation of Mann (135) on the impact of this incident on the characterization of Moses. Moses heroically continues as leader of the people and communicator of YHWH's instructions despite the fact that he himself now has no stake in the Promised Land. In earlier episodes he had protested YHWH's threats to destroy the nation, but he makes no such intervention in his own behalf. In fact, no reaction by Moses to this apparently harsh decision is recorded. Instead, we see him going about his duties as if nothing had happened.

Embassy to Edom (20:14-21)

20:14 The sending of messengers to the king of Edom is a new development in the plot line. Which way will the story go?

20:14 "You know all the adversity . . ." The word *tᵊlāʾâ* last occurred in Exod 18:8 where Moses reports to his father-in-law. If a connection between the two texts is intended, the reader may wonder whether the king of Edom's reaction will be as benevolent as Jethro's.

20:18 "You shall not pass through, or we . . ." The NRSV does not reflect the fact that here "Edom" speaks as an individual to an individual: "You (sg.) shall not cross through *me* lest with sword *I* come out to confront you (sg.)."

20:19 Israel begins speaking in the plural (we) but then shifts to the singular: "They said to him, the children of Israel did, 'On the highway we will go up and if from your (sg.) waters we drink, I or my cattle, I will give their cost. It's nothing, really. Just let me cross on foot [lit: with my feet].' "

Death of Aaron

20:23 "The Lord said to Moses and Aaron at Mount Hor, on the border of the land of Edom." This introduction is given a certain solemnity, being lengthened by the geographical reference.

20:24 "You both rebelled." The Hebrew *mᵊrîtem* ironically echoes Moses' words to the people in 20:10 *(hammôrîm)*. He had called them rebels, but he and Aaron were, in YHWH's estimation, the ones who rebelled (Doob Sakenfeld 1985, 146).

20:28 "Moses stripped Aaron of his vestments," etc. The action is speeded up, i.e., it is told in less time that it took to happen.

Numbers 21

Victory at Hormah

21:3 (YHWH hands over the Canaanites; they are destroyed; the place is called Hormah.) The mention of Hormah recalls the defeat of the Israelites when they tried to take the land even though YHWH was not with them (14:45). Now that defeat is undone and Israel's lost honor is restored (Douglas 1993a, 191).

Fiery Serpents, Bronze Serpent (21:4-9)

21:5 "The people spoke against God and Moses." This is a new development. Until now they have spoken against Moses (and Aaron) but not against God. But, in fact, "you brought us up" is second-person masculine plural *(heʿĕlîtūnû),* addressed (apparently) to God and Moses.

Continuation of the Journey (21:10-20)

21:9-11 Moses is told to make a *śārāp* (something having to do with burning) but he makes a *nᵊḥaš nᵊḥōšet* (a serpent of bronze). These last words sound like words referring to sorcery, but how could Moses be implicated in sorcery? And, as if the ambiguity of this is not enough, the Israelites next move to a place called *ʾōbōt,* which means either "wineskins" or "spirits of the dead consulted in necromancy" and then to a place called "ruins" (also the haunt of spirits). All of this sounds rather ominous, and may be preparing the way for the Balaam story.

21:18 "The well that . . . the nobles . . . dug, with the scepter, with the staff." There is something incongruous about the image of princes digging a well with their scepters. (Is it something like using a gold shovel at a ground-breaking, or does it have to do with magic?)

Defeat of Sihon (21:21-32)

21:22 The language here is similar to 20:17. It begins with the first-person singular but then shifts to plural. It is framed by *ʾeʿbᵊrâ bᵊʾarṣekā,* "let me cross your land," and *naʿăbōr gᵊbûlekâ,* "let us cross your territory."

21:25 "Its villages." Literally "its daughters"—an expression commonly used for villages that are dependent on a city center.

21:26 (Sihon had taken Heshbon from the former king of Moab.) The narrator flashes back in time to fill in the history of Heshbon. What Sihon had taken from another is taken from him.

21:27-30 (The Ballad of Heshbon.) Budd (248) suggests that what we have here is a taunt song in verse 27, which is then extended to apply to Moab in the following verses. One literary characteristic of these verses is the use of ellipsis, in this case one verb doing double duty for every two stichs (Van Seters 193).

21:32 "Captured . . . dependencies." Literally "they seized her daughters." (See note on v. 25 above.)

Defeat of Og (21:33-35)

Numbers 22

Balaam

The Balaam episode is set off by changes of the location of the Israelite camp: to the plains of Moab in 22:1 and then to Shittim in 25:1.

The whole Balaam episode takes place without Israel's knowledge. Only the characters and the reader know about the threat to Israel and how YHWH dealt with it (Mann 138).

22:2 Balak. The name could be heard as meaning "devastator" (Ross, *IDB*), in which case it would be ironic since "Devastator" is foiled in his attempt to live up to his name. There may be a further comic element in that "Devastator" is the son of "little bird" *(ṣippôr)*. Moses, of course, is the husband of "little bird" *(ṣippôrâ)*. But it is not the son of *ṣippôrâ* that Balak is up against. It is YHWH himself.

22:3 "Moab was in great dread of the people . . ." Balak's fear of Israel's numbers makes him Pharaoh redivivus (Exod 1:8-12; Ackerman 86; Mann 136). The verse has a poetic quality:

wayyāgor *môʾāb mippénê* *hāʿām* *mᵊʾōd*

kî rab-hûʾ

wayyāqoṣ *môʾāb mippᵊnê* *bᵊnê yiśrāʾēl*

afraid was Moab before the people greatly

for great it was

dreading was Moab before the children of Israel

22:6 In stating of Israel, "they are stronger than I," Balak becomes a mirror image of the spies, who had said the very same thing about the inhabitants of the land (13:31).

22:7 "Fees for divination." This translation is based on a guess as to the referent of *qᵊsāmîm*. Horowitz has proposed that the word refers to models of omens (like the ceramic sheep livers found by archaeologists). Such a reading would bring with it the nuance that Balak is dissatisfied with the readings of his own diviners and is sending the model to Balaam for a second opinion.

22:8 "I will bring back word to you, just as the Lord speaks to me." It comes as a total surprise that Balaam will respond with the word of YHWH.

22:9 "God came to Balaam and said . . ." The narrator constructs a dialog between God *(ʾĕlōhîm)* and Balaam.

22:11 "'A people has come out of Egypt . . .'" Balaam quotes Balak verbatim except that he substitutes *qâbâ-llî* for *ʾārâ-llî* of verse 6—the first of ten instances of the verb *qbb* in the Balaam story. It occurs nowhere else in the Pentateuch. The possible significance of this is to prepare for the incident at Baal-peor where the Israelite idolater and his female partner are pierced through the belly *(qŏbātāh)* in her tent-shrine (*qubbâ,* Num 25:8).

22:12 "You shall not curse the people, for they are blessed." The combination of the words *ʾrr* (curse) and *brk* (bless) recall verse 6 but put it in a new light. Elohim informs Balaam (and the reader, but not Balak) that Israel is blessed.

22:13 "The Lord has refused to let me go with you." Balaam informs Balak's messengers about what God has told him but withholds the key information that Israel is blessed (Douglas 1993b, 419).

22:14 "Balaam refuses to come with us." Instead of reporting to Balak that YHWH has refused to let Balaam go (v. 13) they say that he refuses to come. They obviously did not take Balaam seriously when he said he was going to consult YHWH (v. 8). The fact that they took such God-talk to be merely a negotiating ploy is the key element in the characterization of these minor characters. After all, what good was he as a sorcerer if he could not manipulate the gods to do or decree as he wanted? (Spero 471).

22:15 "Officials more numerous and more distinguished." Narrative tension is increased by the sending of a more high-powered delegation. *nikbādîm,* "honorable," may connote wealth. The reader is being offered the possibility of construing Balaam's motive as greed, as do the New Testament and rabbinic tradition (and, apparently, Balak).

22:16 "I will do you great honor." The root *kbd* seen in verse 15 is repeated. If Balaam wants to see how well the king rewards those who do his will he has only to look at the wealth displayed by the delegation. Balaam can become like them. He is also being offered great honor *(kābôd),* which will take material form.

22:17, 20 By making God's order to Balaam in 20 ("only what I tell you will you do" *[wᵊʾak ʾet-haddābār ʾăšer-ʾădabbēr ʾēlêkā ʾōtô taʿăśeh]*) echo Balak's words to Balaam in 17: "Whatever you tell me I will do" *[wᵊkol ʾăšer-tōʾmar ʾēlay ʾeʿĕśeh]*, the narrator is making Balak a parody of Balaam (Castello 36).

22:18 The words *yhwh ʾĕlōhay,* "YHWH my God," on the lips of a pagan sorcerer must have sounded strange (or wondrous) to the first hearers of this narrative.

22:20 "Do only what I tell you to do." That Balak is a parody of Balaam is confirmed by the use of *ʿśh* as the last word in this verse. One would logically expect either *dbr* or *ʾmr* ("to speak," "to say"), so the appearance of "to do" is likely to be for the purpose of recalling verse 17 ("Whatever you say to me I will do").

22:22, 24, 26 Balak had sent messengers to Balaam. Now YHWH sends his own messenger to Balaam. Each initiative of the angel is told with an increasing number of words (vv. 6, 9, 13; Rouillard 1980, 223).

22:23 "The donkey saw the angel of the Lord . . ." The ass can see the angel. The reader can see the angel. The only one who cannot is Balaam (Clark 140). Some commentators would add to the last sentence the ironic qualification "Balaam—the seer!" However, the term does not come into use until later in the story and the contrast can only be seen in retrospect. The reader is now given a new piece of information that heightens the narrative tension. The angel is holding a drawn sword in his hand—presumably intending to use it against Balaam.

22:27 "Balaam's anger was kindled . . ." Balaam becomes angry but he does not know (as the reader does) that God is angry with him (v. 22). The mention of the staff (compare vv. 23, 25) is an escalation.

22:28 "The Lord opened the mouth of the donkey . . ." Regarding the characterization of Balaam, St. Augustine remarks:

> There is as great a distance between the prophecy of prophets such as Isaiah and Jeremiah and that transitory passing prophecy as appeared in Saul, as the distance when humans speak and speech as it appeared in Balaam's ass . . . It was not an indication that the beast was permanently to be able to speak with men. If God can make an ass speak, he can certainly make an ungodly man submit to the spirit of prophecy for a short time. (Translation of PL 40, cols. 129-130 by Baskin [1983, 110]).

Whereas Ambrose and Augustine regarded Balaam as wholly evil, Origen and Jerome (following the *Biblical Antiquities*) thought that Balaam started out good, was corrupted by greed, but then eventually repented of his misdeeds. Coats (1973) attempts (unsuccessfully in my opinion) to refute those who maintain that Balaam is not virtuous but is simply compelled by YHWH's prophetic word. Mann (137) sees a change of character.

22:29 "I wish I had a sword in my hand!" The narrator has used knowledge effectively so that the reader perceives the irony of Balaam's expressed desire for a sword with which to kill the ass when the ass has avoided the sword that in fact is in the angel's hand to kill Balaam (Castello 38). The reader knows that the ass has not been making sport of Balaam but saving his life (Laffey).

22:31 "The Lord opened the eyes of Balaam." The narrator uses the same language that was used of the donkey's first vision in verse 23. Such a repetition might suggest that Balaam's sin is blindness, as he himself acknowledges in verse 34 (Rouillard 1980, 217).

22:33 The angel's language now echoes Balaam's threat in verse 29. It would now become apparent to Balaam that the angel had been there all along and had heard Balaam's words to the donkey, and that the fate he wished for the donkey would have been his own at the hands of the angel (Rouillard 1980, 216). Balaam would have killed the donkey, but she saved his life.

22:34 "I have sinned." If Balaam's confession is judged sincere, then the reader must allow for a change of character and a positive evaluation of Balaam. This is why Num. Rab. 20:15 sees the confession as insincere, "He said so because he was a subtle villain and knew that nothing can prevent punishment except repentance, and that if any sinner says, 'I have sinned,' the angel is not permitted to touch him" (quoted in Baskin 1983, 159, note 81).

22:35 "So Balaam went on with the officials of Balak." The concluding words of this act of the drama repeat almost identically the conclusion of the previous act (22:20-21; Castello 38). This word-for-word repetition heightens the difficulty in construing the character of YHWH. (Why attack Balaam for doing what YHWH had permitted? Is YHWH inconsistent?) (Rouillard 1980, 20).

22:36 The fact that Balak goes out to the farthest point on his border to meet Balaam may be construed as an indicator of his anxiety at the presence of Israel—an anxiety that mirrors that of the Israelites in chapter 13.

22:37 "Am I not able to honor you?" Why should Balak think that Balaam's hesitancy was due to doubts about the king's willingness or ability to honor Balaam (22:17)? Apparently the king, like his officials, thinks that Balaam is motivated by greed.

22:38 "I have come to you now." Balaam does not waste time explaining his reluctance. He responds to the king's question with another question. There is some irony in this, first because of all the effort that Balak has had to make to get Balaam to come, but most of all because, as verse 36 informs us, it is Balak who has gone out to the edge of his territory to meet the sorcerer (Rouillard 1980, 6).

22:38 "The word God puts in my mouth . . ." In regard to the characterization of Balaam, Origen remarks on this verse that if Balaam had been a genuine prophet the word of God would not have been in his mouth but in his heart. His heart being filled with greed, God's word could find no place there but only in his mouth (quoted in Baskin 1983, 107–108).

22:41 "He could see part of the people of Israel." Balak had expressed fear at the great number of Israelites (22:3-6, 11). This number is now dramatized in the fact that only the edge *(qᵊṣēh hāʿām)* of the throng can be seen (23:13).

Numbers 23

23:3 "Stay here beside your burnt offerings while I go aside. Perhaps the Lord will come to meet me." It is YHWH, the God of Israel, that Balaam expects to encounter, but not at the site of the sacrifice.

23:7-8 "Come, denounce Israel!" Repetition of the root *zʿm* ("denounce," *zōʿămâ* in v. 7, *ʾezʿōm* and *zāʿam* in v. 8) and word play on the name "Jacob" in the words *māh ʾeqqōb lōʾ qabbōh ʾēl* ("How can I denounce what El has not denounced?") stress the point that Jacob most certainly will not be cursed (Wilson 39; Tosato 101). The first half of Balaam's declamation in verse 7 features a chiastic structure (Tosato 99):

From Aram has brought me	Balak	
The king of Moab		from the hills of the east

23:10 ". . . or number the dust." The NRSV misses the opportunity to represent the ellipsis in the Hebrew (*mānâ* doing double duty).

23:14 "Field of Zophim." *ṣōpîm* could be rendered "lookouts," or even "spies." So, e.g., Luther, *Späherfeld.*

23:17 "What has the Lord said?" Balak's question betrays his resignation to the fact that it is YHWH (the God of Israel) who is doing whatever blessing or cursing there is to be done.

23:20 "He has blessed and I cannot revoke it." Is this an echo of Isaac's words to Esau that the blessing given to Jacob cannot be withdrawn (Gen 27:37-38)? A parallel between Balak and Esau is intriguing, but, while the situation is similar, the language is not. So any possible echo is not verbal.

23:23 "There is not enchantment against Jacob." Others: "There is no divination in Jacob." Both readings are possible, depending on how one reads *bᵊ*, but in the context it seems more likely that Balaam is stating that magic powers are ineffective rather than that the Israelites do not practice divination.

23:24 (Image of a lion rousing itself and not lying down again until it has eaten its prey and drunk its blood.) Balak might well be alarmed, considering that *he* is apparently the lion's prey in this *māšāl.*

Numbers 24

24:1 "He did not go, as at other times, to look for omens." Now the reader learns what it is that Balaam has been doing when he separated himself from Balak—seeking omens *(nᵊḥāšîm)*. Is this information meant to put Balaam's prophetic activity in a new light? Balaam has stated (23:23) that there is no divination *(naḥaš)* that is effective against Jacob. Are we to conclude that he learned this the hard way?

24:4 "With eyes uncovered." Hebrew *gᵊlûy ʿēnāyim* may recall with irony the uncovering of Balaam's eyes in 22:31 (when he finally saw the angel).

24:10 "Balak . . . struck his hands together." What does this mean? Surely he was not applauding. Budd (269) cites Lam 2:15:

> All who pass along the way
> clap their hands at you;
> they hiss and wag their heads
> at daughter Jerusalem;
> "Is this the city that was called
> the perfection of beauty,
> the joy of all the earth?"

and Job 27:23

> It claps its hands at them,
> and hisses at them from its place.

In these verses, clapping seems to be an expression of contempt or derision. Holladay suggests that the gesture is apotropaic (to ward off bad luck, or, in this case, the blessing of Israel).

24:13 "I would not be able to go beyond the word of the Lord." Balaam's final and climactic speech echoes his words to Balak's messengers in 22:18. This contributes to unifying the whole Balaam story (Coats 1973, 26; Rouillard 1980, 8). The final oracle is given without any accompanying sacrifice and against Balak's order to say no more (Harrelson 34). Balaam's speech is not only a frustration of Balak's evil intention for Israel, it is "the most far-reaching and positive vision of Israel's future found in the entire Pentateuch" (Ackerman 87). It comes not from Moses but from a pagan diviner and, in fact, is unknown to Moses or Israel. The fact that it comes from a pagan diviner makes it all the more credible. And this knowledge elevates the reading position of the reader vis-à-vis Moses and Israel in the story.

24:15-16 "The oracle of the one who . . ." The elaborate introduction is similar to that in verses 3-4 above with the addition of *yōdēaʿ daʿat ʿelyôn,* "knowing the knowledge of Elyon." Is Balaam just "hyping" himself or did YHWH really open his eyes (22:31)? Are his words to be taken as empty boasting, comical when one remembers that even an ass could see what he could not? Or are we to see a change in character?

24:18 "Edom will become a possession, Seir a possession . . ." Within the verse there is a chiastic arrangement of *ʾĕdôm yᵊrēšâ / yᵊrēšâ śēʿîr.*

24:21 "Your nest is set in the rock." The Hebrew word for "nest" *(qēn)* plays on the name Cain *(qāyin)* and his descendants, the Kenites (Budd 270).

24:25 (Balaam went to his place; Balak went his way.) The story ends with the departure of the two main characters.

Numbers 25

The Incident at Baal-peor

By placing this story immediately after the Balaam cycle the author has heightened the irony. Immediately after YHWH has saved the people from the king of Moab's hired sorcerer, the people fornicate with Moabite women. The destruction of Israel that Balak had failed to achieve through Balaam's magic will be accomplished by the people themselves.

This chapter marks an important turning point in the story: the transition from the old generation condemned to dying in the wilderness to the new generation, who would take possession of the Promised Land (Olson 1997, 229).

> The Balaam cycle and the final rebellion and apostasy of the old generation are linked in a dramatic contrast. As God is struggling on the mountaintops surrounding the camp of Israel to bless God's people (Num 22–24), the Israelites down on the plains of Moab are reveling in idolatry and disobedience (Num 25). Only one other pentateuchal narrative contains this contrast of two scenes: the story of the golden calf in Exodus 32. . . . The striking similarities between the Baal Peor apostasy and the golden calf story suggest that these two stories function as bookends for the experience of the old generation from Mount Sinai to the edge of the promised land. . . . Moses is commanded by God, in the aftermath of the golden calf story, to avoid exactly what happens in Numbers 25 (Exod 34:15-16). The Levites kill three thousand of those who worshiped the golden calf; similarly, the 'judges' of Israel are instructed to kill those 'who have yoked themselves to Baal of Peor' (Exod 32:28; Num 25:5; Olson 1997, 233).

25:2 "The people ate and bowed down to their gods." The sequence "ate and bowed down" is curious. The only other occurrence of this sequence is in Ps 22:30, which several modern versions emend.

25:8 "The plague stopped." Only now is the reader given the information that there has been a plague that has killed 42,000 persons.

25:14 "Zimri son of Salu." The narrator has withheld the names of the characters until this point. The names may not be part of the strategy of characterization but simply traditional. The name Zimri could be linked to a root meaning "to prune." Some writers have seen significance in the name Cozbi (next verse).

25:15 "Cozbi." Fewer than one name in ten in the Hebrew Bible is a woman's name. Therefore, if the narrator goes to the trouble of naming a woman the name can be presumed to be significant. Lutzky sees a play on two different meanings of the root *kzb:* I *kzb* means "to lie, deceive, disappoint" whereas II *kzb* means "to be voluptuous." Since in Akkadian *kuzbu* (voluptuousness, sexual vigor) is an attribute of Ishtar and Asherah, Lutzky suggests the possibility that our narrative is directed against the worship of fertility goddesses. Part of the rhetoric would be in the word play on the root of Cozbi's name: "Though the goddess may be alluring and full of promise (*kzb* II), she is no more than a delusion (*kzb* I) to whom all pleas for deliverance would be in vain" (Lutzky 548; see also Niditch 45). The root *kzb* has been heard in Num 23:19 "Not a man is El that he should deceive, nor a descendant of Adam that he should repent." Instead of following the God who does not deceive, the people have followed the alluring deceiver.

Numbers 26

The Second Census

26:3, 63 The second census is framed by the specification of the place: the plains of Moab by the Jordan opposite Jericho.

26:64-65 "There was not one of those enrolled . . . in the wilderness of Sinai . . . Not one of them was left . . ." This is undoubtedly the point of the exercise—the demonstration of the fact that the desert generation has died off just as the Lord had said and a new generation has arisen that can now enter the land. The word of YHWH in 14:35 has been fulfilled.

Numbers 27

The Daughters of Zelophehad (27:1-11)

The section of Numbers that deals with the new generation and its future life in the Promised Land is framed by the story of Zelophehad's daughters (27:1-11; 36; Olson 1997, 232; Ackerman 89).

27:7 "The daughters of Zelophehad are right." Putting *kēn*, "well-founded" first emphasizes the rightness of the daughters' claim.

Moses Views the Land, Appointment of Joshua (27:12-23)

27:16 Moses characterizes YHWH as *ʾĕlōhê hārûḥōt lᵊkol-bāśār*, "God of the spirits of all flesh." This may connote his resignation to his impending death.

27:17 "Who shall go out before them and come in before them . . ." This expression has a military connotation and so prepares the way for the appointment of the person who will lead the conquest.

Numbers 28–29

Instruction on Offerings to Be Made at Appointed Times

28:2; 29:39 The two chapters on sacrifices to be made at appointed times are framed by the word *môʿădîm.*

Numbers 30

Instruction on Vows

30:1 [NRSV: 29:40] ("Moses spoke as the Lord commanded.") Since this verse is clearly the end of the previous section, NRSV numbers it as part of the previous chapter.

30:3 [NRSV: 30:2] The mention of vows at the end of the last chapter naturally leads to an instruction on vows. This verse features a series of cognate accusatives: *nādar nēder* "to vow a vow," *nišbaʿ šᵊbūʿâ* "to swear a swearing," *ʾĕsōr ʾissār ʿal nepeš* "to bind a bond on the soul."

30:5 [NRSV: 30:4] Repetition of *ʾāb,* "father," forms an *inclusio* in the protasis; *qwm,* "stand," in the apodosis.

30:6 This verse is framed by repetition of the phrase *hēnîʾ ʾābîhā ʾōtāh,* "her father expresses disapproval."

30:14 [NRSV: 30:13] Milgrom (1990, xxii) points out the following chiastic structure:

A If her husband offers no objection from that day to the next,

  B he has upheld all the vows and obligations she has assumed

  B' he has upheld them

A' by offering no objection on the day he found out

Numbers 31

Revenge Against Midian

31:2 The juxtaposition of statements makes it appear that (by divine decree) revenge is to be Moses' last act before he dies.

> Is there anything about this new generation that might inspire hope that they will not suffer their parents' fate? . . . There is not a single death of an Israelite in chapters 26–36. . . . The new generation's first military encounter with the Midianites (Num 31) results in a God-given victory over a people who had earlier seduced the old generation into apostasy (Num 25) (Olson 1997, 232).

31:14-15 A new crisis arises when Moses discovers that the troops had allowed female prisoners to live.

31:17 "Kill every male." The command to kill the prisoners is framed by the chiastic structure: *hrg zākār . . . zākār hrg* "to kill the male."

31:40 This verse is framed by repetition of the word *nepeš* (duplicated by NRSV "persons").

Numbers 32

The Reubenites and Gadites Ask to Settle in Transjordan

The request creates narrative tension. Will the request be granted? Will it result in conflict or the break-up of the people?

32:1 "The Reubenites and the Gadites owned a very great number of cattle." The narrator's exposition of the tribes' need for grazing land is framed by repetition of the word *miqneh,* "cattle."

32:8 "Your fathers did this . . ." Moses makes a rhetorical reference to the failure of the previous (doomed) generation to take possession of the land (Numbers 13). The inference is that if the Reubenites and Gadites do as their fathers did they will suffer the same fate.

32:13 "He made them wander." One might hear an echo of the condemnation of Cain in Gen 4:12.

32:16, 24 Milgrom (1990, xxii) proposes a split chiastic structure between verses 16 and 24:

A We will build here sheepfolds for our flocks

  B and towns for our children (32:16)

  . . .

  B' Build towns for your children

A' and sheepfolds for your flocks (32:24)

32:20 The Reubenites and Gadites had offered to go before the Israelites (v. 17) but Moses changes this to going before YHWH. Moses also adds the element of battle.

32:21 "Until [the Lord] has driven out his enemies from before him." These words put the conquest on a theological level: YHWH is driving out his enemies (presumably through the instrumentality of the Gadites and Reubenites).

32:24 "What comes from your mouth, do." Moses' words to the Reubenites and Gadites echo 30:2, the instruction on vows, "When a man makes a pledge . . . he shall do according to all that proceeds out of his mouth."

32:25, 27 "Your servants." The petitioners are pictured as adopting a formal courtly style in their petition (Budd 344). They also adopt the language added by Moses in 20 (going before YHWH, and battle). In this whole episode the expression *lipnê yhwh* occurs seven times.

32:28 (Moses gave the command to Joshua, Eleazar, and the heads of houses.) Moses must make these provisions for the future because he himself will not be crossing the Jordan.

32:38 "Nebo . . . they rebuilt." There may be some word play between the word *nᵊbô,* "Nebo," at the beginning of the verse and the last word, *bānû,* which reverses the first two letters of Nebo.

32:41 This verse, both in Hebrew and in the NRSV, begins and ends with the name Jair.

Numbers 33

Exodus Stations

Here we have a temporal flashback rehearsing the whole journey from Rameses in Egypt to the people's present location across the Jordan from Jericho.

33:2 This verse features a chiastic arrangement:

môṣāʾêhem	*lᵊmasʿêhem*		
	masʿêhem	*lᵊmoṣāʾêhem*	
Their going out	their setting forth		
	their setting forth		their going out

33:3 The mention of Rameses might call to mind the settlement there (Gen 47:11), the forced labor (Exod 1:11), and the departure from there at the beginning of the Exodus (Exod 12:37).

33:3-4 This is new information, and it paints a memorable picture: all the Egyptians burying their firstborn as they watch the Israelites set out.

33:8 "[They] passed through the sea." This seems a remarkably matter-of-fact reference to the crossing of the sea. It is, as it were, hidden in the middle of the sentence.

33:9 The monotony of the list is broken up by the notice of the twelve springs and the seventy palm trees.

33:14 The narrator's notice that there was no water is seen as an understatement by anyone who has read the rest of the book. Since the list is said to have been compiled by Moses, are we to take these notices as his greatly understated log entries? There would then be an almost comic disconnect between the narration (in which the people are ready to lynch him, to scrap the journey to the Promised Land, and go back to Egypt) and Moses' own laconic notice of the incident.

33:16 That the departure from Sinai follows immediately the encampment in the previous verse passes over the narrative of Exodus 25–Numbers 10 and the foundational events told in those chapters.

33:53 "You shall take possession . . . to possess." This verse is framed by the chiastic structure *yrš ʾereṣ . . . ʾereṣ yrš.*

33:54 "You shall apportion . . . you shall inherit." This verse is framed by the verb *nḥl,* "to apportion." The mention of the fathers is poignant. The lots of land are those that would have fallen to the previous generation had they not been unfaithful and had to wander until they perished in the wilderness. There is an implicit call not to imitate their folly. This prepares the way for the warning that if any Canaanite inhabitants are allowed to remain in the land they will become a thorn in the side.

Numbers 34

Borders. Another List of Princes

34:19-28 This is a list of leaders of each tribe who will assist in the distribution of the land. If one compares this list with the earlier lists of leaders in chapters 1, 2, 7, and 10, one can see that the names of the fathers of the leaders in chapter 34 do not correspond with the names of the leaders in the earlier lists. This means that the generation of leaders who perished in the wilderness was not succeeded in leadership by their sons, but rather by the sons of men who had not been leaders in the first generation.

Tribe	*Name*	*Father*	*Earlier Lists*
Judah	Caleb	Jephunneh	Nahshon
Simeon	Shemuel	Ammihud	Shelumiel
Benjamin	Elidad	Chislon	Abidan
Dan	Bukki	Jogli	Ahiezar
Manasseh	Hanniel	Ephod	Gamaliel
Ephraim	Kemuel	Shiphtan	Elishama
Zebulun	Eli-zaphan	Parnach	Eliab
Issachar	Paltiel	Azzan	Nethanel
Asher	Ahihud	Shelomi	Pagiel
Naphtali	Pedahel	Ammihud	Ahira

Johnson (*IDB* 2:87 s.v. Elidad) interprets the names in this list (which shows an increased number of names with El compared to earlier lists) as a sign of "Israel's dependence upon God for the new life in Canaan." In other words, the increase in the number of names compounded with "El" is taken as an indication of a change in character in the people as a whole.

Numbers 35

Levitical Cities. Cities of Refuge

35:25 The provision that the slayer live in the city of refuge until the death of the high priest may assume an understanding of the death of the high priest as expiating blood guilt (Budd 384).

35:29 "A statute and ordinance for you throughout your generations wherever you live." The instruction on the cities of refuge and the slayer has been given in the third person but concludes here with direct second-person plural address to the people. The applicability of the statute is extended through time and space.

35:34 ". . . The land . . . in which I also dwell . . ." YHWH concludes the direct address to the people by speaking personally and emphatically.

Numbers 36

The Daughters of Zelophehad—(Fuzzy) Second Thoughts

36:4 The fear that the inheritance of Zelophehad's daughters would be alienated when property was restored at the Jubilee does not square with the instruction on the Jubilee in Leviticus (Douglas 1993a, 237–38). Why does Moses not simply correct the Manassites' misapprehension of the law, or, if not Moses, the narrator?

36:7-9 Verse 9 repeats verse 7, with slight variants, thus forming a frame around verse 8.

36:10-12 "The daughters of Zelophehad did as the Lord had commanded Moses." These verses constitute a rather lengthy fulfillment-of-command statement, marking a return to the equilibrium seen in the narrative at the first part of Numbers, before the murmurings.

FOR FURTHER READING

Abma, R. "Pioniers in het land: De dochters van Selofchad in Numeri 27:1-11." *ACEBT* 13 (1994) 31–47.

Ackerman, James S. "Numbers." Pages 78–91 in *The Literary Guide to the Bible*. Edited by Robert Alter and Frank Kermode. Cambridge, Mass.: Belknap Press, 1987.

Allegro, J. M. "The meaning of the Phrase *šeṯ ūm hāʿayin* in Num. XXIV 3, 15." *VT* 3 (1953) 78–79.

Althann, R. "Numbers 21, 30b in the Light of Ancient Versions and Ugaritic." *Bib* 66 (1985) 568–71.

Arden, E. "How Moses Failed God." *JBL* 76 (1957) 50–52.

Artus, Olivier. *Etudes sur le livre des Nombres. Récit, Histoire et Loi en Nb 13,1-20,13.* OBO 157. Fribourg: Editions Universitaires, 1997.

Bach, Alice. "Good to the Last Drop: Viewing the Sotah (Numbers 5.11-31) as the Glass Half Empty and Wondering How to View It Half Full." Pages 26–54 in *The New Literary Criticism and the Hebrew Bible.* JSOTSup 143. Edited by J. Cheryl Exum and David J. A. Clines. Sheffield: JSOT, 1993.

Barnouin, M. "Les recensements du livre des Nombres et l'astronomie babylonienne." *VT* 27 (1977) 280–303.

Barré, Michael, L. "The Portrait of Balaam in Numbers 22-24." *Int* 51 (1997) 254–66.

Bartlett, John R. "The Conquest of Sihon's Kingdom: A Literary Re-Examination." *JBL* 97 (1978) 347–51.

Baskin, Judith Reesa. *Pharaoh's Counselors: Job, Jethro and Balaam in Rabbinic and Patristic Tradition.* Atlanta: Scholars, 1983.

Baumgarten, Albert I. "The Paradox of the Red Heifer." *VT* 43 (1993) 442–51.

Beirne, D. "A Note on Numbers 11,4." *Bib* 44 (1963) 201–203.

Ben-Amos, Dan. "Comments on Robert C. Culley's 'Five Tales of Punishment in the Book of Numbers.'" Pages 35–45 in *Text and Tradition:*

The Hebrew Bible and Folklore. Edited by Susan Niditch. Atlanta: Scholars, 1990.

Budd, Philip J. *Numbers.* Word Biblical Commentary 5. Waco: Word Books, 1984.

Burrows, E. *The Oracles of Jacob and Balaam.* London: Burns, 1939.

Butler, Trent C. "An Anti-Moses Tradition." *JSOT* 12 (1979) 9–15.

Carroll, R. P., "Is Humor Also Among the Prophets?" Pages 168–89 in *On Humor and the Comic in the Hebrew Bible.* Edited by Yehuda T. Radday and Athalya Brenner. Sheffield: Almond, 1990.

Castello, Gaetano. "Balaam e Balak: Approccio narrativo a Nm 22–24." Pages 29–48 in *Oltre il racconto: Esegesi ed ermeneutica: alla ricerca del senso.* Edited by Cesare Marcheselli-Casale. Naples: M. D'Auria, 1994.

Clark, Ira. "Balaam's Ass: Suture or Structure?" Pages 137–44 in *Literary Interpretations of Biblical Narratives,* Vol. II. Edited by K.R.R. Gros Louis and J. S. Ackerman. Nashville: Abingdon, 1982.

Coats, George W. (1973) "Balaam: Sinner or Saint?" *Biblical Research* 18 (1973) 21–29.

_____. (1977) "Legendary Motifs in the Moses Death Reports." *CBQ* 39 (1977) 34–44.

_____. (1982a) "Humility and Honor: A Moses Legend in Numbers 12." Pages 97–107 in *Art and Meaning: Rhetoric in Biblical Literature.* JSOTSup 19. Edited by J. A. Clines, D. M. Gunn, and A. J. Hauser. Sheffield: Sheffield Academic Press, 1982.

_____. (1982b) "The Way of Obedience: Tradition-Historical and Hermeneutical Reflections on the Balaam Story." *Semeia* 24 (1982) 53–79.

Cohen, Jeffrey, M. "Balaam: Did God Change His Mind?" *Jewish Biblical Quarterly* 20 (1991/92) 159–63.

Culley, Robert C. (1975) "Themes and Variations in Three Groups of OT Narratives." *Semeia* 3 (1975) 3–13.

Culley, Robert C. (1990) "Five Tales of Punishment in the Book of Numbers." Pages 25–34 in *Text and Tradition: The Hebrew Bible and Folklore.* Edited by Susan Niditch. Atlanta: Scholars, 1990.

Davies, Eryl W. "A Mathematical Conundrum: The Problem of the Large Numbers in Numbers i and xxvi." *VT* 45 (1995) 449–69.

Desplanque, Christophe. "Mystère divin et ambuiguïté humaine dans l'historie de Balaam." *Hok* 64 (1997) 1–16.

Douglas, Mary. (1993a) *In the Wilderness: The Doctrine of Defilement in the Book of Numbers.* JSOTSup 158. Sheffield: JSOT Press, 1993.

Douglas, Mary. (1993b) "Balaam's Place in the Book of Numbers." *Man,* n.s., 28 (1993) 411–20.

_____. (1993/94) "The Glorious Book of Numbers." *Jewish Studies Quarterly* 1 (1993/94) 194–216.

Eerdmans, B. D. "The Composition of Numbers." *OTS* 6 (1949) 101–216.

Fishbane, Michael. (1974) "Accusations of Adultery: A Study of Law and Scribal Practice in Numbers 5:11-31." *HUCA* 45 (1974) 25–45.

_____. (1980) "Biblical Colophons, Textual Criticism and Legal Analogies." *CBQ* 42 (1980) 438–49.

Flack, E. E. "Flashes of New Knowledge. Recent Study and the Book of Numbers." *Int* 13 (1959) 3–23.

Frymer-Kensky, Tikva. "The Strange Case of the Suspected Sotah (Numbers v 11-31)." *VT* 34 (1984) 11–26.

Garbini, Giovanni. "L'iscrizione di Balaam Bar-Beor." *Hen* 1 (1979) 166–88.

García López, Felix. (1977) "Analyse littéraire de Deutéronome, V–XI." *RB* 84 (1977) 481–522; 85 (1978) 5–49.

_____. (1978) "Deut., VI et la tradition-rédaction du Deutéronome." *RB* 85 (1978) 161–200.

_____. 1981) "Yahvé, fuente última de vida; análisis de Dt 8." *Bib* 62 (1981) 21–54.

Gevirtz, S. *Patterns in the Early Poetry of Israel.* Studies in Ancient Oriental Civilization 32. Chicago: University of Chicago Press, 1963.

Goldin, Judah. "In Defense of Balak: Not Entirely Midrash." *Judaism* 40 (1990) 455–60.

Gorman, F. H. *The Ideology of Ritual: Space, Time and Status in the Priestly Theology.* JSOTSup 91. Sheffield: JSOT Press, 1990.

Gottcent, John H. *The Bible: A Literary Study.* Boston: G. K. Hall-Twayne, 1986.

Gray, G. Buchanan. *A Critical Exegetical Commentary on Numbers.* ICC. Edinburgh: T & T Clark, 1976.

Greenstein, Edward, L. "Deconstruction and Biblical Narrative." *Prooftexts* 9 (1989) 43–71.

Grindel, John A., C.M. "The Book of Numbers." *TBT* 89 (1977) 1142–50.

Guillaume, A. "A Note on Numbers xxiii 10." *VT* 12 (1962) 335–37.

Guyot, G. H. "The Prophecy of Balaam." *CBQ* 2 (1940) 330–40; 3 (1941) 235–42.

Hackett, Jo Ann. "Some Observations on the Balaam Tradition at Deir *ʿallā*." *BA* 49 (1986) 216–22.

Hanson, H. E. "Num. XVI 30 and the meaning of *bāraʾ*." *VT* 22 (1972) 353–59.

Harrelson, Walter. "Guidance in the Wilderness: The Theology of Numbers." *Interp* 13 (1959) 24–36.

Harrison, R. K. *Numbers.* Wycliffe Exegetical Commentary. Chicago: Moody Press, 1990.

Hartman, Geoffrey H. "Numbers: The Realism of Numbers: The Magic of Numbers." Pages 39–50 in *Congregation: Contemporary Writers*

Read the Jewish Bible. Edited by David Rosenberg. San Diego, Calif.: Harcourt Brace Jovanovich, 1987.

Hoftijzer, J., and G. van der Kooij. *Aramaic Texts from Deir ʿalla.* Leiden: Brill, 1976.

Horowitz, Victor (Avigdor). "The Expression *ûqsāmîm bĕyādām* (Numbers 22:7) in Light of Divinatory Practices from Mari." *HS* 33 (1992) 5–15.

Jobling, David. "A Structural Analysis of Numbers 11–12." Pages 26–62 in *The Sense of Biblical Narrative: Three Structural Analyses in the Old Testament (I Samuel 13–31, Numbers 11–12, I Kings 17–18).* 2 vols. 2nd ed. Sheffield: JSOT, 1986.

Kaiser, Walter C., Jr. "Balaam Son of Beor in Light of Deir ʿallā and Scripture: Saint or Soothsayer?" Pages 95–106 in *"Go to the Land I Will Show You." Studies in Honor of Dwight W. Young.* Edited by Joseph E. Coleson and Victor H. Matthews. Winona Lake, Ind.: Eisenbrauns, 1996.

Kellenberger, Edgar. "Jahwes unerwarteter Widerstand gegen seinen Beauftragten. Erwägungen zur Episode von Bileams Eselin (Num 22, 22-35)." *Theologische Zeitschrift* 45 (1989) 69–72.

Kselman, John S. "A Note on Numbers XII 6-8." *VT* 26 (1976) 500–5.

_____. "The Recovery of Poetic Fragments from the Pentateuchal Priestly Source." *JBL* 97 (1978) 161–73.

Laffey, Alice L. "Ask the Ass." Paper presented at the annual meeting of the Catholic Biblical Association. Atchison, Kansas, August 15, 1993.

LaVerdiere, Eugene A. "Balaam, Son of Peor." *The Bible Today* 89 (March 1997) 1157–65.

Layton, Scott C. "Whence Comes Balaam? Num 22.5 Revisited." *Biblica* 73 (1992) 32–61.

Le Déaut, R. "Une aggadah targumique et les 'murmures' de Jean 6." *Bib* 51 (1970) 80–83.

Lemaire, André. "Fragments from the Book of Balaam Found at Deir Alla: Text Foretells Cosmic Disaster." *BAR* 11 (Sept.–Oct., 1985) 27–39.

Levine, Baruch A. "Offerings Rejected by God: Numbers 16:15 in Comparative Perspective." Pages 107–16 in *"Go to the Land I Will Show You." Studies in Honor of Dwight W. Young.* Edited by Joseph E. Coleson and Victor H. Matthews. Winona Lake, Ind.: Eisenbrauns, 1996.

Loewe, Raphael. "Divine frustration exegetically frustrated—Numbers 14:34 תנואתי." Pages 137–58 in *Words and Meanings: Essays Presented to David Winton Thomas on His Retirement from the Regius Professorship of Hebrew in the University of Cambridge, 1968.* Edited by Peter R. Ackroyd and Barnabas Lindars. Cambridge: Cambridge University Press, 1968.

Lust, J. "Balaam, an Ammorite." *Ephemerides Theologicae Lovanienses* 54 (1978) 60–61.

Lutzky, Harriet C. "The name 'Cozbi' (Numbers xxv 15,18)." *VT* 47 (1997) 546–49.
McEvenue, Sean E. "A Source-Critical Problem in Nm 14,26-38." *Bib* 50 (1969) 453–65.
_____. *The Narrative Style of the Priestly Writer.* Analecta Biblica 50. Rome: Biblical Institute Press, 1971.
McKane, W. "Poison, Trial by Ordeal and the Cup of Wrath." *VT* 30 (1980) 474–92.
Magonet, J. "The Korah Rebellion." *JSOT* 24 (1982) 3–25.
Malamat, A. "'amm le badad yiskon: A Report from Mari and an Oracle of Balaam." *Jewish Quarterly Review* 76 (1985) 47–50.
Malina, Bruce J. *The Palestinian Manna Tradition: The Manna Tradition in the Palestinian Targums and Its Relationship to the New Testament Writings.* Leiden: Brill, 1968.
Mann, Thomas, W. *The Book of the Torah: The Narrative Integrity of the Pentateuch.* Atlanta: John Knox, 1988.
Marx, Alfred. "A propos de Nombres xxiv 19b." *VT* 37 (1987) 100–104.
Milgrom, Jacob. (1983) "Magic, Monotheism and the Sin of Moses." Pages 251–65 in *The Quest for the Kingdom of God: Studies in Honor of George E. Mendenhall.* Edited by H. B. Huffmon, F. A. Spina, and A.R.W. Green. Winona Lake, Ind.: Eisenbrauns, 1983.
_____. (1985) "On the Suspected Adulteress (Numbers V 11-31)." *VT* 35 (1985) 369–72.
_____. (1987a) "The Literary Structure of Numbers 8:5-22 and the Levitic *Kippur*." Pages 205–209 in *Perspectives on Language and Text: Essays and Poems in Honor of Francis I. Andersen's Sixtieth Birthday.* Edited by E. W. Conrad and E. G. Newing. Winona Lake, Ind.: Eisenbrauns, 1987.
_____. (1987b) "The Structures of Numbers: Chapters 11–12 and 13–14 and Their Redaction—Preliminary Groupings." Pages 49–61 in *Judaic Perspectives on Ancient Israel.* Edited by Jacob Neusner et al. Philadelphia: Fortress, 1987.
_____. (1990) *Numbers.* JPS Torah Commentary. Philadelphia: Jewish Publication Society, 1990.
_____. (1992) "Food and Faith: The Ethical Foundations of the Biblical Diet Law." *BRev* 8/6 (1992) 5, 10.
_____. (1996) "A Husband's Pride, A Mob's Prejudice." *BRev* 12 (1996) 21.
_____. (1997) "Encroaching on the Sacred: Purity and Polity in Numbers 1–10." *Int* 51 (1997) 241–53.
Moore, Michael S. (1990a) *The Balaam Traditions: Their Character and Development*. SBLDS 113. Atlanta: Scholars, 1990.
_____. (1990b) "Another Look at Balaam." *RB* 97 (1990) 359–78.
Morag, S. "Layers of Antiquity. Linguistic Studies on the Oracles of Balaam." (English summary) *Tarbiz* 50 (1980/81) 1–24.

Morley, Jean-Paul. "Du Dieu nomade au Dieu centralisateur. Deux lectures de Nombres 9." Pages 227–36 in *Le Livre de traverse de l'exégèse biblique à l'anthropologie.* Edited by Olivier Abel and Françoise Smyth-Florentin. Paris: Cerf, 1992.

Mutius, Hans-Georg von. "Das Verständnis der Verbform נשׂאתי in Numeri 16,15 im Licht des Targums Neofiti 1." *BN* 87 (1997) 34–38.

Newing, E. G. "The Rhetoric of Altercation in Numbers 14." Pages 211–28 in *Perspectives on Language and Text: Essays and Poems in Honor of Francis I. Andersen's Sixtieth Birthday.* Edited by E. W. Conrad and E. G. Newing. Winona Lake, Ind.: Eisenbrauns, 1987.

Niditch, Susan. "War, Women and Defilement in Numbers 31." *Semeia* 61 (1993) 39–57.

O'Connor, M. *Hebrew Verse Structure.* Winona Lake, Ind.: Eisenbrauns, 1980.

Ogdon, G. S. "The Design of Numbers." *BT* 47 (1996) 420–28.

Olson, Dennis T. (1985) *The Death of the Old and the Birth of the New. The Framework of the Book of Numbers and the Pentateuch.* Brown Judaic Studies 71. Chico, Calif.: Scholars, 1985.

_____. (1997) "Negotiating Boundaries: The Old and New Generations and the Theology of Numbers." *Int* 51 (1997) 229–40.

Propp, William H. "The Rod of Aaron and the Sin of Moses." *JBL* 107 (1988) 19–26.

Reif, S. C. "What Enraged Phinehas?—A Study of Numbers 25:8." *JBL* 90 (1971) 200–6.

Reynolds, Carol Bechtel. "Life After Grace: Preaching from the Book of Numbers." *Int* 51 (1997) 267–79.

Riggans, Walter. *Numbers.* Philadelphia: Westminster, 1983.

Rinaldi, G. "Balaam al suo paese." *Bibbia ed Oriente* 20 (1978) 51–59.

Robinson, Bernard P. "The Jealousy of Miriam: A Note on Num 12." *ZAW* 101 (1989) 428–32.

Rouillard, Hedwige. (1980) "L'anesse de Balaam." *RB* 87 (1980) 5–36; 211–41.

_____. (1985) *La Péricope de Balaam (Nombres 22–24). La Prose et les 'oracles.'* Etudes Bibliques n.s. 4. Paris: Gabalda, 1985.

Safren, Jonathan D. "Balaam and Abraham." *VT* 38 (1988) 105–13.

Sakenfeld, Katharine Doob. (1985) "Theological and Redactional Problems in Numbers 20.2-13." Pages 133–54 in *Understanding the Word.* Edited by J. T. Butler, E. W. Conrad, and B. C. Ollenburger. JSOTSup 37. Sheffield: JSOT, 1985.

_____. (1989) "Feminist Biblical Interpretation." *Theology Today* 46 (1989) 154–68.

Schart, Aaron. *Mose und Israel im Konflikt: Eine redaktionsgeschichtliche Studie zu den Wüstenerzählungen.* Fribourg: Universitätsverlag, 1990.

Snijdars, L. A. "The Meaning of *zar* in the Old Testament." *OTS* 10 (1954) 97–105.
Sommer, Benjamin D. "Reflecting on Moses: The Redaction of Numbers 11" *JBL* 118 (1999) 601–24.
Spero, Shubert. "Multiplicity of Meaning as a Device in Biblical Narrative." *Judaism* 34 (1985) 462–73.
Stuart, Douglas K. *Studies in Early Hebrew Meter.* Missoula: Scholars, 1976.
Sturdy, John. *Numbers.* Cambridge Bible Commentary. New York: Cambridge University Press, 1976.
Sutcliff, E. F. "A Note on Numbers 20." *Bib* 18 (1937) 439–42.
Tosato, A. "The Literary Structure of the First Two Poems of Balaam (Num XXIII 7-10, 18-24)." *VT* 29 (1979) 98–106.
Van Seters, J. "The Conquest of Sihon's Kingdom: A Literary Examination." *JBL* 91 (1972) 182–97.
Venter, P. M. "Die krisis van ongeloof in Numeri 13–14." *HTS* 49 (1993) 297–314.
Vosté, J.-M. "Les oracles de Balaam d'après Nom. 22–24." *Bib* 29 (1948) 169–94.
Wenham, Gordon J. (1981a) *Numbers.* Tyndale OT Commentaries. London and Downers Grove, Ill.: InterVarsity Press, 1981.
_____. (1981b) "Aaron's Rod (Numbers 17 16-28)." *ZAW* 93 (1981) 280–81.
Wharton, J. A. "The Command to Bless. An Exposition of Numbers 22:41–23:25." *Int* 13 (1959) 37–48.
Wilson, Johnny Lee. "A Rhetorical Critical Analysis of the Balaam Oracles." Ph.D. diss., Southern Baptist Theological Seminary, 1981.
Yahuda, A. S. "The Name of Balaam's Homeland." *JBL* 64 (1945) 547–51.
Yaure, L. "Elymas-Nehelamite-Pethor." *JBL* 79 (1960) 297–314.
Zannoni, Arthur E. "Balaam: International Seer/Wizard Prophet." *St. Luke's Journal of Theology* 22 (1978) 5–19.
Zimmerli, Walther. "Die Eigenart der prophetischen Rede des Ezechiel. Ein Beitrag zum Problem an Hand von Ez. 14, 1-11." *ZAW* 66 (1954) 1–26.

DEUTERONOMY

INTRODUCTION

Name

The name "Deuteronomy" in English comes from Greek via Latin and means "the second law." This can be understood as either a repetition of the law or as additional law, and "law" can be taken to refer to legislation or to the combination of legislation and storytelling (in Jewish tradition, *halakah* and *haggadah*) that characterized the Pentateuch. All of these interpretations of the name "Deuteronomy" can claim some validity since a summary of past events is given (especially in chapters 1–4), laws that have already appeared in the Pentateuch are repeated (though sometimes with significant variations), and new instructions are given that have not appeared before.

The traditional Hebrew title of Deuteronomy is *ʾēlleh haddᵊbārîm* "these are the words" or just "words" *(dᵊbārîm)* for short. Even this title is somewhat ambiguous since *dᵊbārîm* can refer either to Moses' speeches or, more specifically, to commandments (in Hebrew the "ten commandments" are, literally, "the ten words").

Interest

Deuteronomy in the Roman Catholic Lectionary

Of the 156 Sundays of the three-year Sunday cycle, pericopes from Deuteronomy are read on ten (6.4%) of those Sundays: three in Year A, five in Year B, and two in Year C. The total number of verses covered is 51 or 5.3% of Deuteronomy's 955 verses. In the weekday cycle Deuteronomy fills eight slots in Year I and three in Year II (1.7% of weekday readings). The number of verses from Deuteronomy that are read on weekdays is 45, or 4.7% of the book.

Deuteronomy in the New Testament

The writers of the New Testament assume that their readers will understand their works in reference to the allusions that they make to Deuteronomy. Among these are the following:

Deut 4:2 Nothing must be added to or taken away from what YHWH has commanded. Rev 22:18-19 Nothing must be added to or taken away from the prophecy.

Deut 4:11 (The mountain was blazing; also 5:23.) Heb 12:18 "You have not come to . . . a blazing fire."

Deut 4:12 "You heard the sound of words but saw no form." John 5:37 "You have never heard his voice or seen his form." Acts 9:7 (those traveling with Saul heard the voice but saw no one).

Deut 4:38 (Driving out nations, taking possession of the land.) Matt 5:5 The meek will take possession of the land *[klēronomeō = yāraš]*.

Deut 6:8 (Bind the commandments on hand and forehead.) Matt 23:5 (The Pharisees enlarge their phylacteries).

Deut 11:29 (Blessing on Gerizim; curse on Ebal.) John 4:20 (The Samaritan woman alludes to the dispute between the Samaritans and the Jews about the identity of the one place chosen by YHWH as the place of worship.)

Deut 18:15 (The Prophet like Moses must be listened to.) Matt 17:5 The voice from heaven says of Jesus, "Listen to him." Luke 7:39 "If this man were a prophet . . ." John 1:21 "Are you the prophet?" John 5:46 "If you believed Moses, you would believe me, for he wrote about me."

Deut 21:20 (The parents of an unruly young man will say) "This son of ours . . . is a glutton and a drunkard." (After this the young man is stoned to death.) Matt 11:19 The Son of Man came eating and drinking, and they say, "Look, a glutton and a drunkard . . ."

Deut 21:22 "Hanging on a tree." Acts 5:30 cites Deut 21:22 in reference to Jesus' crucifixion.

Deut 21:23 (The corpse of a convict must not remain all night on the tree.) Mark 15:42-46 (When evening came the body of Jesus was taken down from the cross.)

Deut 22:22-24 (In a case of adultery, both persons are to be stoned.) John 8:5 "Moses commanded us to stone such women."

Deut 23:1 (Exclusion of eunuch from the assembly.) Acts 8:27 (The Ethiopian Eunuch.)

Deut 27:25 "Cursed be anyone who takes a bribe to shed innocent blood." Matt. 27:4 [Judas] said, "I have sinned by betraying innocent blood." But [the chief priests and the elders] said, "What is that to us? See to it yourself."

Deut 28:4 "Blessed shall be the fruit of your womb . . ." Luke 1:42 ". . . blessed is the fruit of your womb."

Deut 30:6 and Rom 2:29 (Circumcision of the heart).

Deut 31:1 "When Moses had finished speaking all these words to all Israel . . ." Matt. 26:1 "When Jesus had finished saying all these things . . ."

Deut 32:21 and 1 Cor 10:22 (Provoking the Lord to jealousy).

Deut 32:39 ". . . I kill and make alive; I wound and I heal . . ." John 5:21 "Indeed, just as the Father raises the dead and gives them life, so also the Son gives life to whomever he wishes."

Delimitation of Text

The book ends with the death of Moses and, in terms of the canon, so does the Torah. This ending has seemed to some unsatisfactory or at least jarring in relation to the larger plot line of the Pentateuch. Specifically, it is asked, how could the Pentateuch end with the promise to the ancestors not yet fulfilled, especially when YHWH's oath is mentioned no less that twenty-four times throughout the book:

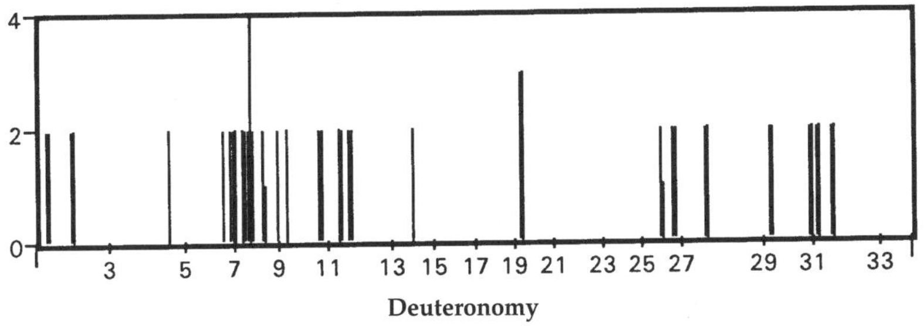

Distribution of *šbʿ* + *ʾāb* in Deuteronomy (MT)

Such an open ending might be compared to the original ending of Mark's Gospel, which ends not with the appearance of the risen Jesus to his disciples but with women running away and saying nothing to anyone.

So, the question is not "where does it end?"—for it is clear that it ends with the death of Moses—but, rather, *why* does it end where it does?

Does the ending reflect the situation of the work's intended audience (Judean exiles in Babylon)? Is the ending part of a rhetorical strategy to persuade exiles to return to Judea?

Language

There are 4983 common nouns in Deuteronomy distributed over 943 verses and employing 679 vocables. Some important nouns: land (197x), people (107), city (57), brother (48), heart (47), gate (34), covenant (27).

There are 3548 verb forms in Deuteronomy, distributed over 933 verses and employing 447 vocables. Some of the more frequently recurring verbs (which indicate the interest of the book) are: to give (176x), to command (88x), to observe (73x), to possess/dispossess (71x), to cross (47x), to bless (39x), to return (35x), to go up (32x), to choose (31x), to love (22x).

At another level Deuteronomy is well known for its power as "preached law." Much of the language is elevated and poetic, spoken in person-to-person address, appealing to the reader through its intradiegetic listeners to take the instruction to heart "so that you may live in the land that the LORD swore to give to your ancestors, to Abraham, to Isaac, and to Jacob" (30:20).

Rhetorical Questions

Although not as numerous as in Numbers, rhetorical questions are found in Deuteronomy as well:

Deut 1:12 But how can I bear the heavy burden of your disputes all by myself?

Deut 1:28 Where are we headed?

Deut 4:7-8 For what other great nation has a god so near to it as the Lord our God is whenever we call to him? And what other great nation has statutes and ordinances as just as this entire law that I am setting before you today?

Deut 4:32-34 . . . has anything so great as this ever happened or has its like ever been heard of? Has any people ever heard the voice of a god speaking out of a fire, as you have heard, and lived? Or has any god ever attempted to go and take a nation for himself from the midst of another nation, by trials, by signs and wonders, by war, by a mighty hand and an outstretched arm, and by terrifying displays of power, as the Lord your God did for you in Egypt before your very eyes?

Deut 5:25 So now why should we die?

Deut 7:17 . . . These nations are more numerous than I; how can I dispossess them?

Deut 9:2 . . . Who can stand up to the Anakim?"

Deut 20:19 . . . Are trees in the field human beings that they should come under siege from you?

Deut 30:12-13 It is not in heaven, that you should say, "Who will go up to heaven for us, and get it [the commandment] for us so that we may hear it and observe it?" Neither is it beyond the sea, that you should say, "Who will cross to the other side of the sea for us, and get it for us so that we may hear it and observe it?"

Deut 31:17 . . . Have not these troubles come upon us because our God is not in our midst?'

Deut 32:6 Do you thus repay the Lord, O foolish and senseless people? Is not he your father, who created you, who made you and established you?

Deut 32:30 How could one have routed a thousand, and two put a myriad to flight, unless their Rock had sold them, the Lord had given them up?

Deut 32:34 Is not this laid up in store with me, sealed up in my treasuries?

Deut 32:37-38 Where are their gods, the rock in which they took refuge, who ate the fat of their sacrifices, and drank the wine of their libations? . . .

Numeruswechsel

Although, as we have seen, both Leviticus and Numbers contain examples of *Numeruswechsel* (change of grammatical number in the second person although the addressee appears to be the same), Deuteronomy has many more by far. These changes can be illustrated by using the King James Version, which features the older English distinction between singular and plural in the second person:

Deut 1:31 And in the wilderness, where *thou* hast seen how that the LORD *thy* God bare *thee,* as a man doth bear his son, in all the way that *ye* went, until *ye* came into this place.

Deut 3:21 And I commanded Joshua at that time, saying, *Thine* eyes have seen all that the LORD *your* God hath done unto these two kings: so shall the LORD do unto all the kingdoms whither *thou* passest.

Deut 4:3 *Your* eyes have seen what the LORD did because of Baal-peor: for all the men that followed Baal-peor, the LORD *thy* God hath destroyed them from among *you.*

Deut 4:21 Furthermore the LORD was angry with me for *your* sakes, and sware that I should not go over Jordan, and that I should not go in unto that good land, which the LORD *thy* God giveth *thee* for an inheritance:

Deut 4:23 Take heed unto *yourselves,* lest *ye* forget the covenant of the LORD *your* God, which he made with *you,* and make *you* a graven image, or the likeness of any thing, which the LORD *thy* God hath forbidden *thee.*

Deut 4:25 When *thou* shalt beget children, and children's children, and *ye* shall have remained long in the land, and shall corrupt *yourselves,* and make a graven image, or the likeness of any thing, and shall do evil in the sight of the LORD *thy* God, to provoke him to anger:

Deut 4:29 But if from thence *ye shall*[1] seek the LORD *thy* God, *thou* shalt find him, if *thou* seek him with all *thy* heart and with all *thy* soul.

Deut 4:34 Or hath God assayed to go and take him a nation from the midst of another nation, by temptations, by signs, and by wonders, and by war, and by a mighty hand, and by a stretched out arm, and by great terrors, according to all that the LORD *your* God did for *you* in Egypt before *thine*[2] eyes?

Deut 6:3 Hear [sg.] therefore, O Israel, and observe [sg.] to do it; that it may be well with *thee,* and that *ye* may increase mightily, as the LORD God of *thy* fathers hath promised *thee,* in the land that floweth with milk and honey.

[1] KJV "thou shalt" presumably assuming diplography of *mem.*
[2] KJV "your" against Heb.

Deut 6:17 *Ye* shall diligently keep the commandments of the LORD *your* God, and his testimonies, and his statutes, which he hath commanded *thee*.

Deut 6:20 And when *thy* son asketh *thee* in time to come, saying, What mean the testimonies, and the statutes, and the judgments, which the LORD our God hath commanded *you?*

Deut 7:4 For they will turn away *thy* son from following me, that they may serve other gods: so will the anger of the LORD be kindled against *you*, and destroy *thee* suddenly.

Deut 7:8 But because the LORD loved *you*, and because he would keep the oath which he had sworn unto *your* fathers, hath the LORD brought *you* out with a mighty hand, and redeemed *thee*[3] out of the house of bondmen, from the hand of Pharaoh king of Egypt.

Deut 7:12 Wherefore it shall come to pass, if *ye* hearken to these judgments, and keep, and do them, that the LORD *thy* God shall keep unto *thee* the covenant and the mercy which he sware unto *thy* fathers:

Deut 7:25 The graven images of their gods shall *ye* burn with fire: *thou* shalt not desire the silver or gold that is on them, nor take it unto *thee*, lest *thou* be snared therein: for it is an abomination to the LORD *thy* God.

Deut 8:1 All the commandments which I command *thee* this day shall *ye* observe to do, that *ye* may live, and multiply, and go in and possess the land which the LORD sware unto *your* fathers.

Deut 8:19 And it shall be, if *thou* do at all forget the LORD *thy* God, and walk after other gods, and serve them, and worship them, I testify against *you* this day that *ye* shall surely perish.

Deut 9:7 Remember, and forget not, how *thou* provokedst the LORD *thy* God to wrath in the wilderness: from the day that *thou* didst depart out of the land of Egypt, until *ye* came unto this place, *ye* have been rebellious against the LORD.

Deut 10:15 Only the LORD had a delight in *thy* fathers to love them, and he chose their seed after them, even *you* above all people, as it is this day.

Deut 11:8 Therefore shall *ye* keep all the commandments which I command *thee*[4] this day, that *ye* may be strong, and go in and possess the land, whither *ye* go to possess it;

[3] KJV "you" apparently assuming haplography of *mem*.

[4] KJV "you."

Deut 11:10 For the land, whither *thou* goest in to possess it, is not as the land of Egypt, from whence *ye*[5] came out, where *thou* sowedst *thy* seed, and wateredst it with *thy* foot, as a garden of herbs:

Deut 11:14 That I will give *you* the rain of *your* land in his due season, the first rain and the latter rain, that *thou* mayest gather in *thy* corn, and *thy* wine, and *thine* oil.

Deut 11:19 And *ye* shall teach them to *your* children, speaking of them when *thou* sittest in *thine* house, and when *thou* walkest by the way, when *thou* liest down, and when *thou* risest up.

Deut 12:1 These are the statutes and judgments, which *ye* shall observe to do in the land, which the LORD God of *thy* fathers giveth *thee* to possess it, all the days that *ye* live upon the earth.

Deut 12:5 But unto the place which the LORD *your*[6] God shall choose out of all *your* tribes to put his name there, even unto his habitation shall *ye*[7] seek, and thither *thou* shalt come:

Deut 12:7 And there *ye* shall eat before the LORD *your* God, and *ye* shall rejoice in all that *ye* put *your* hand unto, *ye* and *your* households, wherein the LORD *thy* God hath blessed *thee*.

Deut 12:9 For *ye* are not as yet come to the rest and to the inheritance, which the LORD *thy* God giveth *thee*.[8]

Deut 12:16 Only *ye* shall not eat the blood; *ye* shall pour it upon the earth as water.

Deut 12:32 What thing soever I command *you*, observe to do it: *thou* shalt not add thereto, nor diminish from it.

Deut 13:3 *Thou* shalt not hearken unto the words of that prophet, or that dreamer of dreams: for the LORD *your* God proveth *you*, to know whether *ye* love the LORD *your* God with all *your* heart and with all *your* soul.

Deut 13:5 And that prophet, or that dreamer of dreams, shall be put to death; because he hath spoken to turn *you* away from the LORD *your* God, which brought *you* out of the land of Egypt, and redeemed *thee*[9]

[5] Possibly due to diplography of *mem*.
[6] Possible diplography of *mem*.
[7] Possible diplography of *waw*.
[8] KJV: "your God giveth you."
[9] KJV: you. Possible haplography of *mem*.

out of the house of bondage, to thrust *thee* out of the way which the LORD *thy* God commanded *thee* to walk in. So shalt *thou* put the evil away from the midst of *thee*.

Deut 13:7 Namely, of the gods of the people which are round about *you*, nigh unto *thee*, or far off from *thee*, from the one end of the earth even unto the other end of the earth;

Deut 13:13 Certain men, the children of Belial, are gone out from within *thy* midst,[10] and have withdrawn the inhabitants of their city, saying, Let us go and serve other gods, which *ye* have not known;

Deut 14:21 *Ye* shall not eat of any thing that dieth of itself: *thou* shalt give it unto the stranger that is in *thy* gates, that he may eat it; or *thou* mayest sell it unto an alien: for *thou* art an holy people unto the LORD *thy* God. *Thou* shalt not seethe a kid in his mother's milk.

Deut 18:15 The LORD *thy* God will raise up unto *thee* a Prophet from the midst of *thee*, of *thy* brethren, like unto me; unto him *ye* shall hearken;

Deut 19:19 Then shall *ye* do unto him, as he had thought to have done unto his brother: so shalt *thou* put the evil away from among *you*.

Deut 22:24 Then *ye* shall bring them both out unto the gate of that city, and *ye* shall stone them with stones that they die; the damsel, because she cried not, being in the city; and the man, because he hath humbled his neighbour's wife: so *thou* shalt put away evil from among *you*.

Deut 23:4 Because they met *you* not with bread and with water in the way, when *ye* came forth out of Egypt; and because they hired against *thee* Balaam the son of Beor of Pethor of Mesopotamia, to curse *thee*.

Deut 24:9 Remember what the LORD *thy* God did unto Miriam by the way, after that *ye* were come forth out of Egypt.

Deut 25:17 Remember what Amalek did unto *thee* by the way, when *ye* were come forth out of Egypt;

Deut 27:2 And it shall be on the day when *ye* shall pass over Jordan unto the land which the LORD *thy* God giveth *thee*, that *thou* shalt set *thee* up great stones, and plaister them with plaister:

Deut 27:4 Therefore it shall be when *ye* be gone over Jordan, that *ye* shall set up these stones, which I command *you* this day, in mount Ebal, and *thou* shalt plaister them with plaister.

[10] KJV: among you.

Deut 28:14 And *thou* shalt not go aside from any of the words which I command *you*[11] this day, to the right hand, or to the left, to go after other gods to serve them.

Deut 28:62 And *ye* shall be left few in number, whereas *ye* were as the stars of heaven for multitude; because *thou* wouldest not obey the voice of the LORD *thy* God.

Deut 28:63 And it shall come to pass, that as the LORD rejoiced over *you* to do *you* good, and to multiply *you*; so the LORD will rejoice over *you* to destroy *you*, and to bring *you* to nought; and *ye* shall be plucked from off the land whither *thou* goest to possess it.

Deut 28:68 And the LORD shall bring *thee* into Egypt again with ships, by the way whereof I spake unto *thee, Thou* shalt see it no more again: and there *ye* shall be sold unto *your* enemies for bondmen and bondwomen, and no man shall buy *you*.

Deut 29:5 And I have led *you* forty years in the wilderness: *your* clothes are not waxen old upon *you*, and *thy* shoe is not waxen old upon *thy* foot.

Deut 29:11 *Your* little ones, *your* wives, and *thy* stranger that is in *thy* camp, from the hewer of *thy* wood unto the drawer of *thy* water:

Deut 30:18 I denounce unto *you* this day, that *ye* shall surely perish, and that *ye* shall not prolong *your* days upon the land, whither *thou* passest over Jordan to go to possess it.

Deut 30:19 I call heaven and earth to record this day against *you*, that I have set before *you* life and death, blessing and cursing: therefore choose [sg.] life, that both *thou* and *thy* seed may live:

Deut 31:6 Be strong [pl.] and of a good courage [pl.], fear not [pl.], nor be afraid [pl.] of them: for the LORD *thy* God, he it is that doth go with *thee*; he will not fail *thee*, nor forsake *thee*.

Deut 31:12 Gather [sg.] the people together, men, and women, and children, and *thy* stranger that is within *thy* gates, that they may hear, and that they may learn, and fear the LORD *your* God, and observe to do all the words of this law:

Deut 31:26 Take this book of the law, and put [pl.] it in the side of the Ark of the Covenant of the LORD *your* God, that it may be there for a witness against *thee*.

[11] KJV: thee.

Deut 31:27 For I know *thy* rebellion, and *thy* stiff neck: behold, while I am yet alive with *you* this day, *ye* have been rebellious against the LORD; and how much more after my death?

Deut 32:6 Do *ye* thus requite the LORD, O foolish people and unwise? is not he *thy* father that hath bought *thee*? hath he not made *thee*, and established *thee*?

Precisely what the aim of this phenomenon is has not yet been determined to the satisfaction of most scholars. People who share a culture that values individualism highly (such as that of the USA) might naturally see this phenomenon as oscillation between appeal to the individual and to the group, but whether this would be the perception of highly dyadic (group-oriented) personalities (such as those of the ancient Mediterranean) may be doubtful.

Time

A noted feature of Deuteronomy is its time-orientation. The reader hears Moses speaking in the present, and often referring to "today" (1:10, 39; 2:18; 4:4, 8, 26, 38-40; 5:1, 3; 6:6; 7:11; 8:1, 11, 18, 19; 9:1, 3; 10:13, 15; 11:2, 8, 13, 26-28, 32; 12:8, 28; 13:18; 15:5, 15; 19:9; 26:17, 18; 27:1, 4, 10; 28:1, 13, 14, 15; 29:9 [NRSV:10], 11-14 [NRSV:12-15]; 30:2, 8, 11, 15, 16, 18, 19; 32:46).

The occurrences of "today" in Deuteronomy can be represented graphically as follows:

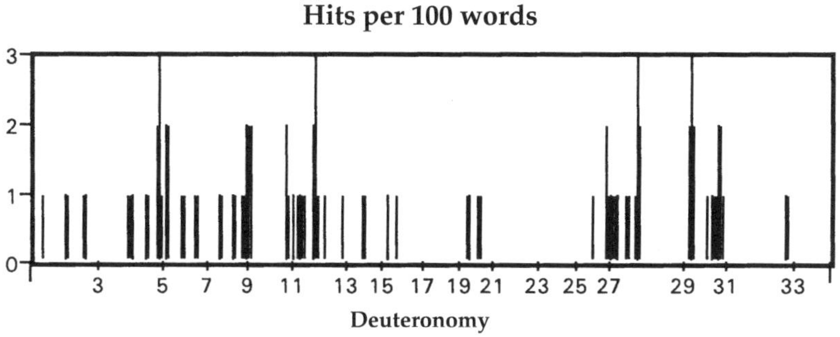

Distribution of "Today" in Deuteronomy (NRSV)

But the present time of Moses' speech is not only the present time of the story world but also the present time of the implied reader—it is the "today" of the worshiping community in any time or place.

Moses' speech looks both to the past and to the future. The past is recalled for the lessons it provides, both of motives for praise of YHWH as benefactor and of mistakes to be avoided. At the same time, Moses' narration looks to the future once the people have crossed over into the Promised Land and taken possession of it.

One can see how allusions to the past history of the people are sprinkled throughout the book by plotting the distribution of the names "Egypt," "Sihon," "Og," and "Amalek" throughout Deuteronomy:

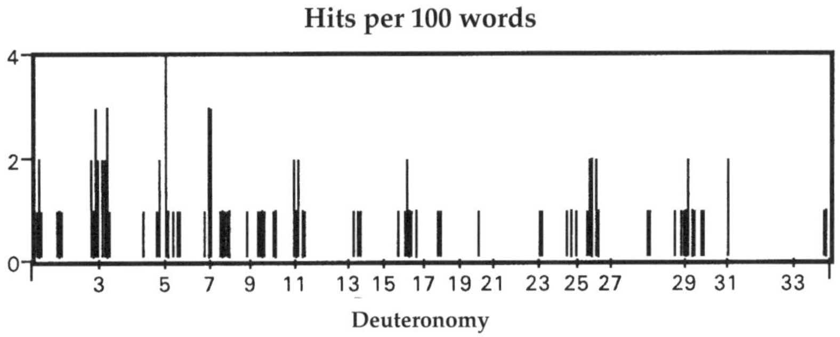

Distribution of the Names "Egypt," "Sihon," "Og," and "Amalek" in Deuteronomy (NRSV)

One can illustrate the future-orientation of Moses' discourse by plotting the phrase "the land that the Lord . . . is giving":

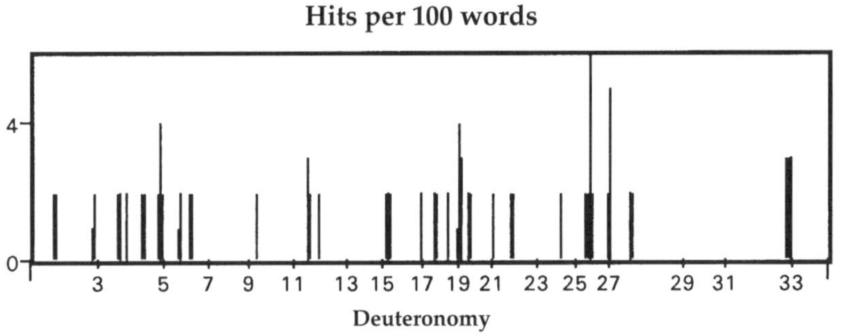

Distribution of the words "land" and "giving" in Deuteronomy (NRSV)

The two temporal phenomena (past and future) are linked. Past victories over apparently insurmountable odds are recalled in order to give hope to a people who are fearful of the future—fearful that they may not be able to overcome the obstacles in their path (or that YHWH will not deliver on his promises).

This relationship among past, present and future time also affects the reader's perception of the pace of the narrative. On one level narrative time equals narration time since most of the book is speech (i.e., it takes the same amount of time to report as it does to happen in real time). On another level the speech (especially in chapters 1–4) summarizes past events very briefly, making narrative time (that is, the time it took for the events to happen in real time) much greater than narration time (the time that telling the story takes up).

Plot

If one asks what has changed between the beginning and the end of this book the obvious answer is that Moses has died. This, in fact, is the event to which the whole book looks forward. Deuteronomy is Moses' last will and testament. This in itself is a dramatic and emotional situation.

But the tension in Deuteronomy does not come from Moses' death—whether or how he will die. What tension there is comes from three sources: 1) the retelling of crises that have already occurred in past time both in reference to the story world and to the implied reader, 2) the anticipation of crises that lie in the future of the story world but are in the past of the implied reader, and 3) the unanswered question as to what choices those who hear the story "today" will make. Moses sets before his hearers (and the reader) two scenarios, as if to say, "Today I set before you two plots." The reader (of whatever time) must choose one or the other.

A recurring theme seems to be the people's fear of superior forces, which implies a lack of confidence in YHWH.

Mann (1988, 145) points out that chapters 6–26 contain laws that have not appeared earlier in the Pentateuch. This recitation of laws concludes with their acceptance by the people in 26:16-19. This means that Deuteronomy can be viewed "as the *completion* of a covenant-making process stretching back to the original events at Sinai."

Tension

The moments of dramatic tension in Deuteronomy come mostly, if not exclusively, from the retelling of past conflicts or from anticipated future conflicts.

1:1-5 These verses are exposition: the narrator's introduction to Moses' speech, setting the time and place. In specifying the context of Moses' speech (v. 4) the narrator refers back to the crisis presented by the aggression of Sihon and Og (Num 21:23, 33). This crisis will afterward be referred to in Moses' speech. It seems to serve as a motive for confidence in the future. If, with YHWH's help, the people were able to defeat Sihon and Og, then they ought not to fear any future adversary.

1:9-18 Moses recalls another drama of the past, this time with more narrative detail and a point of view different from that of Numbers 11. Moses is unable to "bear" the people. This is not due to their complaints (Numbers 11), but to their increase in number, an increase that fulfills the promise to the patriarchs (Gen 15:5; 22:17; 26:4). A further complication comes from the strife among the people (v. 12). The conflict is supposed to be resolved by setting up "heads" over each tribe.

1:26-45 Moses recalls another past crisis: the people refused to enter the land. The complication arises when the people express their fear that YHWH has brought them to the wilderness to destroy them and that the inhabitants of the land cannot be defeated (vv. 26-28). Moses' response is to recall the past deliverance from Egypt and guidance in the wilderness (v. 29). The tension is partly resolved by YHWH's decision that the rebellious generation will have to remain outside the land and die off before their descendants can enter the land. But this creates another tension in that the reader must wait to see this happen before the dynamic that leads to entrance into the land can be played out (v. 34). A further plot development is YHWH's anger with Moses (here said to be on the people's account) (v. 37), resulting in Moses, too, being barred from the land. This raises the question of who will lead the people into the land—a problem resolved by the selection of Joshua as the one who will lead the people after Moses' death (v. 38). The topic then returns to the people's entrance (thus framing Moses' exclusion within the larger context of the rebellious generation's exclusion). Who will enter the land? "Your little ones" (*ṭappᵊkem*, v. 39). Verse 40 literally marks a turning point in the story. The people must turn and return to the wilderness. This leads to a further complication when the people decide to take matters into their own hands by doing the very thing whose refusal had initiated this whole sequence of events, namely, to enter and take possession of the land (v. 41). YHWH warns them not to go up (v. 42), but they pay no attention and so are roundly trounced at Horma (a word meaning "shame," v. 44). Despite the people's weeping, YHWH will not change his mind and the people remain at Kadesh (v. 45).

2:24-36 Moses now recounts more at length the story of the battle with Sihon that was alluded to in 1:4. Tension arises from Sihon's refusal to allow the people to pass through his land (v. 30) but this is countered by YHWH's promise to "give" Sihon and his land to the Israelites (v. 31). The tension reaches a climax in the battle at Jahaz in which Sihon is defeated. Verses 33-36 form the denouement in which Sihon's cities and their inhabitants are destroyed.

3:1-7 A new source of tension arises in the onslaught of Og, but is resolved by the defeat of Og, the capture of his cities, and their distribution to the Transjordanian tribes.

3:23-25 The reader naturally feels tension when the sympathetic character Moses, whom the reader knows to have been sentenced by YHWH to die outside the land, appeals this sentence by asking to be allowed to cross into the land. The tension reaches its highest point when YHWH's anger is provoked (v. 26) and he refuses Moses' request. Verse 27: Denouement: Moses will view the land from Pisgah.

4:25-31 Moses spells out a possible future plot scenario. Problem: The people act corruptly (make idols; do what is evil). Result: YHWH is provoked (v. 25). Problem: The people perish (v. 26), and are scattered (v. 27). Solution: The people seek and find YHWH (vv. 29-31).

5:21 Moses recalls the crisis in which the people feared that they would die from exposure to the divine manifestation. Verses 21-24: Problem: The people ask not to hear the divine voice. Verses 25-26: Solution: YHWH approves. Verses 27-28: Denouement: YHWH sends the people back to their tents. Moses will receive the words and tell them to the people.

6:20-25 Here we have a little dramatization in which a son asks his father the meaning of the things that the Lord has commanded (v. 20). The father ("you" singular) is to respond by telling the story of the Exodus, beginning with the people's status as slaves. This situation of tension for the hearer (the son) is resolved when YHWH brings the people out. Then the narrator (the father) doubles back in time to give further details of the story (vv. 22-25) bringing it up to "this day" (v. 24).

7:4 This verse envisions a possible future plot: The problem comes when Canaanites turn a future generation away from YHWH. The resolution of this tension, or, better, the way to avoid it in the first place is to wipe out the Canaanite population as soon as possible. But this plot line is framed by another scenario in which the Israelites destroy the seven nations (7:1-3) and are blessed for this act of obedience (7:12-16).

7:17 Problem: The Israelites fear their opponents' superior numbers. Solution: They should recall the defeat of Pharaoh and Egypt. YHWH will send pestilence (according to some the word means "hornets") against Israel's enemies (v. 20).

8:3 A past crisis is recalled. Problem: The people were hungry. Solution: YHWH fed them with manna.

8:15 Another past crisis: Problem: There was no water. Solution: Water from the rock.

9:2 Problem: "Who can take a stand in the face of the sons of the Anakim?" Solution: God is a consuming fire.

9:7 Past crisis (Golden Calf). Problem: The people provoked YHWH to the point that YHWH was angry enough to wipe them out (vv. 8, 14) and Moses threw himself down before YHWH. Verse 19: Turning point: YHWH listened to Moses. Verse 20: Further complication: YHWH was angry at Aaron. Solution: Moses prayed for Aaron. Verse 21: Denouement: Moses ritually disposed of the calf.

9:22-29 The people's refusal to take the land is again told (cf. 1:26). Verse 23: YHWH tells them to take the land but they refuse. Verse 25: Moses falls down. Temporal Displacement (flashback): YHWH had said that he would destroy the people. Solution: YHWH's command to Moses to make two new tablets and an ark (10:1) is apparently YHWH's response to Moses' prayer in 9:26 and the resolution of the tension created by YHWH's threat to destroy the people (9:25). But the actual announcement of the resolution does not come until 10:10.

29:21-28 These verses contain a short drama in which either a future generation of Israelites or a group of foreigners see how Israel has become like Sodom and Gomorrah, and ask about the cause of this. The answer represents the people's infidelity and the consequent anger of YHWH and the destruction of the land as having taken place in the past (from the temporal viewpoint of the intradiegetic interlocutor), ending with "as it is this day."

30:1-10 The narrative of the future punishment of the people for breach of covenant begun in the previous chapter now comes to a turning point with the conversion (*wᵊšabtā ʿad-yhwh* (v. 2) of the people, their return from captivity (v. 3) and the gathering and restoration of those who have been scattered (v. 4).

30:11-14 Problem: Where is knowledge of God's will to be found? Solution: It is on your lips and in your hearts.

31:1-8 Problem: The need for new leadership (vv. 1-6). Solution: Joshua (vv. 7-8).

31:16-18 Future problem: After Moses' death, the people will apostatize. Solution (v. 19): The song. Denouement (v. 20): Moses wrote the song and taught it to the children of Israel.

32:10-43 A drama is recounted in which YHWH found Israel in the desert and cared for them. Narrative structure: Life in peril—life saved. But then there is a new twist: An adipose Jeshurun abandons YHWH. This provokes YHWH's jealousy and rejection, climaxing in YHWH's decision to make an end of them (v. 26 JPS) which is only forestalled by YHWH's fear of how such an action might be misinterpreted by other nations.

32:48-52 These verses fulfill earlier plot announcements that Moses would not enter the land (Num 20:12), that he would see the land before he died (Num 27:12-13), and that he would die (Deut 31:14).

33:6 This verse seems to presuppose some crisis in the history of the Reubenites involving the decimation of their population. How this crisis will be resolved is not indicated—only a prayer that Reuben not die out.

33:7 This verse assumes future struggles against opponents in Judah's history.

33:8 This verse refers back to a crisis in Levi's history, set at Meribah, which challenged Levi to put fidelity to YHWH above family loyalty. The outcome was that Levi is rewarded with the privileges of teaching the law to Israel and burning incense in YHWH's presence.

33:17 That Joseph is depicted as a bull whose horns gore peoples *(ʿammîm)* presupposes conflict resulting in victory.

33:20 The enlargement of Gad envisions conflict and the defeat of other peoples.

33:26 YHWH drives out the enemy before Jeshurun.

33:29 The language and images of this verse envision conflict in which Israel is saved from and even treads on enemies because YHWH acts as shield and sword.

34:5 Moses' death is the end to which the whole book has been oriented but also a turning point in the ongoing story of the people.

34:9 The potential crisis of Moses' death has already been resolved by the installation of Joshua. The narrator flashes back to the laying on of hands and also now informs the reader that the people had accepted Joshua as leader.

Implied Formal Structure in Case Law

As in Leviticus, the case law in Deuteronomy, although they prescind from concrete instances, can be actualized as mini-dramas with a problem-solution formal structure. That is, many examples of case law have within them the makings of a gripping drama when actualized. One need only put real people in the situation that the law envisions and narrative tension results. The laws contain the seeds of drama.

The various cases have a certain tension in them; some action provokes a crisis that must be resolved and the resolution is proposed—sometimes the outcome is also specified. In other words, a situation arises that disrupts the equilibrium of the community and a way must be found to restore the balance. The necessary remedy is applied, and peace (*šālôm* = well being) is restored.

13:2-6 In the case law of the false prophet there is implied a narrative with the following elements: Problem: A prophet advocates the worship of other gods (vv. 2-3). Solution: The prophet is executed (v. 6).

13:7-12 The case of the heterodox family member implies a narrative structure similar to that in 13:2-6 above.

13:13-19 Problem: Certain "worthless persons" *(bᵊnê bᵊlîyaʿal)* manage to persuade a whole city to serve other gods. Solution: Tension is resolved by the annihilation of the city.

14:24-25 A little implied drama takes place here in which a person desires to tithe. The problem is that he is too far from the central sanctuary to bring goods there. The solution is to convert the goods into cash and then bring the cash to the central sanctuary.

15:7-8 Problem: A person is in need. Solution: An exhortation to openhanded generosity. This is followed by a negative example in which a person does not give because his eye is evil—i.e., greed holds him back from helping his brother. The needy person cries to YHWH, who counts the refusal of help as a sin.

15:12-17 Problem: A "brother" or "sister" is bought as a slave. Solution: Manumission in the seventh year. Further complication: The person wants to remain in service. Solution: Ear-piercing ceremony at doorpost.

15:21 Problem: A firstborn male animal (which, therefore, ought to be sacrificed) is unsuitable for sacrifice. Solution: Do not sacrifice it.

17:2-7 A small drama:
Someone is caught worshiping a god other than YHWH (v. 23)
This is reported.
An investigation is conducted.
The report is found to be true.
The culprit is stoned to death.

17:6-7 The previous drama raises another question: How to avoid unjust execution? Solution: Require more than one witness, and have the witnesses take part in the execution.

17:8-13 Problem: A case arises that cannot be judged locally. Solution: Take it to the one sanctuary. Further complication: One of the parties to the dispute will not abide by the verdict of the Levites. Solution: Execution of the recalcitrant party. Denouement: The people will hear and fear.

17:14-20 Problem: The people want a king. Solution: Limits (no foreigner, must not acquire horses or wives, must copy the law and read it every day).

18:9-22 Problem: How know the divine will?
Subsection: Diviners claim to know
Solution: Drive them out
Solution: YHWH will raise up a prophet
Past crisis: People did not want to hear God's voice
Solution: (v. 17) YHWH will raise up a prophet
Future crisis: Someone will not listen to the prophet
Solution: YHWH will hold such a person accountable
Another problem: A false prophet
Solution: Criterion: A true prophet is one whose words come true.

19:1-3 Problem: A person who killed another by accident might be unjustly put to death by the avenger of blood. Solution: Provide cities of refuge where the manslayer will be safe from the avenger of blood. This is dramatized in vv. 5-6.

19:11-13 Problem: A guilty person seeks asylum in a city of refuge. Solution: Trial by city elders.

19:16-21 Problem: A person is falsely accused of a crime. Solution: Trial.

20:10-16 Problem: How should warfare be conducted? Solution: Offer a besieged town the opportunity to surrender. If they do not surrender, kill all the males in the town. But if the city is Canaanite, kill everything that breathes. (Do not cut down fruit trees during a siege, 20:19-20.)

21:1-9 Problem: A murder victim is found in an open field. Solution: By measuring, determine which is the nearest city, then have the elders of that city swear to their non-involvement in the death.

21:10-13 Problem: A man wants to marry a female captive. Solution: Prescribed ritual and mourning period.

21:14 Problem: A man does not want the captive he has married. Solution: Let her go.

21:15-17 Problem: The firstborn son (the heir) is the son of the less-loved wife. Solution: Give a double portion to the firstborn.

21:18-21 Problem: Juvenile delinquent. Solution: Execution.

21:22-23 Problem: The corpse of an executed criminal will defile the land if it is left on the gibbet over night. Solution: Bury it the same day.

22:1-3 Problem: Someone sees a brother's animal driven away. Solution: Bring it back. Further complication: The owner is not known. Solution: Board the animal until it is claimed.

22:13-19 Problem: A man falsely charges that his wife was not a virgin on their wedding night. Solution: The woman's father brings the evidence of her virginity.

22:20-21 Problem: A girl given in marriage turns out not to be a virgin. Solution: The girl is stoned to death.

22:22 Problem: A man is found (notice the implied drama) lying with a married woman. Solution: Both die.

22:23-24 Problem: A betrothed virgin is deflowered in a city. Solution: Both persons are stoned to death.

22:25-27 Problem: A betrothed virgin is deflowered outside a city. Solution: The rapist is executed.

22:28-29 Problem: A man deflowers a virgin who is not betrothed. Solution: The man must pay the girl's father an indemnity and marry the girl. He cannot divorce her.

23:11-12 Problem: A state of ritual impurity is incurred due to nocturnal emission. Solution: The unclean person stays outside the camp until sundown and then bathes.

23:13-15 Problem: If the camp is defiled by human waste, YHWH will turn away. Solution: Build a latrine outside camp.

23:16-17 Problem: An escaped slave seeks refuge. Solution: Give him refuge.

23:18-19 Problem: Some persons want to establish sacred prostitution. Solution: Outlaw it.

23:20-21 Problem: Interest ("bite") charged on loans. Solution: Only foreigners may be charged interest.

23:22-24 Problem: A person makes a vow. Solution: Pay it or do not vow.

23:25-26 Problem: Eating another person's crops. Solution: Limits.

24:1-4 Problem: Divorce. Further complication: The ex-wife's second marriage is dissolved by death or divorce. Solution: The ex-wife may not remarry her first husband.

24:5 Problem: A man takes a new wife. Solution: Exemption from military service.

24:6 Problem: A creditor threatens a person's livelihood by seizing a mill (or part of it) in pledge on a loan. Solution: Such seizure is not allowed.

24:7 Problem: A person kidnaps another. Solution: Death penalty.

24:8 Problem: A person contracts leprosy. Solution: Follow the laws; remember Miriam.

24:10-13 Problem: A creditor comes to a debtor's house to claim an item to be taken in pledge. Solution: He may not enter the house. Further complication: The debtor is poor. Solution: The debtor's garment taken in pledge must be returned at sundown.

24:14-15 Problem: Treatment of hired servants. Solution: Pay before sundown.

24:16 Problem: Innocent people are punished for crimes committed by their relatives. Solution: Individual liability.

24:17-18 Problem: How secure justice for the weak? Solution: Specific apodictic prohibitions of abuse of aliens, orphans, and widows.

24:19-22 Problem: The poor have nothing to eat. Solution: Reapers must leave the gleanings for them when harvesting.

25:1-3 Problem: A man is to be punished by being beaten. Solution: Limit the number of strokes and let the judge supervise the beating.

25:5-10 Problem: A man dies childless. Solution: Levirate marriage. Further complication: The brother refuses. Solution: The brother is shamed.

25:11-12 Problem: A wife grabs the genitals of her husband's opponent in a brawl. Solution: Cut off her hand.

25:12 Problem: The Levite, the foreigner, the orphan and the widow have no income. Solution: The tithe.

Structure

Deuteronomy consists in a series of speeches made by Moses. Clements (1989, 13–14) and others think that there are four, each introduced by a superscription (1:1; 4:44-49; 29:1; 33:1), and this is the structure I have followed, though with some reservations since, on the one hand, there seem to be superscriptions at 27:1 and again at 27:9, 11 and, on the other, 4:44-49 seems to serve as a pivot between two sections (see notes). Confusion over whether 28:69 [NRSV: 29:1] is the end or beginning of a section (i.e., whether "these are the words" refers to what has come before or what is to come after) can be seen in the different numbering of the verses in the Hebrew and NRSV. One counts the verse as the end of chapter 28 while the other counts it as the beginning of chapter 29. There are also new introductions of Moses' speech by the narrator in 31:1-2 and 7 and other interjections by the narrator in 31:9-10, 14-16a, 24-25 and a separate introduction to the song in 31:30, plus other interventions in 32:44-46 and 48. In short, blocking the book into four speeches is useful but must be recognized as a rough approximation. There are also new beginnings within Moses' speech, e.g., at 6:1 and 12:1. Christensen (1993, 9) proposes a concentric structure.

Several authors have pointed to a propensity on the part of the author to arrange things in groups of seven or multiples of seven.

Characterization

What YHWH Says about YHWH

Remembering that we are hearing layers of voices (the narrator's first, and then Moses' voice), the text portrays direct speech of YHWH in which this character makes statements in the first person either about his own qualities or about his actions in time.

Self-Description

YHWH describes himself as follows: "I am the LORD your God, who brought you out of the land of Egypt, out of the house of slavery" (5:6). ". . . I the LORD your God am a jealous God, punishing children for the iniquity of parents, to the third and fourth generation of those who reject me, but showing steadfast love to the thousandth generation of those who love me and keep my commandments" (5:9-10).

YHWH's Actions

Other statements that YHWH makes about himself are:

10:11 ". . . the land that I swore to their ancestors to give them. . . ."

34:4 ". . . This is the land of which I swore to Abraham, to Isaac, and to Jacob, saying, 'I will give it to your descendants' . . ."

1:8 "See, I have set the land before you . . ."

2:24-25 ". . . See, I have handed over to you King Sihon . . . This day I will begin to put the dread and fear of you upon the peoples everywhere under heaven . . ."

2:31 . . . "See, I have begun to give Sihon and his land over to you . . ."

3:2 . . . "Do not fear him [Og], for I have handed him over to you . . ."

4:10 . . . "Assemble the people for me, and I will let them hear my words, so that they may learn to fear me . . ."

5:7 ". . . you shall have no other gods before me."

5:28-29 ". . . I have heard the words of this people . . . If only they had such a mind as this, to fear me and to keep all my commandments always . . ."

5:31 "But you [Moses], stand here by me, and I will tell you all the commandments, the statutes and the ordinances, that you shall teach them, so that they may do them in the land that I am giving them to possess."

7:4 "for that [intermarriage] would turn away your children from following me . . ."

9:13-14 ". . . I have seen that this people is indeed a stubborn people. Let me alone that I may destroy them and blot out their name from under heaven; and I will make of you a nation . . ."

9:23 "Go up and occupy the land that I have given you . . ."

10:1-2 "come up to me on the mountain . . . I will write on the tablets the words that were on the former tablets . . ."

29:5 "—so that you may know that I am the LORD your God."

29:13 [NRSV: 14] "I am making this covenant . . ."

32:49 . . . "the land of Canaan, which I am giving to the Israelites for a possession . . ."

1:35-36 "Not one of these—not one of this evil generation—shall see the good land that I swore to give to your ancestors, except Caleb son of Jephunneh. He shall see it, and to him and to his descendants I will give the land on which he set foot, because of his complete fidelity to the LORD."

1:39 "to them [your children] I will give it [the land] . . ."

2:5 "for I will not give you even so much as a foot's length of their [the Edomites'] land, since I have given Mount Seir to Esau as a possession."

2:9 "for I will not give you any of its [Moab's] land as a possession, since I have given Ar as a possession to the descendants of Lot."

2:19 "for I will not give the land of the Ammonites to you as a possession, because I have given it to the descendants of Lot."

11:14-15 "then I [NRSV: he] will give the rain . . . and I [NRSV: he] will give grass in your fields . . ."

11:18 "You shall put these words of mine in your heart and soul . . ."

18:18-20 "I will raise up for them a prophet like you from among their own people; I will put my words in the mouth of the prophet, who shall speak to them everything that I command. (v. 19) Anyone who does not heed the words that the prophet shall speak in my name, I myself will hold accountable. (v. 20) But any prophet who speaks in the name of other gods, or who presumes to speak in my name a word that I have not commanded the prophet to speak—that prophet shall die."

28:20 . . . because you have forsaken me. [See notes.]

31:16-18 "they [Israel] will forsake me, breaking my covenant that I have made with them. My anger will be kindled against them in that day. I will forsake them and hide my face from them; . . . On that day I will surely hide my face . . ."

31:19-21 "that this song may be a witness for me against the Israelites. For when I have brought them into the land flowing with milk and honey, which I promised on oath to their ancestors, and they have eaten their fill and grown fat, they will turn to other gods and serve them, despising me and breaking my covenant. . . . For I know what they are inclined to do even now, before I have brought them into the land that I promised them on oath."

31:23 Then the LORD commissioned Joshua son of Nun and said, "Be strong and bold, for you shall bring the Israelites into the land that I promised them; I will be with you."

32:20 "I will hide my face from them, I will see what their end will be . . ."

32:21 "They made me jealous with what is no god, provoked me with their idols. So I will make them jealous with what is no people, provoke them with a foolish nation."

32:23-24 "I will heap disasters upon them, spend my arrows against them . . . The teeth of beasts I will send against them . . ."

32:26 "I thought to scatter them and blot out the memory of them from humankind." The context seems to refer to the future.

32:34-35 "Is not this laid up in store with me, sealed up in my treasuries? Vengeance is mine, and recompense . . ."

32:39-42 "See now that I, even I, am he; there is no god beside me. I kill and I make alive; I wound and I heal; and no one can deliver from my hand. For I lift up my hand to heaven, and swear: As I live forever, when I whet my flashing sword, and my hand takes hold on judgment; I will take vengeance on my adversaries, and will repay those who hate me. I will make my arrows drunk with blood, and my sword shall devour flesh—with the blood of the slain and the captives, from the long-haired enemy."

Statements Made about YHWH by Others

Statements made by Moses about YHWH are similar to those made by YHWH about YHWH.

Past Actions

There are several references to YHWH's oath, or covenant or "promise" of land and blessing to the ancestors: 1:11, 21; 4:31; 6:3, 10, 18, 23;

7:8, 12, 13; 8:1, 18; 9:5; 10:11; 11:9, 21; 13:17; 19:8; 27:3; 28:11; 29:12 [NRSV: 13]; 30:20; 31:7, 20, 21; 34:4. YHWH set his heart on Israel (*ḥšq* 7:7; 10:15). YHWH loved (*ʾhb* 4:37; 10:15) Israel's ancestors and chose (*bḥr* 4:37; 7:6, 7; 10:15; 12:5; 14:2) their descendants. He has chosen the Levites as his ministers (18:5; 21:5).

Another past action of YHWH that is often referred to is bringing the people out of Egypt: Deut 4:20 "But the LORD has taken you and brought you out of the iron-smelter, out of Egypt, to become a people of his very own possession, as you are now." See also 4:37; 5:6, 15; 6:12, 21, 23; 7:8, 19; 8:14; 9:26, 29; 13:5, 10; 16:1; 26:8; 29:24 [NRSV: 25]. YHWH took a nation for himself from the midst of another nation, by trials, by signs and wonders (6:22; 7:19; 11:3; 26:8; 29:3), by war, by a mighty hand and an outstretched arm, and by terrifying displays of power . . . (4:34), making the water of the Red Sea flow over the Egyptian army (11:4). YHWH redeemed Israel (*pdh* 7:8; 9:26; 13:6 [NRSV: 5]; 15:15; 21:8; 24:18). YHWH fed the people manna (8:3, 16). YHWH guided *(nḥh)* the people (32:12).

YHWH has blessed the people (2:7) and has caused them to multiply (1:10) more than the stars in heaven (10:22).

YHWH destroyed the Anakim (2:21), hardened the spirit of Sihon and made his heart defiant (2:30). YHWH handed over Israel's enemies to them (2:24, 30; 3:3) and destroyed *(hišmîd)* their opponents (2:21-22; 4:3). YHWH turned Balaam's curse into a blessing (23:5).

YHWH spoke out of fire (4:12, 15, 33, 36; 5:4 [face to face], 22, 24, 26; 9:10: 10:4).

YHWH made a covenant with Israel (4:23; 5:2; 9:9; 29:1, 12, 25; 31:16). YHWH wrote the commandments on stone tablets (4:13; 5:22; 9:10; 10:4). YHWH is also frequently the subject of the verb *ṣwh* "to command" and reference is made to his commandments, statutes and judgments, and laws (4:40; 6:2, 17; 7:9; 8:2, 11; 10:13; 11:1; 13:4, 18; 26:17, 18; 27:10; 28:1, 15, 45; 30:8, 10, 16). Naturally, what YHWH demands also characterizes him. Without going through all YHWH's commands, one might simply point to the command to rejoice in YHWH's presence (12:12, 18; 14:26; 16:11; 27:7) or the negative confession prescribed in 26:13-14.

YHWH humbled *(ʿinnâ)* the people to test them (8:2, 3, 16).

YHWH appeared at the tent in a pillar of cloud (31:15). This is the only mention of appearance in Deuteronomy.

YHWH came from Sinai, dawned from Seir, shone forth from Mount Paran (33:2).

YHWH became angry (*ʿnp* or *qṣp*; 1:34, 37; 4:21; 9:7, 8, 19, 20, 22), sometimes to the point where he was ready to destroy Israel (9:8, 19, 20, 25). YHWH's hand was against the rebels to root them out from the camp (2:15).

Non-verbal Descriptions

YHWH is God in heaven above and on earth beneath; there is no other (4:39). Heaven and the heaven of heavens belong to him as well as the earth and everything in it (10:14). YHWH is God of gods and Lord of LORDS, the great God, mighty and awesome, who is not partial and takes no bribe (10:17). YHWH is great and awesome (*gādôl wᵊnôrāʾ* 7:21; 10:17; 28:58 [name]), and does great and awesome things (10:21). YHWH is a devouring fire (*ʾēš ʾōkᵊlâ* 4:24; 9:3). YHWH alone is Israel's God (6:4). YHWH is near *(qārōb)* the people (4:7), as is his word (30:14). YHWH is a jealous God (4:24; 6:15). YHWH is faithful (*neʾĕmān* 7:9) and loyal (*ʿśh/šmr ḥesed* 5:10; 7:9, 12). Sacrifices are his portion (18:1); YHWH is the inheritance of the levitical priests (18:2). YHWH is the God of the ancestors (1:11, 21; 4:1; 6:3; 12:1; 26:7; 27:3; 29:25). YHWH is Israel's father and creator who made and established them (32:6). YHWH is a Rock (32:30). YHWH's eyes are always on the land (11:12).

What YHWH Hates

YHWH abhors the silver and gold that cover idols (7:25; 27:15), child sacrifice (12:31; 18:9-12), defective sacrificial victims (17:1), cross-dressing (22:5), cultic prostitution (23:18), taking back a wife who has remarried (24:4), dishonest weights and measures (25:16). He hates stone pillars (16:22).

What YHWH Demands

What YHWH requires *(šʾl)* of the people is that they fear him, walk in his ways, love him and serve him with all their heart and soul (10:12). He disciplined them (*ysr* 4:36; 8:5 [present]). YHWH commands the annihilation of the present inhabitants of the land (20:17).

What YHWH Will Not Do in the Future

YHWH will not abandon (*rph* 4:31; 31:6, 8) nor destroy (*šḥt* 10:10), or forsake (*ʿzb* 31:6, 8) Israel , nor forget (*škḥ* 4:31) the covenant.

YHWH will not acquit anyone who misuses his name (5:11).

He does not delay in repaying those who reject him (7:10).

He will not inflict illness on Israel (7:15).

He was unwilling to destroy Israel (10:10).

He is not partial *(lōʾ-yiśśāʾ pānîm)* and does not take bribes (10:17).

YHWH does not permit *(lōʾ nātan)* Israel to heed soothsayers and diviners (18:14).

YHWH has not given the people a mind to understand, or eyes to see, or ears to hear (29:4).

YHWH will be unwilling to pardon those who are false to the covenant (29:20).

Present-Future Actions

YHWH hears the words of the people (1:34; 5:28; 26:7) and heeds the words of Moses (9:19; 10:10).

Yhwh's Future Blessings

YHWH will bless Israel (7:13-14; 12:7; 14:24, 29; 15:4, 6, 10, 14, 18; 16:10, 15; 23:20; 24:19; 28:3-6, 8, 12; 30:16). He gives them the power to get wealth (8:18). He will make them abound in prosperity (*hôtîr lᵊṭôbâ* 28:11). He will open his storehouse, the heavens, to give rain (28:12; 11:14). He will set them high above all the nations of the earth (26:19; 28:1). He will establish them as his holy people (28:9; 29:13). YHWH will cause the people (and their livestock) to multiply (*rbh* 6:3; 7:13; 8:1, 13; 13:17; 28:63; 30:5, 16). He will also multiply their days on the land (11:21). YHWH will turn away illness *(hēsîr . . . kōl-ḥōlî)* from Israel and inflict illness and pestilence on those who hate them (7:15, 20). YHWH will show compassion (*rḥm* 4:31; 13:17; 30:3). YHWH will give fruit (26:10) and bounty (*ṭôb* 26:11). YHWH will set Israel high above all nations (28:1). YHWH goes ahead of the people (1:30, 33; 31:8) or with the people (20:4; 23:14; 31:6) and fights for them (1:30; 3:22; 20:4). He carries them (1:31).

One of the most frequently made statements about YHWH is that he is *giving* the land (or towns) to Israel (1:21, 25; 2:29; 3:20; 4:1, 21, 38, 40; 5:16, 31; 9:6; 11:17, 31; 12:9; 13:12; 15:4, 7; 16:5, 18, 20; 17:2, 14; 18:9; 19:1, 2, 10, 14; 20:16; 21:1, 23; 24:4; 25:15, 19; 26:1, 2; 27:2, 3; 28:8; 32:49, 52). YHWH will hand over *(ntn byd)* Israel's opponents to them (7:24; 20:13; 21:10) and give rest to his people (*nwḥ* Hiphil 3:20; 12:10; 25:19). YHWH will destroy Israel's enemies (7:23, 24; 9:3; 31:3-4) and cut them off (12:29; 19:1). He will clear them away (7:1, 22), throw them into a great panic (7:23)—but if Israel is unfaithful, the panic will be theirs (28:20)—and will put fear and dread of Israel among them (2:25; 11:25). YHWH will subdue (*knʿ* Hiphil) Israel's enemies (9:3) and enlarge their territory (12:20). He will fight (*lḥm* Niphal) for Israel (1:30; 3:22; 20:4 [+ give victory]) and give them the spoil *(šll)* of their enemies (20:14). He will fight for the people (1:30). He crosses ahead of them (31:3) as a devouring fire (9:3) and thrusts out Israel's enemies (*hdp* 6:19; 9:4), dispossessing them (4:38; 9:4; 18:12) and causing Israel to take possession *(yrš)* of the land (9:5). He will cause Israel's enemies to be defeated (*ntn niggāpîm* 28:7).

YHWH will choose a place where his name shall dwell (12:5, 11, 14, 18, 21, 26; 14:23, 24, 25; 15:20; 16:2, 6, 7, 11, 15, 16; 17:8, 10; 18:6; 26:2; 31:11). He will also choose a king for Israel (17:15).

YHWH will raise up a prophet like Moses (18:15).

YHWH will hold people to vows that they make (23:21).

Punishment for Unfaithfulness

If Israel is unfaithful, YHWH will scatter them (4:27; 28:64; 30:3), but, when they repent, he will gather them (30:3-4). He will shut up *(ʿṣr)* the heavens so that there will be no rain (11:17). If the people are unfaithful, he will afflict them with illness (28:59, 61). If the people anger YHWH, he will destroy them (6:15; 7:4; 12:30; 28:20, 24, 45, 48, 51, 61, 63). YHWH's anger and passion will smoke against them (29:20). YHWH will hide his face (31:17-18, 20).

A long list of covenant curses can be found in 28:20-44, 48-68; 29:20-29: disaster, panic, frustration, pestilence, consumption, fever, inflammation, blight, mildew, drought, defeat, flight, denial of burial, boils, ulcers, scurvy, itch, madness, blindness, confusion, rapine, frustration, shame, enslavement, abuse, exile, infestation, loss of status, servitude, hunger, thirst, nakedness, a yoke, despoilment, siege, cannibalism of children, disease, decimation, destruction, dispersal, a trembling heart, a languishing spirit, dread, return to Egypt, names blotted out, calamity, devastation, extirpation.

YHWH's Rehabilitation of Israel

YHWH will restore, gather, bring back, circumcise the heart, curse enemies (chapter 30).

Moses

The narrator's assessment of Moses is expressed at the end of the book:

> Never since has there arisen a prophet in Israel like Moses, whom the LORD knew face to face. He was unequaled for all the signs and wonders

> that the LORD sent him to perform in the land of Egypt, against Pharaoh and all his servants and his entire land, and for all the mighty deeds and all the terrifying displays of power that Moses performed in the sight of all Israel (Deut 34:10-12).

The narrator characterizes Moses as "the man of God" in 33:1 and "servant of YHWH" in 34:5.

Although Moses is ostensibly retelling events that have already been narrated earlier in the Pentateuch, and repeating some laws that have already been given, when one compares the laws and retellings of Deuteronomy as recited by the character "Moses" with versions of the same laws and narratives of earlier books, some of which have been attributed directly to YHWH, one notices differences. For example, commentators often say that the laws in Deuteronomy (e.g., those having to do with slaves) are more humane. These differences are often explained by means of a diachronic analysis of the development of Israelite law and narratives. But one may well ask what effect a synchronic reading has on the characterization of Moses—i.e., as a person who, while ostensibly repeating the God-given law, and retelling stories that have already been told, changes the details. Is the reader to think that the character "Moses" oversteps his authority? This might be the conclusion were it not for the fact that Moses' authority as mediator and prophet is so strongly highlighted in the text itself.

See the note on 1:37 for a discussion of the effect on the characterization of Moses that is effected by moving Moses' exclusion from the land from the end to the beginning of the story.

Five times in Deuteronomy, Moses exhorts the people to show no pity *(lōʾ tāḥôs)* in enforcing the law: 7:16; 13:9 [NRSV: 8]; 19:13, 21; 25:12.

In chapter 33 there are several examples of an attempt to portray Moses using language that is reminiscent of the stories of the ancestors. See the note on 33:16.

The narrator tells us that Moses was vigorous up to the time of his death (34:7), although this conflicts with Moses' own statement in 31:2 that he is no longer able to lead the people.

Voices

Although Deuteronomy appears to be almost wholly a Mosaic soliloquy, the layering of voices should not be missed, beginning with the voice of the narrator in the introduction and in a series of historical asides. The next layer is the voice of the intradiegetic narrator, Moses, and then there are the various characters that Moses quotes: YHWH, Moses himself, the Israelites, and others.

Deuteronomy is famous for the apparent melding or blending or fusing of voices (Polzin 1987, 94; Miller 1993, 302; see notes): 7:4; 9:24; 11:13-14; 15:11; 17:3; 19:7; 28:20; 29:5 [NRSV: 6], 13 [NRSV: 14]; 31:23-24; 32:31. See the notes on these verses. (Some of these will not be apparent in the NRSV because the Hebrew text has not been followed.) A feature that contributes to the melding of voices is that YHWH, while speaking in the first person, will refer to himself by name in the third person (1:3, 8, 36). Polzin (1987, 92) thinks that the voices of Moses and the narrator gradually fuse.

The voice of the narrator is very little heard in Deuteronomy (according to Polzin [1987, 92] only 56 verses), but *is* encountered in introductions for speakers and in asides (2:10-11, 20-23; 3:9, 11, 13; 27:11; 29:28 [NRSV: 29]). The narrator also introduces each of the blessings in chapter 33.

Imagery

Some of the more striking and memorable imagery of Deuteronomy are:

YHWH carrying the people as a man carries his son (1:31).

YHWH going ahead of the people in fire by night and in cloud by day (1:33).

Og's 9x4 cubit bed (3:11).

YHWH speaking out of the midst of fire (4:12, 15, 33, 36; 5:4, 22, 24, 26; 9:10; 10:4).

Scattering Israel among the nations (4:27; 28:64).

YHWH writing the commandments on two stone tablets (4:13; 5:22; 9:10; 10:2, 4).

The image of the gate (some 34 times, beginning in 5:14)—the place where the civic life of the community takes place, where justice is administered, where disputes are settled and inside which the life of the community takes place.

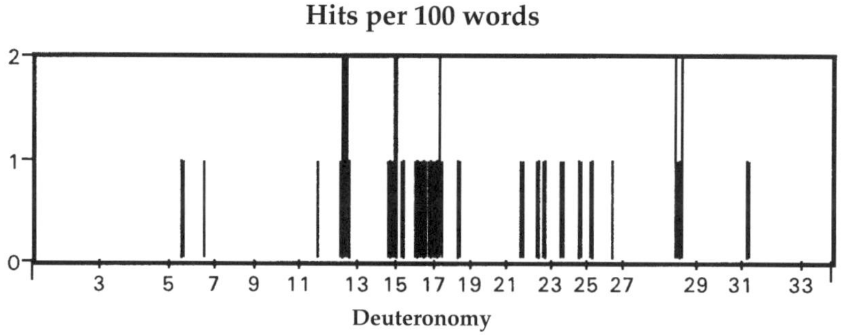

Distribution of the word *šaʿar* (Gate) in Deuteronomy (MT)

Binding the commandments on the hand and between the eyes; writing them on the doorpost of one's gate (6:8-9; 11:18-20).

Eating and being sated (6:11; 8:10, 12; 14:29; 23:24; 26:12; 31:20; 33:23).

Moses' treatment of the Golden Calf (9:21).

People burning their children to their gods (12:31; 18:10).

The king writing a copy of the law and reading from it every day (17:18-19).

Stoning an unruly son (21:19-21).

Setting up a large stone, plastering it and writing on it (27:2, 4).

Six tribes standing on Gerizim and the other six on Ebal (27:12).

An individual fleeing in seven directions (28:25).

Corpses being eaten by birds and beasts (28:26).

Groping at noon like the blind (28:29).

A father and mother eating the flesh of their sons and daughters (28:53-57).

Moses writing the law (31:9, 24).

The law being read to Israel (in the future, 31:11).

Moses putting a song in the people's mouths (31:19).

The eagle (vulture?) stirring up its nest, hovering over its young, spreading its wings and carrying the young on its pinions (32:11).

Sucking honey from a crag and oil from flint (32:13), wealth from the seas, and hidden treasure from sand (33:19).

Moses viewing the land from across the Jordan but not being able to enter (34:1).

YHWH as Rock (32:4, 15, 18, 30, 31).

One person chasing a thousand; two persons routing ten thousand [in battle] (32:30).

YHWH burying Moses in an unknown place (34:6).

Somatic Imagery

Face

The verb *pnh* (to face) occurs sixteen times, in most instances referring literally to turning or heading in a certain direction. It is used metaphorically in 29:18; 31:18 and 20 in the sense of turning away from YHWH to go *(lāleket)* and serve the gods of the nations. In 30:17 the heart is said to turn away. The noun "face" (*pāneh,* usually plural) is found 132 times, most often in the expression *lipnê,* "before the face of x." YHWH sets in front of the people *(ntn lipnê):*

1. The land (1:8, 21)

2. Enemies: Sihon and his land (2:31, 33); the Canaanites (7:2, 23; 31:5); "Enemies" (23:15 [NRSV: 14]) (In these contexts, NRSV renders *ntn lipnê* simply as "give.")

3. The law (4:8; 11:32. See also 4:44 where it is Moses who does this.)

4. Blessing and curse (11:26; 30:1), life and prosperity/death and adversity (30:15), life and death/blessing and curses (30:19)

YHWH goes before *(lipnê)* the people (1:30, 33; 9:3) searching out campground for them and destroying their enemies (11:23). YHWH crosses the Jordan ahead of the people—so will Joshua (31:3, 8).

What the people do before *(lipnê)* YHWH:

1. Weep (1:45)

2. Observe the commandment (6:25)

3. Lie prostrate (Moses 9:18, 25)

4. Eat (12:7, 18; 14:23; 15:20)

5. Rejoice (12:12, 18; 16:11; 27:7)

6. Get credit (24:13)

7. Set down the basket of first fruits (26:4)
8. Recite "creed" (26:5)
9. Stand (*yṣb* 29:10)

To stand before *(ʿmd lipnê)* or serve:

1. Joshua before Moses (1:38)
2. Moses before YHWH (4:10)
3. Levi before YHWH (10:8; 18:7)
4. The people before YHWH (29:13 [NRSV: 14])

Other expressions involving the face:

YHWH brought the people out of Egypt "with his own presence" (*bappānāyw* 4:37). YHWH spoke with the people face to face (5:4) and knew Moses face to face (34:10). YHWH repays "to his face" *(ʾel-pānāyw)* a person who rejects him (7:10) and will have no other gods before him (*ʿal-pānāy* 5:7). When Israel becomes unfaithful, YHWH will hide his face in anger (31:17, 18).

YHWH drives out or causes fear among their enemies in the face of *(mippᵊnê)* the Israelites (4:38; 6:19; 7:1, 20, 22; 8:20; 9:4, 5; 12:29, 30; 18:12; 33:27).

Eyes

YHWH's Eyes

YHWH guards Israel as the apple (*ʾîšôn*, "little man," i.e., reflected image) of his eye (32:10).

The eyes of YHWH are always on the land (11:12).

The people are exhorted to do what is right and just in the eyes of YHWH (6:18; 12:25, 28; 13:18; 21:9) and warned of the consequences of doing what is evil in his eyes (4:25; 9:18; 17:2; 31:29).

YHWH looks down *(šqp)* from his heavenly dwelling (26:15).

The People's Eyes

Repeated emphasis is put on the things that YHWH has accomplished in the eyes of the people. This is, perhaps, best summarized by 4:34, "Or has any god ever attempted to go and take a nation for himself from the midst of another nation, by trials, by signs and wonders, by war, by a mighty hand and an outstretched arm, and by terrifying displays of power, as the LORD your God did for you in Egypt before your very eyes?" (also 1:30; 3:21; 4:3; 6:22; 7:19; 10:21; 11:7; 29:2, 3). But if the people are not faithful, their eyes will have to look upon maddening sights (28:32, 34, 67). One's eye must never be blinded by a bribe (16:19).

Nose

YHWH's Nose

YHWH's nose means YHWH's anger, which is kindled by the people's unfaithfulness (6:15; 7:4; 9:19; 11:17; 13:18 [NRSV: 17]; 29:19 [NRSV: 20], 22 [NRSV: 23], 23 [NRSV: 24], 26 [NRSV: 27]; 31:17; 32:22).

It is the office of the Levitical priest to place incense before YHWH's nose (Hebrew: *bᵊʾappᵊkā* 33:10).

Ears

The law is read in the ears of the people (31:11, 28) as is the song (31:30; 32:44). Despite all the wonders that they had witnessed, the people did not have ears to hear (29:4).

Heart

Note that sometimes NRSV renders Hebrew "heart" as "mind," since, in Hebrew, the heart is regarded not as the seat of emotion but of thought and will.

The people must take to heart that YHWH is God (4:39). They must have a heart to fear YHWH (5:29). YHWH's word is or must be in the heart of the people (6:6; 10:14; 11:18; 32:46). They must not let the things their eyes have seen slip from their hearts (4:9), but must keep in their hearts the blessing and curse that YHWH has set before them (30:1). The people must seek (4:29), love (6:5; 30:6), serve (10:12; 11:13; 28:47), obey (30:2), and turn to (30:10) YHWH and observe his ordinances (26:16) with all their heart. YHWH sometimes tests the people (as a man tests his son [8:5]) to know what is in their heart (8:23; 13:4 [NRSV: 3]).

The people's heart must not turn away (29:18; 30:17; also 17:17 in reference to the king) nor become haughty (8:14; 17:20 [the king]) nor be deceived (11:16), nor become timid (20:3) or stubborn (29:19). The foreskin of their heart must be circumcised (10:16; 30:6). Otherwise YHWH will bring about events that will put terror (28:67) or confusion (28:28) in their heart, causing it to tremble (28:65).

The image of the heart melting is used in reference to the dread that enemies feel at Israel's approach (1:28; 20:8).

Hand/Arm/Palm/Sole/Foot/Finger

"Hand," used literally, easily conjures up an image in the mind of the reader:

YHWH lifts his arm to take an oath (32:40). The tablets of the law are written with the finger of God (9:10).

Moses takes the tablets of the covenant in his two hands (9:15) and throws them from his two hands (9:17). Later, he goes up the mountain with two (new) tablets in his hands (10:3).

Moses lays hands on Joshua (34:9). People are to lay hands on a person to be executed (13:9; 17:7).

Contraband must not "stick" to anyone's hand (13:17).

People come to the temple with money in hand (14:25); the priest takes a basket of offerings from the hand of the offerer (26:4); a man wields an ax in his hand (19:5); people pluck grain with their hands (23:25); and the elders of a city wash their hands and state that their hands have not shed the blood of a corpse found in a nearby field (21:6-7). The talion demands a hand for a hand (19:21); a woman stretches out her hand to help her husband in a brawl (25:11); and a man puts a bill of divorce in his wife's hand (24:1, 3).

"Hand" is also frequently used in a figurative sense to represent power or control. This usage is strikingly illustrated in 28:32 where, as a result of infidelity, the people cannot prevent the loss of their children to the enemy. "It is not in the power of your hand" *(ʾên lᵊʾēl yādekā).*

YHWH's Hand

YHWH brought Israel out of Egypt "with a strong hand and an outstretched arm" (4:34; 5:15; 7:19; 11:2; 26:8; "hand" without "arm": 6:21; 7:8; 9:26; "arm" without "hand": 9:29). He has begun to show his strong hand (3:24). No one can deliver from YHWH's hand (32:29). His hand takes hold of judgment (32:41) and is against rebels (2:15).

The Hands of Enemies

Israel is "handed over" to the Amorites (1:27). When Israel's adversaries triumph over them they say "our hand is triumphant *(rāmâ)*" (32:27). But Israel was redeemed from the hand of Pharaoh (7:8) and has taken land from the hands of the two kings of the Amorites (3:8).

Other Characters

In 34:12 the expression "strong hand" *(yad haḥăzāqâ)*, which is so often used of YHWH, is apparently applied to Moses.

In 33:7 YHWH is asked to strengthen the hand of Judah.

A closed or open hand is used to represent miserliness or generosity towards one's needy neighbors (15:2, 3, 7, 8, 11).

The expression "the works of one's hands" (*mʿśh yd* 2:7; 14:29; 24:19; 28:12; 30:9) or "what the hand reaches for" (*mšlḥ yd* 12:7, 18; 15:10; 16:15; 23:20; 28:8, 20) or "the deeds of one's hand" (*pʿl yd* 33:11) are used in the sense of "undertakings." If the people keep the law, their undertakings will be blessed. But if, instead, they worship the works of their hands (*mʿśh yd* used in reference to idols 4:28; 27:15; 31:29), their undertakings will fail.

YHWH hands Sihon, Og, and other enemies over to Israel (2:30; 7:24; 20:13; 21:10), but Israel must not attribute their victory to the strength of their own hands (8:17).

When YHWH came from Sinai, he put his holy ones in the hands of the "favorite among peoples" (33:3).

Foot

The image of the foot is used several times. Noteworthy among these is that of the foot not slipping (32:35) and dipping one's foot in oil (33:24).

Mouth

YHWH's mouth is mentioned about five times (but is rightly rendered as "command" in four of those). Moses puts the song in the mouths of the people and it will not be lost from their mouths (31:19, 21). Figurative use is made of the expression "mouth of the sword" (31:19, 21), and the story of the earth opening its mouth to swallow rebels is recalled (11:6).

Throat *(nepeš)*

The *nepeš* is the seat of appetite or desire (12:15, 20, 21; 14:26; 18:6; 21:14; 23:24). One is to love and serve YHWH with all one's heart and soul (4:29; 6:5; 10:12; 11:13; 13:4 [NRSV: 3]; 26:16; 30:2, 6, 10) and put YHWH's words in their heart and soul (11:18).

Neck

The stiff neck (*qāšeh ʿōrep* 9:6, 13; cf. 10:16; 31:27) conveys the notion of stubbornness. But if the people are unfaithful, YHWH will put an iron yoke on their neck (28:48).

Voice

Frequent mention is made of the voice of YHWH. This usage does not always show up in the NRSV because the idiom "heed the voice," which occurs about eighteen times, is rendered "obey" (but "obey the voice" in 8:20; 13:4, 18). YHWH's voice is said to be heard out of darkness in 5:23, but out of fire in the next verse. At Sinai the people saw no form, but only heard a loud voice (4:12, 36; 5:22). They feared that they would die (5:25-26; 18:16).

YHWH hears the voice of the people when they cry out in affliction (26:7) and Moses prays that YHWH will hear the voice of Judah (33:7).

Head

An interesting figurative use of head is, "YHWH will make you the head, and not the tail" (28:13)—an image that is reversed in 28:44.

Loins

Moses prays that YHWH will crush the loins of Levi's adversaries (33:11).

Womb

YHWH is the subject of the verb *rḥm* in 13:17 and 30:3. This image suggests the tender love of a mother for her baby.

Walk

YHWH walks (continuously, *mithallēk*) in the midst of the camp (23:14). The people must walk in the way that YHWH has commanded (5:33; 8:6; 10:12; 11:22; 13:5 [NRSV: 4]; 19:9; 26:7, 17; 28:9; 30:16). They are not to walk after other gods (6:14; 8:19; 11:28; 13:3 [NRSV: 2]; 28:14; 29:17 [NRSV: 18], 25 [NRSV: 26]), nor turn from the way or the commandment (*swr* 5:32; 7:4; 9:12, 16; 11:16; 11:28; 17:17, 20; 28:14; 31:29), nor be led astray (*ndḥ* 4:19; 13:6 [NRSV: 5], 11 [NRSV: 10], 14 [NRSV: 13], 30:17). Otherwise, YHWH will cause them to walk to an unknown nation (28:36).

Blood

Some striking figurative uses are "the avenger of blood" (*gōʾēl haddām* 19:6, 12), "innocent blood" (*dām nāqî* 19:10, 13; 21:8, 9; 27; 25), wine called "the blood of grapes" (32:14), and arrows "drunk with blood" (32:42). A particularly difficult legal case to decide is one between blood and blood (*bên-dām lᵊdām* 17:8)—an expression the meaning of which has been variously interpreted.

Other Images Used in Deuteronomy

Other images: a population as numerous as the stars (1:10; 10:22; 28:62), cities fortified to the sky (1:28), girding on weapons (1:41), being chased by bees (1:44), peoples trembling in fear (2:25), sticking to YHWH (4:4; 10:20; 11:22; 13:5 [NRSV: 4], 30:20), a burning mountain (4:11; 9:15), from one end of heaven to the other (4:32), a land flowing with milk and honey (6:3), breaking down altars, smashing pillars, cutting down Asherim and burning carved images (7:6), the fruit of the body (*pᵊrî beṭen* 7:13), grain, wine and oil (7:13; 11:14; 12:17; 14:23; 18:4; 28:51), being ensnared by idolatry (7:16, 25), thirsty ground (8:15), water from flint rock (8:15), the land drinks water (11:11), YHWH shuts heaven (11:17), pouring out blood on the ground (12:16), cutting off the nations (12:29; 19:1), "the wife you embrace" (13:6 [NRSV: 7]), gathering spoil (13:17), a city becomes a heap (13:17), self-laceration (14:1), thrusting an awl through a slave's ear and into a doorpost (15:17), putting a sickle to standing grain (16:9), planting an Asherah and setting up a pillar (16:21), a judgment between stroke and stroke (17:8), to extirpate evil (17:12), to multiply horses or wives (17:16-17), making a son or daughter pass through fire (18:10), removing a boundary marker (19:14), building a new house (20:5), planting a vineyard (20:6), not leaving alive anything that breathes (20:16), axing trees (20:19), the corpse of a man hanged on a tree (21:23), a man hiding from his neighbor's stray ox or sheep (22:1), the elders of a city measuring the distance from a corpse found in a field to the nearest city (21:2), the elders of a city washing their hands over a heifer whose neck has been broken (21:6), an ass or ox that has fallen (22:4), the tokens of virginity (22:15), a man uncovering his father's skirt (23:1), returning an escaped slave to his master (23:16), cult prostitutes (23:18), interest (literally, "bite") on a loan (23:20), a man sending his wife out of his house (24:1), a judge overseeing a beating (25:2), a widow removing the shoe of her husband's brother and spitting in his face (25:9), a wife grabbing the genitals of her husband's opponent in a brawl (25:11), cutting off the wife's hand (25:12), Amalek cutting off Israel's "tail" (25:18), blotting out the remembrance of a person (25:19), leading the blind astray (27:18), killing a neighbor in secret (27:24), setting Israel above all nations (28:1), opening a rich storehouse of rain (28:12; 11:11, 14), pestilence sticking to a person (28:21), heaven becoming brass and earth becoming iron (28:23), rain changed into powdery dust (28:24), locust and worm devouring crops (28:38-39), being pursued and overtaken by curses (28:45), a vulture swooping (28:49), high, fortified walls come down (28:52), the diseases of Egypt stick to a person (28:60), "YHWH will scatter you (sg.) from one end of the earth to the other" (28:64), gods of wood and stone (28:64; 29:16), Israel passing through other nations (29;15), extirpating people from one land and throwing them into another (29:27), gathering those who were scattered (30:3), going up to heaven or beyond the sea (30:12), a pillar of cloud standing over the door of the tent (31:15), a crooked (*ʿiqqēš*) generation (32:5), finding a person [lost] in the howling wilderness (32:10), a fire that consumes the underworld, devours the earth, and sets fire to the foundations of the mountains (32:22), heaping evils on a person (32:23), wasting hunger (32:24), the teeth of beasts and the venom of things that crawl in the dust (32:24), the sword that bereaves (32:25), gods eating the fat of sacrifices and drinking the wine of libations (32:38), whetting a flashing sword (32:41), being gathered to one's ancestors (32:50, 2x), YHWH dawning from Seir/shining from Paran (33:2), the Deep couching beneath (33:13), the produce of the sun and the yield of the moons (33:14), the One who dwells in the bush (33:16, see notes), the horns of a wild ox gore people (33:17), the lioness tearing arm and head/the young lion springing (33:21-22), treading on the backs of defeated enemies (33:29).

Knowledge

As in Numbers, we see examples of reader elevation in relation to Israel's enemies (2:32). When Sihon takes the field against Israel, both the reader and Moses (and Israel?) know that YHWH has delivered Sihon into the hands of the Israelites (2:24, 31; 29:6). The same holds true for Og (3:1, 2). Similarly, the nations do not know what Joshua and the Israelites know, namely that YHWH will do to them what he did to Sihon and Og (2:11). The seven nations do not know that YHWH is throwing them out of the land (7:1, 19-20, 22-24; 12:29; 19:1; 33:27) and wiping them out (20:16-17; 31:3). The sons of Anak do not know that YHWH will destroy them (9:3). Future potential enemies do not know that YHWH is on Israel's side (20:1) and that they will be defeated (21:1; 28:7) and will come fawning to Israel who will tread on their backs (33:29). Amalek does not know that he is to be rubbed out (*mḥh* 25:19). The peoples to the ends of the earth do not know that they will be gored (33:17).

Israel not only knows that its enemies will be defeated, they know YHWH's will and covenant with Israel promised blessings and curses

(28). Israel will know the law because it will be read to them every seven years (31:11) and the song will insure that they know (31:19). Despite the command to remain ignorant about the local gods (11:30; 20:18), Israel will serve gods that it did not know (29:25; 32:17) and does not know the gods that it will serve in exile (28:64), nor the people who will consume their produce (28:33), nor the place to which they will be exiled (28:36). When the nations witness Israel's destruction, they will inquire about its cause, and learn that it was due to abandonment of the covenant (29:23).

Other passages where knowledge plays a role:

1:26 There is some character elevation here: the reader does not know why the people refused to go up into the land. The reason is held back until verse 28.

5:27-28 Moses is to hear the law from YHWH and then teach it to the people, who do not want to hear the voice of YHWH directly. Moses' knowledge will be greater, at least for a time.

8:2, 16 The people and the reader now learn the reason for the wanderings: YHWH was testing them to see what was in their heart and to know whether or not they would keep the commandments.

In retelling the story of the Golden Calf, Moses indicates that both the people (9:14) and Aaron (9:20) were in mortal danger, even though they didn't know it, due to YHWH's anger at such a provocation. They would have been destroyed were it not for Moses' intervention.

In two cases the reader may wonder why the characters do not know something that the reader knows: Doesn't the rebellious son know that he will be stoned to death? (21:19). Doesn't the husband who falsely accuses his wife of not being a virgin on their wedding night know that her father has proof to the contrary? (22:13-19).

In three instances a person who commits an offense in secret is nevertheless subject to the covenant curse: a person who secretly sets up an idol (27:15), a person who leads the blind astray (27:18) (the blind, of course, do not know that they are being led astray), and a person who kills his neighbor in secret (27:24).

Another act that takes place in secret is a graphic illustration of the application of the covenant curses. During a time of siege a desperately hungry woman secretly eats the child she has born along with the afterbirth (28:57).

31:21 YHWH knows the inclination *(yēṣer)* of Israel's seed.

34:6 No one knows where Moses is buried.

Point of View

Some observations of shift of viewpoint occur in the notes.

The combination of *hinnēh* and *rʾh* occurs only twice in Deuteronomy: 9:13, where the focus is through YHWH's perception, and 9:16 where it is through Moses.

The phrase "beyond the Jordan" in 1:1 indicates Cisjordan point of view.

19:14 adopts a post-conquest temporal point of view (see note on this verse).

29:24 [NRSV: 23] adopts a point of view that is after the destruction of the land in punishment for unfaithfulness to the covenant.

A Note on the Numbering of Verses

Please note the following differences in the numbering of verses between the MT and the NRSV:

MT	NRSV
13:1	12:32
13:2	13:1
13:19	13:18
23:1	22:30
23:2	23:1
23:26	23:25
28:69	29:1
29:1	29:2
29:28	29:29

In all other chapters the numbers of verses are the same in both versions.

NOTES

Deuteronomy 1

Moses' First Discourse: Recapitulation of the People's Story (1–4)

1:1 "These are the words that Moses spoke to all Israel . . ." The expression "all Israel" frames the entire book (Craigie 1976, 89; Christensen 1991, 7), occurring a total of thirteen times, including the first and last verses of Deuteronomy.

1:1 "Beyond the Jordan" Although Moses is east of the Jordan, the narrator's point of view is from the other (Cisjordan) side of the river. From the narrator's point of view, Moses is on the other side of the Jordan (Mayes 1981, 114).

1:1–3:29 Christensen (1991, 1) sees these verses as the initial unit, which summarizes the past. He proposes the following chiastic structure:

A Summons to Enter the Promised Land (1:6b-8)

  B Organization of the People for Life in the Land (1:9-18)

    C Israel's Unholy War (1:19–2:1)

      D The March of Conquest (2:2-25)

    C' YHWH's Holy War (2:26–3:11)

  B' Distribution of the Land in Transjordan (3:12-17)

A' Summons to Take the Promised Land (3:18-22)

1:2 " . . . eleven days to reach Kadesh-barnea from Horeb." The notice may serve two purposes: 1. It connects the events of the end of the journey with those of its beginning (Christensen 1991, 7). 2. It contrasts the short travel time from Horeb to Kadesh-barnea with the forty years spent in the wilderness (next verse)—a time that would have been unnecessary if the older generation had not rebelled (Thompson 1974, 82).

1:3 11/1/40 is the only exact date in Deuteronomy. Moses and Aaron each die two and half months before one of the two feasts that are at opposite ends of the liturgical cycle: Moses before Passover and Aaron before Sukkoth (Christensen 1991, 8; Thompson 1974, 82). The mention of the fortieth year presupposes the story of how the people ended up remaining in the wilderness all that time.

1:3 "Moses spoke . . ." Speaking is going to be what characterizes Moses in Deuteronomy.

1:4 Sihon and Og, whose stories are told in Numbers 21 and again in Deuteronomy 2–3 are mentioned together three times in Deuteronomy (here and 29:6; 31:4) and an additional six times in other parts of the Old Testament (Num 32:33; Josh 2:10; 9:10; 1 Kgs 4:19; Ps 135:11; Neh 9:22). The purpose of mentioning them here seems to be to give the people confidence that YHWH is with them and that they should not be afraid in the future. Since the name YHWH is closest to "defeated" in the Hebrew, it is presumably YHWH who defeated Sihon (rather than Moses).

1:5 The beginning of Moses' speech is somewhat solemnly introduced not by the more prosaic *waydabbēr lēʾmōr* (he spoke saying), but by *hôʾîl . . . bēʾēr,* ("he undertook to expound") the latter being a rare word.

Leaving Horeb (1:6-8)

1:6 "The Lord . . . spoke to us at Horeb . . ." Moses begins by jumping back in time and space to the end of the people's stay at Horeb. Moses quotes YHWH, who commands the people to go directly into the land as far as the Euphrates.

1:7 The dimensions described go far beyond any possible historical Israelite empire (Christensen 1991, 12). They are highly idealized—a Hebrew mirror image of the empires that successively oppressed them.

1:8 "Go and take possession . . ." The verb *yrš* has the connotation of possessing by dispossessing (Christensen 1991, 12). In other words, Israel takes possession of the land by taking it away from its present inhabitants.

1:8 "The land that I swore . . ." Hebrew "The land that YHWH swore . . ." The NRSV here follows textual variants found in the Samaritan

Pentateuch and in some Greek recensions. However, it is not unusual in Deuteronomy for YHWH to refer to himself by name in the third person. This is possibly due to a deliberate strategy on the part of the author to blend the voices of YHWH, Moses, and the narrator.

Setting up the Judges (1:9-18)

1:9-10 "I said to you, 'I am unable by myself to bear you . . .'" The character Moses uses the same language as in Num 11:11-15 but represents himself as having said these words to the people rather than to YHWH (Christensen 1991, 20; Mayes 1981, 118). Here YHWH quotes himself.

Num 11:14	*lōʾ ʾûkal*	*ʾānōkî lᵊbaddî*	*lāśēʾt*	*ʾet-kol-hāʿām hazzeh*
Deut 1:9	*lōʾ ʾûkal*	*lᵊbaddî*	*śᵊʾēt*	*ʾetkem*

1:10 "Like the stars of heaven" recalls the promise to the patriarchs in Gen 15:5; 22:17; 26:4 and recalled in Exod 32:13. The fact that the promise to the ancestors has manifestly been fulfilled ought to give the people confidence in YHWH's ability to fulfill his other promises.

1:12 "How can I bear the . . . burden?" *ṭōraḥ,* "burden," carries with it a possible nuance of wearisome toil.

1:13 When this monologue is compared with Num 11:10-17 it appears that Moses omits to mention that the establishment of the "heads" was done at YHWH's command.

1:16 "Members of your community . . . one person and another." The NRSV translation rightly generalizes the term "brother" but loses the implicit appeal to view one's fellow citizens as family. One might notice here the layering of voices: the narrator quotes Moses quoting himself.

1:17 "Not be partial": literally "not recognize the face."

1:17 "Any case that is too hard for you, bring to me . . ." Moses is characterized as someone capable of judging cases too difficult for others to judge.

The Crisis at Kadesh (1:19-46)

Sending the Scouts (1:19-25)

1:21 Here the second-person address switches from plural to singular, thereby making the appeal more personal.

1:22 (The people want to send spies into the land.) In Num 13:2, 17 the initiative to send the spies comes from YHWH. In this retelling it comes from the people—all of them *(kullᵊkem)*. Such a demand is now seen as an indication of lack of faith in YHWH (Mann 1979, 490; Mayes 1981, 126).

1:25 Moses depicts the report of the spies as being only positive, in contrast with Num 13:32. Moses, in retelling the incident, ignores the negative part of the report.

The People Refuse to Enter the Land (1:16-40)

1:27 "It is because the Lord hates us . . ." The placement of the word "hate" in the Hebrew gives it special emphasis: "Out of hatred of YHWH for us he brought us out . . ."

1:28 "We actually saw there the offspring of the Anakim." There is a contrast developed between the mighty works of YHWH, which the people have seen (1:19, 30, 31) and which ought to give them courage, and their fear at *seeing* the Anakim (Miller 1990, 35). This contrasts with Moses' invitation to the people to *see* in verse 21.

1:31 "The Lord your God carried you . . ." The father-son imagery used here is part of the theme of the love of God developed in Deuteronomy (Christensen 1991, 30).

1:33 (YHWH goes ahead to seek out a place.) The use of the verb *twr* here ("seek"—the same word used of the spies in Num 13:2) is ironic, since in the view of Deuteronomy the sending of the spies was not YHWH's initiative (as it is in Numbers), but the people's. This creates a tension between the people taking it upon themselves to search out the land, on the one hand, and God reconnoitering a place for them to encamp, on the other (Christensen 1991, 30). But there is tension even within Numbers; see 10:33, where the ark goes a three days' journey ahead of the people to search out a resting place.

1:37 (YHWH is angry with Moses. Moses will not enter the land.) The narrative in Numbers had located YHWH's prohibition of Moses' entrance into the land in chapter 20, where Moses berates the people and strikes the rock twice. This comes after a series of confrontations between Moses and those who rebel against his authority. By moving YHWH's rejection of Moses' entrance to the first crisis (the story of the spies), the author of Deuteronomy has increased the irony in two ways. 1. The rejection of Moses is tied to what amounts to Israel's rejection of the land. 2. The character Moses must now continue as leader throughout the wilderness era without any hope of entering the land himself: in fact, with the knowledge that his own death draws nearer with every step that the people take toward the land (Mann 1979, 491).

1:39 "And as for your little ones . . ." Even though YHWH is supposed to be speaking to Moses, his words here are really addressed to the people.

1:40 "Journey back to the wilderness . . ." The order to turn recalls 1:7, where the people are commanded to resume their journey. But now the people are sent in the opposite direction.

The Unsuccessful Attempt to Take the Land without YHWH (1:41-46)

1:41 "*We* are ready to go up . . ." The emphatic "we" means "we and not our descendants" (Driver 1901, 29). The people are contradicting YHWH's sentence that not they but their children will enter the land.

1:46 The repetition of the verb *yšb* forms an *inclusio* that frames this verse.

Deuteronomy 2

The Desert Journey

Edom (2:1-7)

2:2 "You have gone around this mountain long enough" echoes 1:6.

2:4 YHWH tells Moses what he is to say, but the speech is YHWH's since the "I" of the next verse is YHWH, not Moses.

2:7 "The Lord your God has blessed you . . ." Despite the fact that the forty years of wandering were a punishment, YHWH caused the people to prosper there. The argument is that as a result of the blessings that have flowed from YHWH's presence with them the people can afford to purchase food and water from the Edomites. If the "I" of verse 5 is YHWH, then this same YHWH must be referring to himself in the third person. Alternatively, the voice has shifted to that of Moses, in which case there has been a melding of the two voices (as Polzin has pointed out regarding other verses).

Moab (2:8-15)

2:8 "So we passed by our kin, the descendants of Esau . . ." No mention is made of the Edomite force that came out against them (Num 20:20). The execution of YHWH's command in verse 4 sets up a command-fulfillment formal structure that may prepare for either the continuation of this pattern or its violation.

2:10-11 The purpose of some of this sidebar seems to be to show that the people's fear of the land's (giant) inhabitants was groundless since in other lands that YHWH had given to other peoples the giants had been replaced by others (presumably not giants). What is more, in the case of the non-giants (Horites in 2:12) one people had been replaced by another.

If the sidebars are regarded as part of the divine speech (rather than asides of the narrator) then they would be quite pointed reminders that the people's fear of the present inhabitants of Canaan was groundless.

2:14 "Warriors." They are called what they should have been but were not (Christensen 1991, 42; Craigie 1976, 112).

2:15 This verse features a rhyme: *gam bām lᵊhummām ʿad tummām.*

Ammon (2:16-23)

2:20-23 Another sidebar, this time about races of giants that had been destroyed by other peoples settling in their respective lands. Israel should not fear to do what others have been able to accomplish.

Confrontation with Sihon (2:24-37)

2:24 "Begin to take possession . . ." This verse marks a turning point in the story—the first divine order to engage a foe militarily and dispossess them. What had been forbidden against the Edomites is here enjoined. The older generation had shown its lack of faith by saying that YHWH would deliver them into the power of the Amorites (1:27). But now the Amorites are given over to the new and obedient generation (Craigie 1976, 113).

2:29 Here Moses says that the descendants of Esau allowed Israel to pass through their land. This is at variance with Num 20:21, where the people had to go around Edom. One may solve this problem by means of source criticism (conflicting traditions), but what is the narrative effect of seeing the character "Moses" bend the truth? Is the reader meant to perceive him as a shrewd negotiator who bolsters his argument by saying that other peoples have already granted the same request that he is now making to Sihon?

2:36 The statement that no citadel was too high for the people contradicts that of the murmurers in 1:28 that the Canaanite cities were fortified to the heavens. Once the people trusted in YHWH, no fortress could withstand them (Christensen 1991, 54).

Deuteronomy 3

Conquest and Allotment of Transjordan; Moses Excluded

Og (3:1-11)

3:1-3 The language here is almost identical to Num 21:33-35—more identical than is reflected by the NRSV, which renders *lammilḥāmâ* as "to battle" in Num 21:33 but "for battle" in Deut 3:1. Similarly, *ntn* is "given" in Num 21:34 but "handed over" in Deut 3:2; in the same verse, *yôšēb* is "ruled" in Numbers but "reigned" in Deuteronomy. Since Moses has now become the intradiegetic narrator, the "they" of Numbers becomes "we" in Deuteronomy (Thompson 1974, 97).

3:3 "The Lord . . . handed over . . . We struck . . . down." God's action is mentioned first, followed by human action (Craigie 1976, 119). Moses' report of the defeat of Og echoes the language of YHWH's promise in verse 2:

> *2 bᵊyādᵊkā nātattî ʾōtô wᵊʾet-kol-ʿammô*
>
> into your hand I give him and all his people
>
> *3 wayyittēn . . . bᵊyādēnû . . . ʾet-ʿôg . . . wᵊʾet-kol-ʿammô*
>
> he gave into our hand Og and all his people.

This echo effect stresses the point that YHWH has kept his promises—and that therefore he ought always to be trusted to do so.

3:4 A twofold negation is used here for rhetorical effect: There was not a city that we did not take.

3:5 "Fortress town with high walls." The mention of the walls belies the people's fear of "cities fortified up to heaven" expressed in 1:28.

3:6 ". . . destroying men, women, and children *(ṭap).* It is not the "little ones" of the Israelites that perish (as the people feared, 1:39), but those of their enemies (see also 2:34).

3:9 A narrator's aside concerning the nomenclature of Mt. Hermon.

3:11 Another narrator's aside, this time on Og and his bed (not sarcophagus [Hübner, 1993]). Only Og remained of the Rephaim—they had all been wiped out, mostly by other peoples. Fear of them was groundless. Pointing to Og's iron bed emphasizes that the last of the giants is no longer. Certainly, the aside on Og's bedstead is intended to stress the great size of the defeated enemy and thereby to allay the people's fear of the size of their future opponents.

Distribution of Amorite Land in Transjordan (3:12-22)

3:12 "I gave the Reubenites and Gadites the territory north of Aroer." Moses avoids narrating the circumstances under which the Transjordan territory was given to Reuben, Gad, and half Manasseh as a crisis (which it is in Numbers 32). Moses omits mention of his confrontation with the Reubenites and Gadites (Num 32:1-42; see also Deut 3:18-20).

3:13 (The region of Argob used to be called a land of Rephaim.) The point of this sidebar is, once again, that the giants whom the people feared have been defeated.

3:20 "Across the Jordan," i.e., from a Transjordanian perspective—a shift in viewpoint from 1:1.

3:21 "Your own eyes have seen." Deuteronomy puts much emphasis on what the people have seen with their own eyes (the expression occurs some sixteen times) even though at least some of the events referred to were witnessed only by those who are now dead. But this is part of the narrative strategy of making the reader of any age a witness of these events. See 5:3. The point is made that what YHWH has done in Transjordan he will do in Cisjordan.

Moses Excluded (3:23-29)

3:24 Here, what YHWH is beginning to show is not the land or the way, but his greatness and his strong hand.

3:25-26 "Let me cross over . . . The Lord was angry." Moses' words here *(ʾeʿbᵊrâ-nāʾ wᵊʾerʾeh)* are similar to his words at the burning bush *(ʾāsūrâ-nāʾ wᵊʾerʾeh,* Exod 3:3). Here there is word play on *ʿbr*, "cross." Moses says "let me cross," but this makes YHWH "cross" with him

(Mann 1979, 481, n. 1; Christensen 1991, 65). Moses' request certainly creates some narrative tension. The reader knows how forgiving YHWH can be, especially on those occasions when Moses has interceded for the people. Will YHWH give in to Moses' intercession in his own behalf?

3:26 "Enough from you!" Hebrew: *rab-lāk*. The expression has occurred in 1:6 and 2:3 to say that the people had remained long enough in a particular place. It also echoes the story of the overreaching of the Levites in Num 16:3, 7.

Deuteronomy 4

Conclusion of Moses' First Discourse

The Baal-peor Incident (4:1-8)

4:1 "So now, Israel . . ." *wᵊʿattâ* introduces the point to be made from the previous summary.

4:6 (What other peoples will say when they hear of Israel's statutes.) The instructions that YHWH has given are grounds for a claim to honor among the nations.

Recollection of the Events at Horeb (4:9-14)

4:12 "Saw no form; there was only a voice." Therefore there can be no justification for fashioning a plastic representation of the deity (Driver 1901, 67).

Exhortation (4:15-40)

4:17 "The likeness of any animal . . ." The names of the various types of creatures recall both the creation story and the dietary laws. YHWH has created these animals, but not in his image. They are not to be worshiped.

4:20 "But the Lord has taken you . . ." The "you" here is emphatic: "And (speaking of allotting) *you* the Lord has taken . . ."

4:28 "You will serve gods that neither see, nor hear, nor eat, nor smell." Idols are not even capable of what animals can do (Driver 1901, 73).

4:29 (You will seek the Lord and you will find him.) This verse seems to mitigate the gloom of the preceding text.

4:35 "To you it was shown . . ." Hebrew: *horʾētā*. This is the only example of theological passive in Deuteronomy, an indirect way of saying that it was YHWH who showed the people his power in the Exodus events.

4:36 Heaven and earth: a merismus. Note the pairing:

heaven	hear	voice
earth	see	fire

4:38 "To drive out nations greater and stronger" picks up on the point of the sidebars (2:10-11, 20-23; 3:9, 11, 13).

The Cities of Refuge (4:41-43)

Narrator's Pivot Text (4:44-49)

4:44-49 These verses have been viewed in two different ways: 1. They serve as a conclusion of the first four chapters of Deuteronomy. They seem to form an *inclusio* with 1:1-5 with which they share a similar content. They also summarize what had come before (Lundbom 1996, 302, 304). 2. Alternatively, since no instructional material has been given in chapters 1–4, the words "This is the instruction that Moses set before Israel" must point forward to what follows (Driver 1901, 79).

Perhaps the best solution would be to see these verses as both conclusion and introduction—a pivot-text that both links and separates the two discourses.

Moses' Second Address (5–28)

Deuteronomy 5

The Covenant at Horeb (5:1-33)

The Decalogue (5:6-21)

Moses' Mediation (5:22-33)

5:24-27 This speech is important for the characterization of the people and of Moses. Obviously, the story is told to justify Moses' mediation. But what does it say about the people? If they have seen that someone can hear God's voice and not die, why do they fear to die?

5:25 "Why should we die . . . we shall die." The verse is framed by the word "die" (*mwt*). This has the effect of stressing the people's fear of dying.

5:29 "If only they had such a mind . . ." The expression *mî yittēn*, literally, "who will give," used conventionally in the sense of "would that . . ." sounds strange coming from YHWH, who does not have to rely on any higher power to fulfill his wishes.

Deuteronomy 6

Exposition of the First Commandment (6:1-25)

6:16 (Do not test as at Massah.) Word play on the word *nsh*, "to put to the test" and the place name Massah (taken to be from the same root) forms an *inclusio* as well as a play on words.

Deuteronomy 7

Destruction of the Canaanites (7:1-11)

Repetition of the root *ḥrm* ("destroy," 7:2, 26) and the common subject matter (destruction of the Canaanites) both at the beginning (7:1-6) and end of the chapter (7:17-26) forms an *inclusio* that binds the whole together (Hall 1998, 96). This *inclusio* frames two discourses (7:7-11, 12-16) on the love of YHWH for the people. Deut 7:7-11 recalls YHWH's great act of love in the past—the Exodus, while 7:12-16 looks to the blessings to come in the future once the people are settled in the land. The framing device links the two themes: driving out the Canaanites and obliterating their cult will be both a sign of YHWH's love (Hall 1998, 97) and an act of obedience on the part of Israel.

Hall (1998, 97) proposes the following structure for chapter 7:

A Destroy the Canaanites from the land (7:1-6)

  B God chose you because of his promise to the fathers, so obey the law (7:7-11)

  B' When you obey, God will keep the promise to the fathers and bless you (7:12-16)

A God will destroy the Canaanites from before you (7:17-26).

7:3 "Do not intermarry" literally "become each other's in-laws." Marriages in this society are not only between individuals but also between families. Intermarriage with Canaanites would involve the whole family in the possible pollution of idol worship.

7:4 "From following me . . ." Here is another case where Moses' speech melds into YHWH's, only to be followed by YHWH referring to himself in the third person (see Driver 1901, 99; Thompson 1974, 81).

7:7 "Fewest of all peoples." One may contrast this statement with those in which the number of Israelites is compared to the stars of heaven (1:10; 10:22) or in which the people are described as "a great nation" (4:6; 26:5) or in which others fear them because of their numbers (Num 22:3-4) or can only perceive a part of them due to their vastness (Num 23:13).

7:10 Repetition of the verb *šlm* forms an *inclusio* that frames this verse, reinforcing the point that YHWH repays rejection.

Rewards for Obedience (7:12-26)

7:12–8:20 This section focuses on memory and forgetfulness (Christensen 1991, 179).

7:13 "Issue of your flock." The Hebrew word for "issue" here is unusual and apparently related to the goddess Ashtoreth (Driver 1901, 103). Perhaps the implication is that fertility is not to be sought in the worship of the Canaanite gods but only in the worship of YHWH—who alone can grant increase.

7:13 "The fruit of your womb." The "your" here is masculine.

7:17 "If you say to yourself, 'These nations are more numerous than I . . .'" Again, the problem of the people's fear of their adversaries arises—this time as regards numbers.

7:22 (YHWH will clear away the nations little by little.) An explanation of why the extermination of the inhabitants will not be immediate. One may wonder why such a rationalization was thought necessary.

7:23 (YHWH will throw the Canaanites into a great panic.) *hāmām mᵉhûmâ gᵉdôlâ,* "panic them a great panic." The use of cognate accusative (a verb and its object taken from the same root) reinforces the image.

7:24 (You will blot out the names of kings.) Since acquired honor is conceived of as a limited good, causing the kings' names to perish implies a gain in Israel's honor at the expense of the defeated kings.

Deuteronomy 8

Divine Providence in the Wilderness (8:2-4)

8:1-20 O'Connell (1990, 437), following Lohfink (1965, 76) has proposed the following chiastic structure:

1	A-Exhortation
2-6	B-Wilderness
7-10	C-Arable Land
11	D-Exhortation
12-13	C'-Arable Land
14-17	B'-Wilderness
18-20	A'-Exhortation

Hall (1998, 90) proposes a more detailed analysis of the chiastic structure:

1	A Keep the commandments so you can possess the land the Lord swore to your (pl.) fathers
2-3	B Remember what God did for you—testing, humbling, feeding, manna
4	C You were sustained in the wilderness
5	D Know in your heart God disciplines you
6	E Therefore, keep the commandments
7-9	F The good gifts of the land
10	G When you have eaten and are satisfied
11	E' Beware lest you forget God and do not keep his commandments
12	G' Lest when you have eaten and are satisfied
13	F' The good gifts of the land
14	D' Don't let your heart become proud and forget
15	C' You were sustained in the wilderness
16-17	B' God fed you manna in the wilderness to humble and test you
18	A' Remember God who swore to your fathers
19-20	D' If you forget you shall surely perish

Hall maintains that E' is displaced for emphasis and that D' is placed outside the chiasmus, also for emphasis. In other words, he supposes that the hearers would have been attuned to the chiastic structure and impacted when it was rearranged.

8:2-6 García López (1981, 50) points out the following elements of chiastic structure:

2 A *derek ʾăšer hōlîkăkā*

B *lādaʿat ʾet-ʾăšer bᵊlibbᵊkā . . .*

hătišmōr miṣwōtō

3 C *lōʾ . . . wᵊlōʾ*

lᵊmaʿan hôdīᵃʿkā . . . lōʾ . . . yiḥyeh hāʿādām

kî ʿal-kol-môṣāʾ pî-yhwh yiḥyeh hāʾādām

4 *lōʾ . . . lōʾ*

5-6a B' *wᵊyādaʿtā ʿim-lᵊbābekā . . .*

wᵊšāmartā ʾet-miṣwōt . . .

6b A' *lāleket bidrākāyw*

2 A the way by which he caused you to walk

B to know what was in your heart . . .

whether you would observe his commandments

3 C not . . . and not

so as to make you know . . . not . . . lives one

but on all that comes from mouth of YHWH . . . lives one

4 not . . . not

5-6a B' know in your heart

observe the commandments

6b A' to walk in his ways

The common elements in A and A' are also arranged chiastically: *drk hlk/hlk drk* (way walk/walk way).

The Temptation to Self-sufficiency (8:6-20)

8:7 "Underground waters"(*təhōmōt,* sometimes associated by commentators with the Tiamat of Mesopotamian mythology, especially the *Enuma Elish;* Driver 1901, 109). The same word occurs in Gen 1:2; 7:11; 8:2; but see also 49:25. The forces of chaos will not manifest themselves in flood but in the temptation to self-sufficiency.

8:16 "Israel is represented as an individual . . . whose training in early life has been severe for the purpose of fitting him better for the position which he has to fill in riper years" (Driver 1901, 110).

8:19 This verse begins and ends with an infinitive absolute plus a finite form; both reinforce the words "forget" and "perish," and associate them closely together.

Deuteronomy 9

Success not Merited (9:1-6)

9:2 "Who can stand up to the Anakim?" This seems to be a proverbial rhetorical question, but, ironically, it will be shown to have an answer—YHWH will enable Israel to stand up to them.

The Golden Calf (9:7-29)

9:7 "Remember and do not forget." The twofold, positive/negative formulation adds punch to the saying.

9:7 "You have been rebellious . . ." In the previous verse Moses has called the people "stiff-necked." Now he illustrates this by citing cases (Thompson 1974, 139).

9:12 "The people you brought out of Egypt." It is YHWH who brought them out but here YHWH speaks as if to distance himself from that action (Mayes 1981, 199).

9:13 The characterization of the people as stiff-necked was made by Moses in verse 6 but is now even more authoritatively made by YHWH (Christensen 1991, 190).

9:16 "Then I saw that you had indeed sinned . . ." Moses' perception now corresponds to YHWH's in verse 12. Moses' use of YHWH's very words from verse 12 confirms the accuracy of YHWH's prediction.

9:17 (Moses smashes the tablets.) Moses spells out his actions in detail, thereby slowing the pace of the narrative—something like the effect of slow motion in film. Archaeological discoveries of Ancient Near Eastern treaty texts confirm that his gesture means that the covenant has been broken (Mayes 1981, 200).

9:17 "Before your eyes" *(lᵊʿênêkem).* Appeal is made to the people's perception. But, in fact, the people being addressed (the new generation) had not been eyewitnesses to these events. This is a rhetorical device directed at the reader of whatever time.

9:18 "Then I lay prostrate before the Lord . . ." The order of events as narrated here is not the same as in Exodus 32. Moses' first intercession (Exod 32:11-14) is passed over (Driver 1901, 114–15). Logically, smashing the calf ought to come before Moses' intercession.

9:19 "That time also." Note the rhetorical force of the *gam happaʿam hahīʾ*.

9:21 "Then I took the sinful thing you had made, the calf, and burned it with fire and crushed it, grinding it thoroughly, until it was reduced to dust; and I threw the dust of it into the stream that runs down the mountain." In Exod 32:20 Moses grinds the calf into dust and sprinkles the dust on water which he makes the people drink. This suggests an ordeal—something similar to that of the suspected adulteress in Num 5:16-28. But in the Deuteronomic version of the story the drinking is dropped and more ways of destroying the calf are added—ways that could not all be applied to one and the same object. This would seem to indicate that the list of destructive measures is rhetorical rather than realistic. Begg (1985, 229) points to similar lists of impossible destructive processes in "a number of ANE texts." This opens up the possibility that Deuteronomy has changed what was an ordeal into either an enacted *rîb* (suit for breach of covenant) or a rite of purification—i.e., the defiling object is carried away by the water of a running stream, in a way similar to the expiation for an unsolved homicide (Deut 21:1-9; Mayes 1981, 201).

9:24 Driver (1901, 116) observes that this verse repeats verse 7 but with sharper reproach:

> 7: you have been rebellious against the LORD from the day you came out of the land of Egypt until you came to this place.
>
> 24: You have been rebellious against the LORD as long as he has known you.

9:24 "As long as he has known you." The Hebrew here has "I knew," which is followed by some modern translations. The reading "he knew" follows the LXX and Samaritan versions and assumes that the words do not fit on the lips of Moses (Mayes 1981, 202). Is this another example of the melding of voices?

9:25-29 The wording here does not correspond to the parallel passage in Exod 34:9 but instead echoes the words of Moses' intercession on other occasions (Exod 32:11-13; also some of Num 14:16; Driver 1901, 116). Moses' prayer is framed by repetition of the phrase "Your people, your possession" *(ʿammᵊkā wᵊnaḥălātᵊkā)* (Christensen 1991, 189). The reader may note the layers of quotes within quotes. Here "the narrator is quoting Moses who, in the valley of Beth-Peor, is quoting what he (Moses) had said at Horeb to the effect that he had prayed that the Egyptians would not say 'such and such' at some time subsequent to the events at Horeb" (Polzin 1993, 363).

9:28 "What will the Egyptians say?" Moses appeals to YHWH's sense of the honor that YHWH has acquired as a good patron.

9-10 Mayes (1981, 195), following Lohfink (1963, 207 ff.), divides these two chapters into five sections, each beginning with a reference to forty days and nights.

9:9-10	covenant making
9:11-17	covenant breaking
9:18-21	atonement for breach of covenant
9:25–10:5	renewal of covenant
10:10-11	consequences of renewal

Deuteronomy 10

Moses' Second Ascent of Horeb (10:1-11)

10:1 (Moses is ordered to put the stone tablets in an ark of wood.) Mayes (1981, 203–204) thinks that the aim of Deuteronomy here is to counter a more elaborate notion of the ark as a platform for the invisible YHWH. Rather than see it as the footstool of the invisible deity, Deuteronomy reduces it to a coffer to hold the commandments.

10:1-3 The order of the command (tablets-ark) is reversed in the execution (ark-tablets), thus forming a chiastic arrangement.

10:1-5 As a result of Moses' intercession the people are restored to YHWH's favor (Driver 1901, 117) and the tension that arose over the threat to destroy them is resolved.

10:4 "Then he wrote on the tablets the same words as before . . ." Whereas in Exod 34:28 Moses is the one who writes the second copy of the Decalogue, our present text has God do it, as in Exod 24:12; 31:18 (Mayes 1981, 205).

10:9 "Levi has no allotment or inheritance with his kindred." What was said of Aaron in Num 18:20 is here extended to the Levites.

10:11 "Get up and go on your journey . . ." The key moment when the people break camp and leave Sinai, which is narrated in such detail in Numbers 10, is here summarized in a single verse.

What YHWH Requires (10:12-22)

10:12 "So now, . . ." *(wᵊʿattâ)* signals the statement of the conclusion that the speaker wants his audience to draw from the preceding narration. Repetition of *wᵊʿattâ* in verses 12 and 22 frames the passage (Christensen 1991, 205).

10:16 This key verse in the exhortation is highlighted by a chiastic structure:

circumcise	foreskin of	your heart and	
		your neck	do not stiffen.

10:17 (YHWH does not take sides in judgment.) The great Lord cannot be bribed. The implication is that human judges can be, especially in cases against the weak in society.

10:22 The reference to descendants as numerous as the stars recalls the promise to Abraham in Gen 15:5 and 22:17, and to Isaac in Gen 26:4. Because they can see for themselves that God has fulfilled the promise to Abraham and Isaac, the people ought to have confidence in God's ability to fulfill the rest of the covenant commitments to them.

Deuteronomy 11

Recall the Exodus (11:1-9)

11:6-7 Recounting the punishment of those who revolted despite having seen God's deeds with their own eyes implicitly warns the hearers that they, too, will be punished for any similar revolt. One may wonder why Korah (Num 16:35-50) is not mentioned here (Driver 1901, 128).

YHWH Gives Rain (11:10-17)

11:10 (A land irrigated by foot). Most authors think of some kind of mechanical device used to convey water from the Nile river, but one author, taking "foot" to be a euphemism, has suggested that the narrator intends to show contempt for Egypt by portraying the Egyptians as watering their gardens with urine (Eslinger 1987).

11:13 "If you will only heed his every commandment that I am commanding you . . ." The Hebrew has here: ". . . my commandments that I am commanding you." The NRSV here follows a variant found in the Septuagint (though one Greek manuscript reads "my"). If the Hebrew were followed, this would be another example of the melding of the voice of YHWH into the voice of Moses. It is now YHWH who is speaking even though there has been no indication of change of speaker (compare verse 8 above) and the text will go on to speak of YHWH in the third person (see note on 1:8).

11:14 "Then he will give . . ." Confusion as to the identity of the speaker continues. The Hebrew here has first person "I will give," in which case the speaker is clearly YHWH, since Moses cannot make it rain. The NRSV here follows the Samaritan and the Greek versions.

Promised Reward (11:18-25)

Choose Blessing or Curse (11:26-32)

11:28 "Gods that you have not known." What is the implication of the statement that the people have not *known* the other gods that they might follow? Sometimes in the Bible, knowledge refers not to intellectual knowledge but to experience. Does our present verse refer to the *experience* of the Exodus, i.e., that Israel has experienced salvation from no other god? This point will be made in the poem at the end of our book: no other god was with YHWH when YHWH delivered Israel.

11:30 "Some distance to the west . . ." More literally, "after the way of the setting of the sun." Why such an extended (poetic) way of saying "west"? Is there more to this choice of expression? Two of the words (*ʾaḥărê* and *derek*) echo what has come just before about abandoning the *way* that has been commanded and going *after* other gods.

Deuteronomy 12

Lundbom (1996, 307) proposes the following rhetorical structure for chapter 12:

These . . . *statutes and ordinances* . . . *you shall be careful to do* (12:1)

  Beware of *other gods* (12:2-3)

    Instructions on tithes and offerings (12:4-14)

    Instructions on clean and unclean food (12:15-28)

  Beware of *other gods* (12:29-31)

Every word that I command you *you shall be careful to do* (13:1 [12:32]).

The One Sanctuary (12:1-14)

12:1 "These are the statutes . . ." This verse is the superscription to chapters 12–26 (Driver 1901, 138).

12:2 (Canaanite cult sites to be obliterated.) The implied question here is where YHWH ought to be worshiped and, if this is not at existing cult places, what to do with them. The demand made to destroy the Canaanite sites is repeated from chapter 7 (Lohfink 1995, 112).

12:12 "The Levite who resides in your towns" (Heb: within your gates). The use of this expression (45x, most often with the suffix meaning "your") is characteristic of Deuteronomy (Driver 1901, 144).

Non-Sacrificial Slaughter (12:15-28)

12:15 "You may slaughter and eat meat within any of your towns . . ." This instruction responds to the (unstated) question, "How can those who are too far away from the one place of sacrifice eat meat?" The answer is non-sacrificial slaughter.

12:20-28 This repeats vv. 15-16 while adding more explanation (Driver 1901, 147).

12:22 This verse is framed by an *inclusio* formed by the repetition of *ʾkl*.

12:23-25 These verses repeat v. 16 while adding basis and motives (Driver 1901, 148).

12:25 A third repetition for emphasis (Driver 1901, 149).

How Did the Canaanites Worship? Don't Ask (12:29-31)

Deuteronomy 13

Warnings Against Being Led into Idolatry

"The sermon is polemical, putting into the mouths of individuals words they would not likely say: 'Let us go after other gods and serve them, which you (and your fathers) have not known'" (Lundbom 1996, 307).

False Prophet (13:1-5)

Kin (13:6-11)

13:7 *ʾēšet ḥêqekâ* This colorful expression means "the wife of your bosom."

A City (13:12-19)

13:18 [NRSV: 13:17] "So that the Lord may turn from his fierce anger." Patrick (1995, 425) sees the motive clause of this verse as bringing out the thinking behind all cases involving the *môt yûmat* ("be put to death") penalty. "The major offenses threaten to involve the whole community in guilt and only quick and thorough purgation will avert communal judgment."

Deuteronomy 14

Mourning (14:1-3)

14:1 "You must not shave your forelocks" Heb: "You shall not put baldness between your eyes." Instead of having baldness between one's eyes, one should have the Torah (6:8; 11:18).

Diet (14:4-20)

14:13 The use of *mîn* "kind" here recalls the creation account (Gen 1:11, 12, 21, 24, 25), thereby indicating that the dietary laws are seen as part of the structure of the cosmos. God's ordering of the world through separation includes Israel's separation from the nations and Israel's separation of the clean from the unclean.

Tithes (14:22-29)

Deuteronomy 15

Hamilton (1995, 31–4) points out that the author's choice of words here is highly evocative, "The three primary somatic or body terms used in this passage to arrest the attention of the audience are *yād* (hand), *lēbāb* (heart, soul, etc.) and *ʿayin* (eye)." Hand connotes power. The hand is shut or opened to one's poor kin. "The word 'hand' is used to cover all the actions of the one to whom the *šᵉmiṭṭâ* -year law is addressed . . . . The use of the verb *ʾmṣ* (to harden) with *lēbāb* is particularly noteworthy . . . for the powerful to harden their hearts against the poor is for them to find themselves in the same camp with Sihon, who was given over for conquest." One's eye must not be evil (Hamilton 1992, 31–4).

The Year of Release (15:1-11)

15:2-3 Hamilton (1992, 17) proposes the following chiastic structure:

A-remit *šmṭ*

B-the claim *maššēh yādô*

C-not exact *lōʾ yiggōś*

D-neighbor/kin *rēaʿ/ʾaḥ*

E-for one has called a remission by YHWH *qrʾ šᵊmiṭṭâ*

D'-foreigner *nokrî*

C'-may exact *tiggōś*

B'-what is yours *wᵊʾăšer yihyeh lᵊkā*

A'-remit *tašmēṭ yādekā*

The balance is upset by the occurrence of *yad* in B and A' and of *ʾaḥ* in D and A'.

15:3 "Any member of your community" Heb: "brother" (7x in this chapter). The obligation toward one's "brothers" is emphasized by the contrasting lack of obligation to foreigners and other nations (Hamilton 1992, 37–8).

15:11 "I therefore command you . . ." Who is the speaker here?

15:12 Hamilton observes:

> As with the pairing of *ʾāḥ* and *rē(a)ʿ* in the *šĕmiṭṭāh*-year law, *ʾāḥ* is paired with another term [*ʿibrî* "Hebrew" which connotes the experience of being slaves in Egypt] in the manumission law. The second term spells out the identity of the one who sells self into slavery. It underscores the emotional tie to the audience which that term is meant to evoke. (Hamilton 1992, 38).

Slaves (15:12-18)

15:12-18 Tsevat (1994, 594–5) thinks that five laws designed to protect the unfortunate have been gathered together between 14:22 and 15:18. These laws move from the least to the most miserable in society. 15:12-18 is the last of these laws and covers the most wretched persons in society—slaves. The five laws are bound together by seven references to God's blessings in the past, present and future, which constitute the motivation for kindness towards the downtrodden. The release of slaves is in imitation of what God did for Israel in the Exodus (Hamilton 1992, 39-40). The giving of gifts takes the Deuteronomic legislation a step beyond Exod 21:1-11.

Sacrifice of Firstlings (15:19-23)

Deuteronomy 16

The Liturgical Calendar

Passover (16:1-8)

16:4 "No leaven shall be seen . . ." The command is rather intense: not only shall leaven not be eaten, it shall not even be seen, and not just within the house, but in the whole territory.

16:6 "In the evening at sunset," i.e., at the time of day when you left Egypt.

Weeks (16:9-12)

16:9 In the Hebrew, this verse is arranged chiastically:

šibʿâ šābūʿôt tispor-lāk

lispōr šibʿâ šābūʿôt

seven weeks to count

to count seven weeks

Booths (16:13-15)

Administration of Justice (16:18-20)

16:18 This verse is framed by the *inclusio špṭ-mišpāṭ,* "judge"-"judgment."

16:19 In verse 18 above, an individual (thou) is addressed and told to set up judges. This verse continues the direct address but (without notice) shifts the addressee from the person setting up the judges to the judge himself (Patrick 1995, 428).

16:19 "You must not show partiality" Heb: *lōʾ takkîr pānîm* "you shall not recognize faces."

Pagan Poles and Pillars (16:21-22)

16:21 "You shall not plant any tree as a sacred pole . . ." Based on the placement of this prohibition, one may wonder whether, in the minds of the Israelites, there is a logical connection between perverting justice and planting an asherah?

Deuteronomy 17

17:3 Are the words "which I have forbidden" spoken by Moses, or do they represent a sudden change to the divine first person? If the latter, then YHWH would be speaking very personally here (Driver 1901, 206; Thompson 1974, 81). This may be another case of the melding of voices.

The High Court (17:8-13)

17:4 "You make a thorough inquiry." In this translation, "thorough" seems to represent Hebrew *hêṭēb* (roughly, "do good") used adverbially. This forms a balancing contrast with *ʿśh ʾet-hāraʿ* ("do evil") in verse 2.

The Law of the King (17:14-20)

Deuteronomy 18

Rights of Levites (18:1-8)

Prohibition of Magic (18:9-14)

18:9 The close similarity in language between this verse and 17:14 (the establishment of the monarchy; Lohfink 1995, 113, n. 12) may indicate that the speaker (Moses) wants to draw a parallel between the establishment of the monarchy and the imitation of the abhorrent practices of the nations.

The Prophet Like Moses (18:15-22)

18:15 "The Lord will raise up for you a prophet like me." Driver (1901, 227) suggests that the purpose of the prophet was to substitute for the forbidden diviners mentioned earlier in the chapter. Hence, "you shall heed such a prophet" implies "and not diviners, soothsayers, etc., as your neighbors do."

18:20 This verse features an *inclusio* formed by repetition of *nābîʾ*.

Deuteronomy 19

Cities of Refuge (19:1-13)

19:7 "Therefore I command you . . ." Who is the speaker?

Boundary Markers (19:14)

19:14 "You must not move your neighbor's boundary marker, set up by former generations . . ." The temporal viewpoint here is some time after the settlement. The "former generations" *(rīʾšōnîm)* surely does not refer to the Canaanites (Driver 1901, 235).

19:15 Repetition of the verb *qwm* frames this verse in an *inclusio.*

Witnesses (19:15-21)

Deuteronomy 20

Holy War (20:1-20)

Non-Palestinian Cities (20:10-15)

20:15 "Thus you shall treat all the towns that are very far from you . . ." Only now is the information given that the rules given thus far only apply to cities outside the promised land.

Palestinian Cities (20:16-18)

Treatment of Fruit Trees in Time of Siege (20:19-20)

20:19 This verse is framed by the *inclusio tāṣûr-māṣôr*.

Deuteronomy 21

Unsolved Homicide (21:1-9)

21:1-9 Wright (1987, 403) calls this text, "A rite of elimination: the killing of the cow is a reenactment of the murder which removes impurity of bloodguilt to a place where it will not threaten the community and its concerns; the flowing wadi further removes the evil to distant bodies of water."

Marriage with a Female Captive (21:10-14)

21:10-14 Since marriages with Canaanite women are outlawed in 7:3, what seems to be envisioned here is warfare with surrounding nations after settlement in the land (Driver 1901, 244).

Inheritance (21:15-17)

21:17 The *inclusio bᵊkōr-bᵊkōrâ* sets this verse off.

The Rebellious Son (21:18-21)

21:18-21 (The Incorrigible Son.) Bellefontaine (1979) suggests that this prescription is aimed at Israel as a whole. Deuteronomy often uses the father-son image to portray the relationship between YHWH and Israel (1:31; 8:5; 14:1). Just as the unruly son is accused of being a glutton and a drunkard, Israel in the desert sinned with regard to food (Exod 16; Num 11; Deut 8:3, 16) and drink (Exod 17:1-7; Num 20:2-13; Deut 8:15). Eating and drinking also accompanied idol worship (Exod 32, especially v. 6; Deut 9:8-21). Just as the rebellious son is put to death and serves as a warning to others, so the rebellious generation died in the desert to serve as a warning to future generations (Deut 1:31-40).

21:19-20 Hebrew: ". . . to the elders of his city and to the gate of his place. And they shall say to the elders of his city . . ." Notice that the suffixes refer not to the parents ("their city, their place") but to the son: his place, his city. Stulman (1990, 630) sees the author's purpose as conveying power to city elders in a reformed [post-exilic] society.

Burial of a Person Who Has Been Executed (21:22-23)

Deuteronomy 22

Stray Animals (22:1-3)

Fallen Animals (22:4)

Cross Dressing (22:5)

Bird's Nest (22:6-7)

Parapet on House (22:8)

Forbidden Mixtures

Seed (22:9)

Ox and Donkey Yoked Together (22:10)

Wool and Linen Woven Together (22:11)

Tassels (22:12)

Sexual Morality (22:13-29)

22:13-29 Wenham and McConville (1980) call attention to structural elements that tie these verses together: 1. each is made up of the same five elements (below); 2. the cases are arranged in logical order; 3. the six punishments are arranged in chiastic order; and 4. the six cases are arranged in two groups of three each—a triadic division that is used in both Leviticus and Deuteronomy.

The five elements that make up each case are:

1. the woman's marital status
2. circumstances
3. specification of the evidence required for the case
4. what punishment is appropriate to the circumstances
5. a comment explaining the purpose of the punishment

Logical order: Three cases deal with married women (vv. 13-22); three with unmarried girls (23-29).

		married	*unmarried*
case introduced by	*kî*	(vv. 13,	23)
sub-case introduced by	*wᵊʾim*	(vv. 20,	25)
case introduced by	*kî*	(vv. 22,	28)

Chiastic ordering of punishments:

19	A	damages of one hundred shekels to father, no divorce
21	B	woman executed
22	C	man and woman executed
24	C^1	man and woman executed
25	B^1	man executed
29	A^1	damages of fifty shekels to father, no divorce

"The combination of parallel paneling and chiasmus give this section a notable coherence and compactness suggestive of careful drafting" (250).

The Tokens of Virginity (22:13-21)

22:15 (Parents bring out tokens of their daughter's virginity to the city elders.) The solution presupposes an earlier narrative in which the tokens of virginity were created and then handed over to the parents. That being the case, how could the husband be so foolish as to accuse his wife when he knew that her father could produce proof of her virginity? But the text also presupposes a narrative of the alienation of the husband from his wife.

22:17 "I did not find evidence of your daughter's virginity." Here the father represents the husband's allegation as directed at himself (not at his daughter).

Adultery (22:22)

Rape (22:23-29)

22:28 This verse is framed by repetition of the verb *mṣʾ* "find."

Deuteronomy 23

Exclusion from the Assembly (23:1-8)

More on Holy War (23:9-14)

Miscellaneous Laws (23:15-25)

23:20 "You shall not charge interest on loans . . ." The colorful word translated "interest" *nšk* literally means "bite." The appearance of this word both at the beginning and end of this verse forms an *inclusio.*

Deuteronomy 24

Marriage (24:1-5)

24:5 This verse is framed by repetition of *lqḥ* "take."

Justice and Charity (24:6-22)

24:6 The repetition of the root *ḥbl* "to take in pledge" frames this verse in an *inclusio.*

24:11 This verse is framed by the word *ḥwṣ* "outside."

24:16 This verse features an *inclusio* using the word *mwt* "die." Yaron (1986, 158) points out what he calls "a climactic tricolon 'not A, nor B, but C'":

> Parents shall not be put to death for their children,
> nor shall children be put to death for their parents;
> only for their own crimes may persons be put to death.

Deuteronomy 25

Flogging (25:1-3)

25:2 "If the one in the wrong deserves to be flogged . . ." more colorfully in Hebrew: "If the wicked person is a son of beating."

Don't Muzzle the Ox (25:4)

25:4-12 Eslinger (1984, 222–23) proposes a chiastic structure for 25:4-12

4	A	*lōʾ taḥsōm*	you shall not muzzle
5	B	*yaḥdāw . . . ʾēšet*	together . . . wife
6	C	*šəmô miyyiśrāʾēl*	his name from Israel
7-8	D	*yébimtô . . . hazzəqēnîm*	brother's widow . . . elders
9	D'	*yəbimtô . . . hazzəqēnîm*	brother's widow . . . elders
10	C'	*šəmô bəyiśrāʾēl*	his name in Israel
11	B'	*yaḥdāw . . . ʾēšet*	together . . . wife
12	A'	*lōʾ tāḥôs*	you shall not pity

Levirate Marriage (25:5-10)

25:7-8 Eslinger (1984, 226 n. 6) further proposes a smaller chiastic structure in 25:7-8:

7 A *lōᶜ yaḥpōṣ . . . lāqaḥat* he has no desire . . . to take

B *hazzᵊqēnîm* the elders

C *mēʾēn yᵊbāmî* my husband's brother refuses

C' *lōʾ ʾābâ yabbᵊmî* my husband's brother not willing

8 B' *ziqnê* the elders

A' *lōʾ ḥāpaṣtî lᵊqaḥtāh* I have no desire to take her

25:5-10 The law of levirate marriage is dramatized by the speeches of the characters involved as well as by the tension created by the brother's refusal and the attempt made by the city elders to persuade him to change his mind.

25:9 (Widow removes brother-in-law's sandal, spits in his face, says . . .) After reviewing four interpretations of the rite of removing the sandal (by a widow), Kruger (1996) interprets the gesture as a rite of passage which dissolves the marriage bond between the widow and her brother-in-law (which is automatic upon the death of the husband). This, however, does not explain the spitting. Wilson suggests that the purpose is to induce shame. The re-naming amounts to a public humiliation.

Wife Grabs Husband's Assailant by His Genitals (25:11-12)

Honest Weights and Measures (25:13-16)

Amalek (25:17-19)

25:18 "Struck down all who lagged behind" *(wayzannēb)* literally, cut off the tail.

Deuteronomy 26

First Fruits (26:1-11)

26:5 "A wandering Aramean was my ancestor . . ." *ʾbd* here can be understood either as "wandering," as in NRSV, or as "perishing" (Janzen 1994). The latter interpretation would fit with the tradition expressed in 32:10 q.v.

Tithes (26:12-15)

26:13-15 Of particular interest in this speech, which is prescribed for "thou" to recite, is the so-called "negative confession" in verses 13b and 14a.

Exhortation (26:16-19)

26:19 "Set you high." "High" here = *ʿelyôn*, "uppermost."

Deuteronomy 27

Future Ceremony at Shechem (27:1-26)

27:8 "You shall write . . . very clearly." The rare word *bʾr* is used here and in 1:5. Moses makes the law clearly perceptible either by explaining it or by carving it on stone tablets (Miller 1993, 303).

Deuteronomy 28

Blessings (28:1-14)

28:2 The blessings are almost personified as pursuing and overtaking the people (Driver 1901, 304). The word *nśg* has been used previously (19:6) in reference to the avenger of blood pursuing the manslayer and so forms a powerful contrast: being overtaken by blessings and not by someone who is out to kill one.

28:12 "The Lord will open for you his rich storehouse . . ." The limited good that is available will not be withheld from Israel. The language here recalls the Joseph story (Gen 41:33-36, 48-49, 54-57) in which Joseph stored the grain of bountiful years and rationed it in time of famine.

Curses (28:15-68)

28:15 The image of being pursued and overtaken, use of the blessings in 28:2 above is here reversed. The unfaithful people are overtaken by curses as by enemies.

28:20 The expression "until you are destroyed" is repeated "with knell-like effect" (Driver 1901, 307) in vv. 24, 45, 51, and 61. It reverses the "until they [Israel's enemies] are destroyed" of 7:23 (see also 7:24). The expression "because of your evildoing in forsaking me" seems to fit better on the lips of YHWH than of Moses—another melding of voices?

28:23 The failure of rain and crops is conveyed by the image of the sky turning to bronze and the earth to iron.

28:25 Reverses the blessing of v. 7 (Driver 1901, 308) and then goes on to make it worse for Israel.

28:29 Another powerful image, with people having to grope as if in darkness even at high noon.

28:37 (Israel will become a byword among the nations.) "Byword" *(šᵊnînâ)* comes from the word for "tooth"—they will lose all honor and become the object of biting remarks. The verse is framed by repetition of *šammâ*.

28:40 An *inclusio* is formed by the word *zyt*.

28:43-44 The ascent of the aliens is the reversal of the imagery in vv. 12b-13a.

28:50b A chiastic structure reinforces the gravity of the breakdown of even the most fundamental social structures:

lōʾ-yiśśāʾ pānîm	*lᵊzāqēn*	
	wᵊnaʿar	*lōʾ yāḥōn*
not respect	elder	
	youth	not favor

28:54 "Will begrudge food" Hebrew: "His eye will be evil." Similarly in verse 56 below and earlier in 15:9.

28:55 ". . . Giving to none . . . the flesh of his children whom he is eating." Powerful image of the horrors of the siege: a man so desperately hungry that he eats his own children. Instead he should be eating all the good things mentioned in the blessings.

28:59 ". . . Severe and lasting afflictions and grievous and lasting maladies." The word here rendered "lasting" *(neʾĕmān)* carries with it a great deal of irony. It is the same word that elsewhere means "faithful" or "dependable." The only other instance of this form of this verb (*ʾmn*

Niphal) in Deuteronomy comes at 7:9: the people must know that YHWH is the *faithful* God who maintains covenant loyalty with those who love him and keep his commandments. Another form of the same verb (Hiphil) occurs twice in reference to the people's lack of trust in YHWH (1:32; 9:23). The implication is that because the people have failed to regard YHWH as dependable, they can depend on suffering afflictions and maladies.

28:60 "He will bring back upon you the diseases of Egypt . . ." In 7:15 God had promised the people (assuming their obedience) to remove the diseases of Egypt. Now these diseases will not only be brought back, but will *cling (dbq)* to the people (Driver 1901, 317) who failed in their duty to *cling* to YHWH (4:4; 10:20; 11:22; 13:4).

28:62 "As numerous as the stars in heaven . . . left few in number" a reference to the promise to the patriarchs (Gen 15:5; 22:17; 26:4), which is seen here as having once been fulfilled in the past but now cancelled out. Israel will return to the state of affairs when Jacob came down to Egypt (26:5 ". . . A wandering Aramean was my ancestor; he went down into Egypt and lived there as an alien, *few in number*" (Driver 1901, 317).

28:65 "The Lord will give you a trembling heart . . ." In 2:25 YHWH had promised to make peoples everywhere under heaven tremble in fear of Israel. Now it is Israel that will tremble. These are the only two instances of *rgz* in Deuteronomy and so are unquestionably meant to balance each other.

28:65 (Imagery: Failing eyes.) "The eyes are said to 'fail' when they long eagerly for something, especially if the longing be disappointed" (Driver 1901, 318). By way of example, Driver cites Jer 14:6 (the eyes of wild asses fail because there is no herbage); Job 11:20; 17:5; Lam 2:11; 4:17 ("Our eyes failed, ever waiting vainly for help . . ."); Ps 69:4; 119:123, and Deut 28:32.

28:66 The word *ḥyym* "life" frames this verse.

28:67 The horrors seen as a result of the curses contrast with all the good things that the people have *seen with their own eyes* (Deut 3:21; 4:9; 7:19; 10:21; 11:7; 29:2-3).

28:68 "YHWH will bring *thee* back to Egypt in ships." A plurality of ships would not be needed for an individual. It is clear that the "thee" here is collective.

"There will be no buyer," no one to acquire you. The use of *qōneh* here may play on a title used of God elsewhere in the Pentateuch (Gen 14:19,

22) which will appear in 32:6. The play is on the word *qōneh* which can mean both "maker" and "acquirer." Having been abandoned by their maker *(qōneh),* they will return to Egypt but not find anyone to acquire *(qōneh)* them there.

28:69 [NRSV: 29:1] This verse is taken to be a colophon in the Hebrew text and is treated as such in JB, NAB, and NJV. The Septuagint and Vulgate treat it as the first verse (superscription) of the following chapter, a division followed by NRSV, NEB, NIV and REB (Lundbom 1996, 313).

Deuteronomy 29

Moses' Third Address (29-30)

Exhortation

29:5 [NRSV: 6] "So that you may know that I am the Lord your God." The speaker here is supposed to be Moses (verse 1 [NRSV: 2]) but it is obvious that the voice has melded into that of YHWH. Moses' voice returns in the next verse ("We defeated them").

29:6 [NRSV: 7] "When you came . . . Sihon . . . came out against us . . ." There is a shift from "ye" to "we" and so it seems that the speaker is once again Moses.

29:10 [NRSV: 29:11] "The aliens," literally "*your* aliens" as also in 5:14; 24:14; 31:12 (Driver 1901, 322).

29:11 [NRSV: 29:12] "An oath, which the Lord . . . is making" Literally, cutting a curse. This is the only instance of this combination in the Hebrew Bible. Usually, the expression is "to cut a covenant" *(krt bryt).*

29:11 [NRSV: 29:12] "To enter into the covenant . . ." The use of *ʿbr* for entering into the covenant parallels the use of the same word in reference to crossing (the Jordan) to enter the promised land. But in view of the expression "cut a curse" used in this same verse, the "crossing" in question here may refer to passing through the halves of slaughtered animals (Gen 15:17; Jer 34:18). There may be some irony involved as well, since *ʿbr bryt* is used in 17:2 to refer to the transgression of the covenant.

29:13 [NRSV: 29:14] "I am making this covenant . . ." Who is the "I"? From the context, it would appear to be Moses. Is he speaking here in YHWH's name?

29:13-14 [NRSV: 29:14-15] The one who is not "here today" is the reader.

29:15-17 [NRSV: 29:16-18] These verses seem to explain the passage through other nations as an opportunity for the Israelites to see for themselves the idols of other peoples and so know what poisonous root to avoid.

29:18 [NRSV: 19] "Moist and dry," an example of merismus.

29:19 [NRSV: 29:20] The curses will descend on them. The use of *rbṣ* seems to conjure up the image of a predator crouching and then pouncing on its prey. The obliteration of Israel's name which Moses' intercession had dissuaded YHWH from carrying out in 9:14 will not be prevented now.

29:20 [NRSV: 29:21] Throughout Leviticus, Numbers, and Deuteronomy, one of the strongest characteristics of Israel (if not the chief characteristic) is supposed to be their separation (indicated by *hibdîl*) from other nations—a separation that parallels the act of creation. Now, with the greatest irony, the people are separated out not for God's favor but for calamity.

29:22 [NRSV: 29:23] "Unable to support any vegetation." The story of Sodom and Gomorrah is recalled, but also Gen 1:11-12 or perhaps 2:5 when there was as yet no herb *(ʿēśeb)* of the field. The destruction will return the land to its state before creation.

29:24 The drama of vv. 21-27 envisions a future time when nations inquire about a past destruction of the land (an event that is future in relation to the intradiegetic narrator and narratee).

29:26 [NRSV: 27] "Every curse written in this book." The words "this book" are strange on the lips of foreigners and represent an incursion of the author's point of view (Driver 1901, 329).

29:28 [NRSV: 29] This verse appears to be added comment from the extradiegetic narrator.

Deuteronomy 30

Future Repentance in Exile (30:1-10)

30:1 "The 'blessing' might be deemed not strictly appropriate in a context which contemplates entirely the case of the nation's disobedience: but it seems that the writer has in view Israel's future as a whole, which would not be throughout of a uniform character, but would present examples both of national obedience and of national apostasy" (Driver 1901, 328–29).

Knowledge of the Divine Will Is Within Reach (30:11-14)

The Two Ways (30:15-20)

30:15 "See, I have set before you today life and prosperity *(haṭṭôb)*, death and adversity *(hārāʿ)*." Compare 11:26-28 where the alternatives are blessing and curse. "You" here is singular.

30:20 "Holding fast to him." *dbq* means both to stick to and to hold on to. This is the last of five occurrences of this image in Deuteronomy.

Deuteronomy 31

Final Charge to Joshua and the People (31:1-8)

31:3 This verse is framed by repetition of the divine name YHWH.

31:1-8 Much of the language of these verses echoes chapters 1–3 (Driver 1901, 333) and thus forms a frame for the three discourses given by Moses.

31:3 "The Lord your God . . . The Lord promised." This verse is framed by the divine name YHWH (the first and last words of this verse in the Hebrew). There is a parallelism in the two similarly constructed statements:

yhwh ʾlhyk	*hwʾ ʿbr lpnyk*	and
yəhwšʿ	*hwʾ ʿbr lpnyk*	

YHWH your God,	he is crossing before you
Joshua	he is crossing before you

Provision for Covenant Renewal Ceremony (31:9-13)

Joshua Commissioned (31:14-15)

31:14 "Your time to die is near." There are echoes here of Gen 47:29.

Gen 47:29	*wayyiqrᵊbû*	*yᵊmê-yiśrāʾēl*	*lāmût*	*wayyiqrāʾ*
Deut 31:14	*qārᵊbû*	*yāmẹkā*	*lāmût*	*qᵊrāʾ*
	they approached,	the days for Israel	to die	and he called
	they approached,	your days	to die	call

The expression occurs only in these two places in the Pentateuch (Sonnet 1997, 205, whose chapter 6 points out many echoes of the patriarchal narratives in Deut 31–34). Sonnet refers to this phenomenon as *déjà lu.* As we will see from other examples below, the intention here is apparently to draw a parallel between the ancestors and Moses.

Moses Writes the Song (31:16-30)

31:16 "Soon you will lie down with your ancestors." This verse reminds one of Gen 47:30 (Sonnet 1997, 205).

Gen 47:30		*wᵉšākabtî*	*ʿim-ʾăbōtay*
Deut 31:16	*hinnẹkā*	*šōkēb*	*ʿim-ʾăbōtẹkā*
		lie	with ancestors

Aside from these two passages, this expression is only seen in 1 Kgs 14:20. The author's intention seems to be to draw a parallel between Moses and Joseph.

31:16-22 (YHWH tells Moses about the people's future unfaithfulness and punishment; tells him to write the song.) These verses serve to give a negative interpretation to the song (chapter 32), namely that it stands as a witness against the people—an interpretation that Mayes thinks does not fit 32:36-38 (Mayes 1981, 376).

31:18 There is word play here on *pānāh* (to face) and *pānîm* (face). God hides his face because the people face other gods.

31:19 "Write this song." Even though the command is addressed to Moses, the forms are plural *(kitbû lākem).*

31:23-24 "Then the Lord commissioned Joshua . . ." The identification of YHWH as speaker is not in the Hebrew and the last person mentioned is Moses. So, contextually, the speaker should be Moses. The Septuagint supplies "Moses," but modern versions either do not identify the speaker or supply the Lord as the speaker (Driver 1901, 342). This could be another example of the melding of voices that we have seen before. Why is the commissioning of Joshua mixed in with the story about the song? Both are oriented to the time when Moses will no longer be leading the people. The same can be said of the writing of the Torah scroll (Sonnet). It will also function as a witness against the people in a future without Moses.

31:24-30 Lundbom (1996, 300) observes that these verses are held together by a concentric arrangement of key words:

law	words	song
song	words	law

31:27 (If the people are rebellious while Moses lives, what will they be like when he dies?!) This picks up and reinforces a motif already introduced in 31:21 and will continue through verse 29.

31:27-29 Sonnet (1997, 168-9) lays out the many echoes to be found in these verses of Deuteronomy 9, where Moses retells the story of the Golden Calf.

31:29 There is an echo here of Gen 49:1 (Sonnet 1997, 206). This particular combination of words is unique to these two passages.

Gen 49:1	*yiqrāʾ*	*ʾetkem*		*bᵊʾaḥărît hayyāmîm*
Deut 31:29	*wᵊqārāʾt*	*ʾetkem*	*hārāʿâ*	*bᵊʾaḥărît hayyāmîm*
	what will befall	you		in later days
	there will befall	you	evil	in later days

31:29 "Provoking him to anger through the work of your hands." Sonnet (1997, 169) sees an ironic contrast between "the works of your hand" here and the same phrase used in 2:7 (NRSV: "Surely the Lord your God has blessed you in all your undertakings;" Heb: "the work of your hand").

Deuteronomy 32

The Song of Moses (32:1-43)

Mayes (1981, 380) sees the song as a *rîb* (a lawsuit for breach of covenant) consisting in the following parts:

1. vv 1-3 introduction, summoning of witnesses
2. 4-6 introductory statement of case

3. 7-14 prosecution speech, recalling YHWH's benefits
4. 15-18 indictment for apostasy
5. 19-25 judgment of guilt and threat of destruction

Nigosian (1996, 12) has pointed out the overlap and correlation of two different kinds of structure in the song:

> So far, two sorts of structure have been mainly considered: a generic pattern, that of the *Rîb* (invocation of witnesses, accusation, plaintiff's benefits to the accused, statement of breach of covenant, judgement), and a stylistic pattern, that of concentrically structural antithesis (e.g., election, protection, plenty reversed by famine, terror, annihilation). What has also been noted is that these patterns correlate: the hinge or pivot of the concentrically structured antithesis (stylistic pattern) is precisely the opening of the final element of the *Rîb:* judgement (generic pattern).

The fact that the song contains elements that cannot be explained as part of a *rîb* pattern led G. E. Wright to designate Deuteronomy 32 as "a broken *ribh*" (Geller 39).

32:1 "Give ear, O heavens . . . let the earth hear . . ." Calling heaven and earth to witness implies a covenant context.

32:10 "He found him" *(yimṣāʾēhû)* conjures up the image of some poor soul in the wild or of an exposed infant or abandoned child (Gen 21:16-17; Ezek 16:5-7; Hos 9:10). The menacing situation is highlighted both by the unusual expression "wilderness land" *(ʾereṣ midbār),* and by the description *ûbᵊtōhû yᵊlēl yᵊšīmōn* ("in a howling wilderness waste") in which *tōhû* supplies an element of primeval chaos and *yᵉlēl* (hapax) the wailing of helpless people or the howling of wild animals (Geller 1982, 51–2; Nigosian 1996, 17).

32:11 The appearance of *rḥp* "hover" in such close proximity to *tōhû* "waste" seems to indicate a deliberate evocation of the creation story in which the earth was formless *(tōhû)* and the wind/spirit of God hovered *(mᵉraḥepet)* over the waters (Gen 1:2). The rescue of Israel from the wilderness parallels the creation of the world.

32:11 (An eagle bears its young aloft on its pinions.) Just what image is implied here is the subject of much discussion, depending on what kind of bird it is (*nešer* = vulture or eagle), and whether we are dealing here with something that these birds actually do with their young or something that the ancients (without the benefit of binoculars) thought that the birds do. Neither vultures nor eagles take their young for rides on their wings.

32:12 Verse 12b restates negatively what has been said in 12a (Geller 1982, 50). Geller (1982, 55) also points to the ambiguity of *ʿimmô* "with him." It can mean both that no strange god assisted YHWH in rescuing the people and that Israel had not yet taken up the worship of any strange god (as it soon would).

32:15 Jeshurun from *yšr* meaning upright (American colloquial: "on the level"). "Designating the nation under its ideal character . . . as the *Upright one*" (Driver 1901, 360).

32:18 Just as, on the human level, a son would err grievously in not honoring his father and mother, so Israel has failed towards YHWH, who is here represented as both father and mother—"the Rock that engendered you; El who writhed in labor to deliver you *(mᵊḥōlᵊlekā)*" (Driver 1901, 363).

32:20 "I will hide my face from them . . ." YHWH is quoted speaking in the first person.

32:31 Nigosian (1996, 11) points up the difficulty of distinguishing voices here:

> It is clear that the poet is speaking in v. 31. Can the speeches of YHWH be delimited? YHWH begins to speak in v. 20, and his words run at least to v. 27, possibly to v. 30. . . . It seems that despite punctuating the text with the catchword "say" . . . the poet has made little effort to distinguish his words from the words of YHWH.

32:35 "Their foot shall slip." An image of reversal of fortune (Driver 1901, 374; Ps 38:17 [NRSV: 16]; 94:18).

32:38 "Let them [Israel's gods] rise up." The text plays on the fact that the Hebrew word for "God," *Elohim,* is plural in form even though it refers to one Being. But the same word can be (and is) used in reference to a plurality of non-Israelite gods. From the perspective of the nations, Israel's Elohim must be a plurality but the reader knows that that is not the case—or at least should not be.

32:39 "I am he." YHWH speaks in the first person.

32:40 The image of YHWH lifting his hand to heaven to swear an oath is engaging since there is no higher power to enforce the oath.

32:41 "My flashing sword" Hebrew: "the lightning of my sword."

32:43 "He will avenge the blood of his children." Here (and beginning as far back as 39) the topic seems to be YHWH's vengeance on those who destroy the people. NRSV here is a reconstruction based on the evidence of the Dead Sea Scrolls and the versions, which are quite different from the traditional Hebrew text at this point.

Exhortation (32:44-47)

32:44-47 The same concentric key-word structure,

law . . . words . . . song

song . . . words . . . law

that appeared in 31:24-30 recurs here (Lundbom 1996, 300).

YHWH Tells Moses to Ascend Mount Nebo (32:48-52)

32:50 "You shall die there . . ." Hebrew: "die" (imperative verb form). The command to die and to be gathered to one's kindred is striking.

Deuteronomy 33

The Blessing of Moses

33:1 Moses is qualified as "man of God" by the narrator.

33:2 "The Lord came from Sinai." The name YHWH occurs in the poem only at the beginning (v. 2), the divider (v. 21) and the end (v. 29) (Freedman 1980, 37–8), thus forming a structuring element. Here it is in emphatic position.

33:3 "In your charge (Heb: hand) . . . at your heels (Heb: feet)." "Hand" and "foot" are a linked word-pair—a kind of merismus meaning "in every way," "entirely" (Freedman 1980, 41).

33:7 "And this he said of Judah" Each blessing, except the first, is introduced by the voice of the narrator (Driver 1901, 386).

33:12 "Between his shoulders" plays on the use of "shoulders" to refer also to the sides of mountains (Driver 1901, 404).

33:13 "The deep that lies beneath." There is an echo here of Gen 49:25.

Gen 49:25	*tᵊhôm*	*rōbeṣet tāḥat*
Deut 33:13	*ûmittᵊhôm*	*rōbeṣet tāḥat*
	the deep	crouching beneath
and from	the deep	crouching beneath (Sonnet 1997, 213)

The intended effect of this and other echoes of the blessing of Jacob seems to be to draw a partial parallel between Moses and the patriarch.

33:14 "The fruits of the sun and the rich yield of the months." "Months" plays on the pairing of sun and moon (Driver 1901, 406). The word for "month" in Hebrew, as in English, is derived from the word for "moon."

33:15 This verse contains an echo of Gen 49:26 in the expression "everlasting hills *(gibʿôt ʿôlām),*" (Sonnet 1997, 213) which is only found in one other place in the Bible (Hab 3:6), it forms another parallel between Moses and Jacob.

33:16 "Who dwells on Sinai." This reading emends the Hebrew text. Most modern versions follow the MT (traditional Hebrew text) in reading "Who dwells in the bush"—an apparent reference to Exod 3:2-4.

33:16 The second half of this verse echoes Jacob's blessing of Joseph in Gen 49:26. The phrase *lᵊrōʾš yôsēp ûlᵊqodqōd nᵊzîr ʾeḥāyw* "on the head of Joseph, on the brow of him who was set apart from (Deuteronomy: the prince among) his brothers" is identical in both, though differently translated in NRSV). The repetition of this phrase here seems aimed at a characterization of Moses as a dying patriarch (even though he is not physically the progenitor of the people). This, in turn, makes the Exodus story one of the birth of a people.

33:28 Besides echoes of Jacob's blessing of Joseph in Gen 49, Sonnet (1997, 215) hears allusions to the Balaam story, e.g., the location, and, in this verse, the expression *škn bdd* "to dwell apart" (Num 23:9).

Deuteronomy 34

The Death of Moses

34:1 (Moses goes up Mount Nebo. YHWH shows him the whole land.) This fulfills the command in 32:49. Here, there is an association of the patriarch Abraham with Moses. In Gen 13:15, YHWH promises to give all the land that Abraham sees to Abraham and his "seed" for ever (see notes on verse 4 below). In our present verse, YHWH causes Moses to see the whole land. The phrase "all the land/the whole land" *(kôl-hāʾāreṣ)* as the object of "to see" only occurs in these two verses and in Jer 40:4.

34:4 "I have let you see [the land] with your eyes, but you shall not cross over there." George Coats (1977) points out the contrast between a heroic motif associated with the account of Moses' death (his vigor, his spirit, his unique face-to-face relationship with YHWH, and the attribution to him of "mighty acts"), on the one hand, and, on the other hand, the motif of Moses as a rebel who is being punished by YHWH by being excluded from the promised land (Deut 32:48-52). Coats' solution is diachronic: he thinks that 34:1-12 reflects a tradition that knew nothing of a sinful Moses. But a synchronic approach to the text would see the irony that results from the juxtaposition of the two motifs.

34:4 "Abraham, Isaac, and Jacob." In blessing the tribes before his death, Moses echoes the gesture of Jacob blessing his twelve sons (Genesis 49). But whereas Jacob, after his death is brought back to the Promised Land and buried by his sons, Moses remains outside. He does not die surrounded by his sons but alone with the God whom he knew face to face, and it is YHWH who buries him (Sonnet 1996, 493).

34:4 "I will give it to your descendants." The paralleling of Moses with Abraham is reinforced by allusion to Gen 12:7 (Sonnet 1997, 219):

Gen 12:7	*lᵊzarʿăkā ʾettēn ʾet-hāʾāreṣ hazzōʾt*	to your seed I will give this land
Deut 34:4	*lᵊzarʿăkā ʾettᵊnennāh*	to your seed I will give it [this land]

34:5 "At the Lord's command" literally "at the mouth of YHWH." The Targum paraphrases "at the kiss of the Memra of the Lord" from which comes the rabbinic legend that Moses died by the kiss of God (Driver 1901, 423).

34:5 Moses is characterized as "servant of YHWH."

34:6 "He was buried." Literally "He buried him." The Samaritan and Greek versions offer the possibility of reading "they buried him." NRSV has read the verb as impersonal, but, taken at face value, the text could mean that YHWH buried Moses.

34:6 "Opposite Beth-peor." The word *mûl* "opposite" (which occurs 8 times in Deuteronomy) may form an inclusion with 1:1 (there pointed *môl*).

34:7 "His sight was unimpaired and his vigor had not abated." This verse can be contrasted with Gen 27:1 (Isaac's blindness) and 48:10 (Israel's [Jacob's] blindness). It also contrasts with Moses' own words in 31:2, "I am now one hundred twenty years old. I am no longer able to get about" (Coats 1977, 36; Mayes 1981, 413). Although the author has drawn parallels between Moses and the patriarchs, Moses is in this respect unlike Isaac and Jacob (Sonnet 1997, 220). Moses was in fact what Balaam claimed to be (Num 24:3-4, 15-16). The Ugaritic cognate of the Hebrew word rendered "vigor" connotes the force of life as opposed to the weakness manifested in death (Thompson 1974, 319-20). "Death comes, not because of natural decay, or at least not very much of it, but because the appointed time for the end of a man's life has arrived" (Coats 1977, 36).

34:9 (The Israelites obeyed Joshua.) If the "prophet like Moses" is Joshua, then this verse narrates the fulfillment of the command given in 18:15 ("to him you shall listen"). The fulfillment relieves some narrative tension, gives hope for the future, and implicitly exhorts the reader to do the same.

34:10 "Moses was a prophet, but in his epitaph it is not Moses' knowledge of God that is stressed, but the Lord's knowledge of him" (Craigie 1976, 406).

34:11-12 The language used here of Moses is usually reserved for YHWH (Coats 1977, 38; Mayes 1981, 414).

34:12 Last words: *lᵊʿênê kol-yiśrāʾēl,* forming an *inclusio* with the "all Israel" in 1:1.

FOR FURTHER READING

Albright, W. F. "The 'Natural Force' of Moses in Light of Ugarit." *BASOR* 94 (1944) 32–35.

Anderson, John G. "Leprosy in Translations of the Bible." *BT* 31 (1980) 207–12.

Barstad, Hans M. "The Understanding of the Prophets in Deuteronomy." *SJOT* 8 (1994) 236–51.

Begg, Christopher T. (1975) "The Significance of the *Numeruswechsel* in Deuteronomy: The 'Pre-history' of the Question." *ETL* 55 (1979) 116–24.

_____. (1985) "The Destruction of the Calf (Exod 32,20/Deut 9,21)." Pages 208–51 in *Das Deuteronomium: Entstehung, Gestalt und Botschaft.* Edited by Norbert Lohfink. Leuven: Leuven University Press, 1985.

Bellefontaine, Elizabeth. "Deuteronomy 21:18-21: Reviewing the Case of the Rebellious Son." *JSOT* 13 (1979) 13–31.

Bergen, David A. "Bakhtin Revisits Deuteronomy: Narrative Theory and the Dialogical Event of Deut 31:2 and 34:7." *Journal of Hebrew Scriptures* 2 (1998–1999) http://www.arts.ualberta.ca/JHS/Article 4.

Bosman, H. L. "Redefined Prophecy as Deuteronomic Alternative to Divination in Deut 18:9-22." *AcT* 16 (1996) 1–23.

Boston, J. R. "The Wisdom Influence upon the Song of Moses." *JBL* 87 (1968) 198–208.

Brekelmans, C. "Deuteronomy 5: Its Place and Function." Pages 164–73 in *Das Deuteronomium: Entstehung, Gestalt und Botschaft.* Edited by Norbert Lohfink. Leuven: Leuven University Press, 1985.

Cairns, Ian. *Word and Presence: A Commentary on the Book of Deuteronomy.* ICC. Grand Rapids: Eerdmans, 1992.

Callaway, Phillip R. "Deut 21:18-21: Proverbial Wisdom and Law." *JBL* 103 (1984) 341–52.

Carmichael, Calum M. "Forbidden Mixtures in Deuteronomy XXII 9-11 and Leviticus XIX 19." *VT* 45 (1995) 433–48.

Carrière, J.-M. "L'organisation des lois en *DT 19-26:* les lois sur le mariage." *NRT* 114 (1992) 519–32.

Christensen, Duane L. (1984) "Two Stanzas of a Hymn in Deuteronomy 33." *Bib* 65 (1984) 382–89.

_____. (1985a) "Form and Structure in Deuteronomy 1–11." Pages 135–44 in *Das Deuteronomium Entstehung, Gestalt und Botschaft.* Edited by Norbert Lohfink. Leuven: Leuven University Press, 1985.

_____. (1985b) "Prose and Poetry in the Bible: The Narrative Poetics of Deuteronomy 1, 9-18." *ZAW* 97 (1985) 179–89.

_____. (1991) *Deuteronomy 1–11.* Word Biblical Commentary 6a. Dallas: Word, 1991.

_____, ed. *A Song of Power and the Power of Song: Essays on the Book of Deuteronomy.* Sources for Biblical and Theological Study 3. Winona Lake, Ind.: Eisenbrauns, 1993.

_____. (1993) "Deuteronomy in Modern Research." Pages 3–17 in *A Song of Power and the Power of Song: Essays on the Book of Deuteronomy.* Sources for Biblical and Theological Study 3. Edited by Duane L. Christensen. Winona Lake, Ind.: Eisenbrauns, 1993.

Clements, R. E. *Deuteronomy.* Old Testament Guides. Sheffield: JSOT, 1989.

Coats, G. W., "Legendary Motifs in the Moses Death Reports." *CBQ* 39 (1977) 34–44. Repr. pages 181–91 in *A Song of Power and the Power of Song: Essays on the Book of Deuteronomy.* Sources for Biblical and Theological Study 3. Edited by Duane L. Christensen. Winona Lake, Ind.: Eisenbrauns, 1993.

Craigie, Peter C. *Deuteronomy.* Grand Rapids: Eerdmans, 1976.

Dahman, Ulrich. "Weitere Fälle von Siebenergruppierungen im Buch Deuteronomium." *BN* 72 (1993) 5–11.

Dion, P.-E. "'Tu feras disparaître le mal du milieu de toi.'" *RB* 87 (1980) 321–49.

Driver, S. R. *A Critical and Exegetical Commentary on Deuteronomy.* ICC. 3d. ed. Edinburgh: T&T Clark, 1901.

Eslinger, Lyle. (1984) "More Drafting Techniques in Deuteronomic Laws." *VT* 34 (1984) 221–26.

_____. (1987) "Watering Egypt (Deuteronomy xi 10-11)." *VT* 37 (1987) 85–90.

Freedman, David Noel. "The Poetic Stucture of the Framework of Deuteronomy 33." Pages 25–46 in *The Bible World: Essays in Honor of Cyrus H. Gordon.* Edited by Gary Rendsburg, et al. New York: KTAV, 1980.

García López, Felix. (1977–78) "Analyse littéraire de Deutéronome, V-XI." *RB* 84 (1977) 481–522; 85 (1978) 5–49.

_____. (1978) "Deut., VI et la tradition-rédaction du Deutéronome." *RB* 85 (1978) 161–200.

_____. (1981) "Yahvé, fuente última de vida; análisis de Dt 8." *Bib* 62 (1981) 21–54.

Geller, Stephen A. "The Dynamics of Parallel Verse—A Poetic Analysis of Deut. 32:6-12." *HTR* 75 (1982) 35–56.

Giles, Terry. "Knowledge as a Boundary in the Organization of Experience—Deut 8:3,16." *IBS* 13 (1991) 155–69.

Glatt-Bilad, David A. "The Re-interpretation of the Edomite-Israelite Encounter in Deuteronomy II." *VT* 47 (1997) 441–55.

Görg, Manfred. "Die 'Astarte des Kleinviehs.'" *BN* 69 (1993) 9–11.

Gottcent, John H. *The Bible: A Literary Study.* Boston: G. K. Hall-Twayne, 1986.

Hall, Gary. "Rhetorical Criticism, Chiasm, and Theme in Deuteronomy." *SCJ* 1 (1998) 85–100.

Halpern, Baruch. "The Centralization Formula in Deuteronomy." *VT* 31 (1981) 20–38.

Hamilton, Jeffries M. *Social Justice and Deuteronomy: The Case of Deuteronomy 15.* SBLDS 136. Atlanta: Scholars, 1992.

Heller, Jan, "Sjemaᶜ als fundament van 'monotheïsme'?" *ACEBT* 10 (1989) 37–44.

Höffken, Peter. "Eine Bemerkung zum religionsgeschichtlichen Hintergrund von Dtn 6,4." *BZ* 28 (1984) 88–93.

Holladay, W. L. "Jeremiah and Moses: Further Observations." *JBL* 85 (1966) 17–27.

Hoppe, Leslie J. "The Levitical Origins of Deuteronomy Reconsidered." *BR* 28 (1983) 27–36.

Houtman, C. "Another Look at Forbidden Mixtures." *VT* 34 (1984) 226–28.

Hübner, Ulrich. "Og von Baschan und sein Bett in Rabbat-Ammon (Deuteronomium 3,11)." *ZAW* 105 (1993) 86–92.

Janzen, J. Gerald. "The 'Wandering Aramean' Reconsidered." *VT* 44 (1994) 359–75.

Knowles, Michael P. "'The Rock, His Work is Perfect': Unusual Imagery for God in Deuteronomy xxxii." *VT* 39 (1989) 307–22.

Kruger, Paul A. "The Removal of the Sandal in Deuteronomy xxv 9: 'A Rite of Passage'?" *VT* 46 (1996) 534–39.

Kselman, J. "The Recovery of Poetic Fragments from the Pentateuchal Priestly Source." *JBL* 97 (1978) 161–73.

Labuschagne, Casper J. (1971) "The Song of Moses: Its Framework and Structure." Pages 85–98 in *De Fructu Oris Sui: Essays in Honor of*

Adriannus van Selms. Edited by I. H. Eybers, et al. Pretoria Orienta Series, 9. Leiden: E. J. Brill, 1971.

_____. (1993) "Divine Speech in Deuteronomy." Pages 375–93 in *A Song of Power and the Power of Song: Essays on the Book of Deuteronomy.* Sources for Biblical and Theological Study 3. Edited by Duane L. Christensen. Winona Lake, Ind.: Eisenbrauns, 1993.

Lasserre, Guy. "Lutter contre la paupérisation et ses conséquences. Lecture rhétorique de Dt 15/12-18." *ETR* 70 (1995) 481–92.

Leeuwen, Raymond C. Van. "What Comes Out of God's Mouth: Theological Wordplay in Deuteronomy 8." *CBQ* 47 (1985) 55–57.

Lenchak, Timothy A. *"Choose Life!" A Rhetorical-Critical Investigation of Deuteronomy 28,69-30,20.* Analecta Biblica 129. Rome: Biblical Institute, 1993.

Levine, Baruch A. *Leviticus wyqrʾ The Traditional Hebrew Text with the New JPS Translation.* JPS Torah Commentary. Philadelphia: The Jewish Publication Society, 1989.

Lohfink, Norbert. (1963) *Das Hauptgebot, Eine Untersuchung literarischer Einlietungsfragen zu Dtn 5–11.* Analecta Biblica 20. Rome: Biblical Institute, 1963.

_____. (1965) *Höre Israel: Auslegung von Texten aus dem Buch Deuteronomium.* Düsseldorf: Patmos-Verlag, 1965.

_____. (1995) "The Destruction of the Seven Nations in Deuteronomy and the Mimetic Theory." *Contagion: Journal of Mimesis, Violence and Culture.* 2 (1995) 103–17.

Lundbom, Jack R. (1976) "The Lawbook of the Josianic Reform [Dt 32]." *CBQ* 38 (1976) 293–302.

_____. (1996) "The Inclusio and Other Framing Devices in Deuteronomy I–XXVIII." *VT* 46 (1996) 296–315.

Lux, Rüdiger. "Der Tod des Mose, als 'besprochene und erzählte Welt.'" *ZTK* 84 (1987) 395–425.

Luyten, J. "Primeval and Eschatological Overtones in the Song of Moses (Dt 32,1-43)." Pages 341–47 in *Das Deuteronomium: Entstehung, Gestalt und Botschaft.* Edited by Norbert Lohfink. Leuven: Leuven University Press, 1985.

McNamara, Martin. *Targum Neofiti 1, Leviticus.* Michael Maher, *Targum Pseudo-Jonathan, Leviticus.* The Aramaic Bible 3. Collegeville, Minn.: The Liturgical Press, 1994.

Mann, Thomas W. "Theological Reflections on the Denial of Moses." *JBL* 98 (1979) 481–94.

Mayes, Andrew D. H. *Deuteronomy.* New Century Bible Commentary. Grand Rapids: Eerdmans, 1981.

Miller, Patrick D. (1970) "Apotropaic Imagery in Proverbs 6:20-22." *JNES* 29 (1970) 129–30.

_____. (1993) "'Moses My Servant': The Deuteronomic Portrait of Moses." Pages 301–12 in *A Song of Power and the Power of Song: Essays on the Book of Deuteronomy.* Sources for Biblical and Theological Study 3. Edited by Duane L. Christensen. Winona Lake, Ind.: Eisenbrauns, 1993.

Moran, William L. "Ancient Near Eastern Background of the Love of God in Deuteronomy." *CBQ* 25 (1963) 77–87.

Nielsen, Kirsten. "Intertextuality and Biblical Scholarship." *SJOT* 2 (1990, #2) 89–95.

Nigosian, Solomon A. (1996) "The Song of Moses (Dt 32): A Structural Analysis." *ETL* 72 (1996) 5–22.

_____. (1997) "Linguistic Patterns of Deuteronomy 32." *Bib* 78 (1997) 206–24.

Norin, Stig. "Ein Aramäer, dem umkommen nahe—ein Kerntext der Forschung und Tradition." *SJOT* 8 (1994) 87–104.

O'Connell, Robert H. (1990) "Deuteronomy viii 1-20: Asymmetrical Concentricity and the Rhetoric of Providence." *VT* 40 (1990) 437–52.

_____. (1992a) "Deuteronomy VII 1-26: Asymmetrical Concentricity and the Rhetoric of Conquest." *VT* 42 (1992) 248–65.

_____. (1992b) "Deuteronomy IX 7–X 7, 10-11: Paneled Structure, Double Rehearsal and the Rhetoric of Covenant Rebuke." *VT* 42 (1992) 492–509.

O'Connor, M. *Hebrew Verse Structure.* Winona Lake, Ind.: Eisenbrauns, 1980.

Ohlsen, Woodrow. *Perspectives on Old Testament Literature.* New York: Harcourt Brace Jovanovich, 1978.

Olsen, Dennis T. *Deuteronomy and the Death of Moses: A Theological Reading.* OBT. Minneapolis: Fortress, 1994.

Patrick, Dale, "The Rhetoric of Collective Responsibility in Deuteronomic Law." Pages 421–36 in *Pomegranates and Golden Bells: Studies in Biblical, Jewish, and Near Eastern Ritual, Law, and Literature in honor of Jacob Milgrom.* Edited by David P. Wright, et al. Winona Lake, Ind.: Eisenbrauns, 1995.

Peels, Hendrik G. L. "On the Wings of the Eagle (Dtn 32,11)—An Old Misunderstanding." *ZAW* 106 (1994) 300–3.

Polzin, Robert M. (1980) *Moses and the Deuteronomist: A Literary Study of the Deuteronomic History, Part One: Deuteronomy, Joshua, Judges.* New York: Seabury, 1980.

_____. (1987) "Deuteronomy." Pages 92–101 in *The Literary Guide to the Bible.* Edited by Robert Alter and Frank Kermode. Cambridge, Mass.: Belknap Press, 1987.

_____. (1993) "Reporting Speech in the Book of Deuteronomy: Toward a Compositional Analysis of the Deuteronomic History." Pages

355–74 in *A Song of Power and the Power of Song: Essays on the Book of Deuteronomy.* Sources for Biblical and Theological Study 3. Edited by Duane L. Christensen. Winona Lake, Ind.: Eisenbrauns, 1993.

Porter, J. R. "The Interpretation of Deuteronomy xxxiii 24-5." *VT* 44 (1994) 267–70.

Richler, Mordecai. "Deuteronomy." Pages 51–58 in *Congregation: Contemporary Writers Read the Jewish Bible.* Edited by David Rosenberg. San Diego, Calif.: Harcourt Brace Jovanovich, 1987.

Rosenbaum, M., and A. M. Silbermann. *Pentateuch: With Haphtaroth and Rashi's Commentary.* 5 vols. New York: Hebrew Publishing Co., 1965.

Roth, Wolfgang. "The Deuteronomic Rest Theology: A Redaction-Critical Study." *BR* 21 (1976) 5–14.

Schley, Donald G., Jr. "'Yahweh Will Cause You to Return to Egypt in Ships' (Deuteronomy xxviii 68)." *VT* 35 (1985) 369–72.

Skehan, Patrick W. "The Structure of the Song of Moses in Deuteronomy (Deut. 32:1-43)." *CBQ* 13 (1951) 153–63.

Sonnet, Jean-Pierre. (1996) "Le Deutéronome et la modernité du livre." *NRT* 118 (1996) 481–96.

_____. (1997) *The Book Within the Book: Writing in Deuteronomy.* Biblical Interpretation Series 14. Leiden: Brill, 1997.

Steiner, Richard C. (1996) "דָּת and עֵין Two Verbs Masquerading as Nouns in Moses' Blessing (Deuteronomy 33:2,28)." *JBL* 115 (1996) 693–98.

_____. (1997) "The 'Aramean' of Deuteronomy 26:5: *Peshat* and *Derash.*" Pages 127–38 in *Tehillah le-Moshe: Biblical and Judaic Studies in Honor of Moshe Greenberg.* Edited by Mordechai Cogan et al. Winona Lake, Ind.: Eisenbrauns, 1997.

Stulman, Louis. "Encroachment in Deuteronomy: An Analysis of the Social World of the D Code." *JBL* 109 (1990) 613–32.

Thompson, J. A. *Deuteronomy.* Downers Grove, Ill.: InterVarsity Press, 1974.

Tigay, Jeffrey H. *Deuteronomy.* The JPS Commentary. Philadelphia: The Jewish Publication Society, 1996.

Tournay, R. J. "Le psaume et les bénédictions de Moïse." *RB* 103 (1996) 196–212.

Tsevat, Matitiahyu. "The Hebrew Slave According to Deuteronomy 15:12-18: His Lot and the Value of His Work, with Special Attention to the Meaning of מִשְׁנֶה." *JBL* 113 (1994) 587–95.

Vanoni, Gottfried. "Der Geist und der Buchstabe: Überlegungen zum Verhältnis der Testamente und Beobachtungen zu Dtn 30,1-10." *BN* 14 (1981) 65–98.

Veijola, Timo. "Höre Israel! Der Sinn und Hintergrund von Deuteronomium vi 4-9." *VT* 42 (1992) 528–41.

Vogels, Walter. "The Literary Form of the 'Question of Nations.'" *ETh* 11 (1980) 159–76.

Weinfeld, Moshe. "Deuteronomy's Theological Revolution." *BRev* 12 (1, 1996) 38–41, 44–45.

Wenham, G. J., and J. G. McConville. "Drafting Techniques in Some Deuteronomic Laws." *VT* 30 (1980) 248–52.

Wilson, P. Eddy. "Deuteronomy xxv 11-12—One for the Books." *VT* 47 (1997) 220–35.

Wright, David P. "Deuteronomy 21:1-9 as a Rite of Elimination." *CBQ* 49 (1987) 387–403.

Wright, G. E. "The Lawsuit of God: A Form-Critical Study of Deuteronomy 32." Pages 26–67 in *Israel's Prophetic Heritage: Essays in Honor of James Muilenburg*. Edited by B. Anderson and W. Harrelson. New York: Harper, 1962.

Yaron, Reuven. "The Climactic Tricolon." *JJS* 37 (1986) 153–59.

Zohar, Noam. "Repentance and Purification: The Significance and Semantics of חטאת in the Pentateuch." *JBL* 107 (1988) 609–18.

Zwickel, Wolfgang. "'Opfer der Gerechtigkeit' (Dtn. xxxiii 19; Ps. Iv 6, li 21)." *VT* 45 (1995) 386–91.

INDEX OF AUTHORS

SCRIPTURE INDEX